BLOOD IN THE SAND

MORE FORGOTTEN WARS OF
THE NINETEENTH CENTURY

BLOOD IN THE SAND

MORE FORGOTTEN WARS OF THE NINETEENTH CENTURY

IAN HERNON

SUTTON PUBLISHING

First published in 2001 by
Sutton Publishing Limited · Phoenix Mill
Thrupp · Stroud · Gloucestershire · GL5 2BU

British Library Cataloguing in Publication Data
A catalogue record for this book is available from the British Library.

ISBN 0-7509-2614-7

Dedication

For my family, as always

Typeset in 10/12pt Plantin Light.
Typesetting and origination by
Sutton Publishing Limited.
Printed in Great Britain by
J.H. Haynes Co. Ltd, Sparkford.

Contents

Preface and Acknowledgements

This is the third book in my trilogy on the forgotten wars of the nineteenth century. My aim was two-fold: to commemorate some of the countless unsung heroes and heroines of arguably the most exciting era in British history, and to nail the myth of Pax Britannica – the belief that the Empire was largely at peace between the great conflicts of the Napoleonic, Crimean and Boer wars. In fact there was not a single month in that century when British forces were not engaged somewhere across the globe. My intention was not to try to rival the sweep and erudition of the great histories of the Empire, or to judge with modern hindsight either the evils or the bounty of an Imperialist age. It was rather to tell, with a reporter's eye, some of the astonishing stories of heroism, self-sacrifice, greed, cruelty and stupidity behind the epic tale of colonial expansion.

There was no conscious theme in each volume of the trilogy beyond the desire to relate these often mind-boggling stories from the viewpoint of the participants themselves, whether they were medal-bedecked generals or semi-literate privates, war-painted warriors or jewel-laden heathen monarchs. But inevitably some themes did emerge. The first book, *Massacre and Retribution*, focused on those stories where events did not always turn out as expected, telling how a modern European army was fought to a standstill by Christian Maoris armed with the latest rifles; how British troops successfully stormed an unassailable mountain fortress in Abyssinia; how redcoats were slaughtered in paradise. The second, *The Savage Empire*, was criticised in some quarters for painting too dark a picture of the Empire. It focused on how Britain increasingly took advantage of the technology of warfare to crush native resistance, using machine-guns and flying columns in Benin, a scorched earth policy on the North-West Frontier, armed steamships in China and ironclads in Zanzibar. Both featured some of the most indelible stains on the British flag: the massacre of ex-slaves in Jamaica, the extinction of an entire race in Tasmania, the execution of rebels in Canada.

This volume highlights the courage of the men and women on all sides, and the respect given to brave enemies. Amid the brutal carnage there was honour to be found and, in the case of the Sikhs and the Gurkhas, foes became long-time friends and allies. Another theme is the incompetence of many leaders, military and civil, rebel and Imperial, which betrayed the heroism shown by the led.

My definition of a forgotten war may also raise some people's hackles. Military historians and the Sikh population may know all about the brutal wars in the Punjab, but the general population does not. People may know the Gurkhas through their peerless reputation fighting alongside British forces, but few are aware that they once fought a ferocious war against Britain. The Eureka Stockade may be famous in Australia, but it is barely remembered here. Some schools still teach children about Napoleon and the Boer War, and most people know about the Zulu Wars because they see the film on television every other Christmas. But for the majority of the British population the wars, policing operations and skirmishes that created an Empire are largely forgotten. And that is a terrible injustice. Interestingly, many of the scenes of conflict of that age remain troublespots today.

Many people have given me invaluable help, encouragement and advice. They include my wife Pauline, my daughters Joanna and Kim; my agent Mike Shaw of Curtis Brown; Jonathan Falconer, Commissioning Editor at Sutton Publishing; editor Sarah Cook; Jamie Cann, who suggested Belize; Simon Mares, who suggested Kars; and the late Sir Robert Rhodes James who helped me start my journey. To these, and others, I give sincere thanks.

Introduction

The common soldier was rarely honoured in Britain in the first half of the nineteenth century. The accolades, medals and fame went mainly to aristocratic officers and generals who planted the flag in the far corners of the world. Ordinary men were not eligible for most medals of valour and battlefield promotions were rare. The vast majority of heroes went unrecognised. The best they could hope for was a decent pension – the worst was a beggar's bowl.

The Crimean War changed all that, and not just with the introduction of the Victoria Cross, the highest honour of all and open to all ranks. The British administration, faced with undeniable evidence of poor generalship and official incompetence, needed heroes from all strata of society. An early example was Private John Penn of the 17th Lancers.

Penn was born into the 14th Regiment of Light Dragoons around 1820, and spent his childhood moving between barracks and stables where his father was a farrier-major. He was orphaned at the age of eight and later was taken as a servant into the household of Lady John Bethell. Discontented with that form of service, he joined the cavalry as soon as he had grown to the required standard height.

He saw much action in the Afghanistan campaign under General Pollock and in the First Sikh War under Lord Gough. He was severely wounded at the bloody battle of Mudki, having been struck on the head by a Sikh artilleryman's sponge-staff during hand-to-hand fighting. Despite his injury he slew the gunner and captured his cannon before wandering dazed into the night. He was found the following day, cold, confused and close to death. His wounds were dressed and just a few weeks later he was in action again at the battle of Sobraon, where the great Sikh army was wiped out.

In the Second Sikh War he saw more action with the 3rd Light Dragoons, taking part in the shambles at Ramnuggar, the crossing of the Chenab, the attack on Soodoolapore, the bloodbath of Chillianwalla and the final battle of Gujerat. His regiment arrived back in England in July 1853. Within days Penn heard that the 17th Lancers were ordered for Turkey and he immediately volunteered to join them. His detachment, including fifty-seven horses, arrived in Varna in July 1854 under the command of Captain the Honourable Hercules Rowley, shortly to become Lord Langford. They arrived in the Crimea on 1 September.

Penn fought at the battle of Alma and at Mackenzie's Farm where a quantity of Russian baggage and stores was captured. By now he had an array of campaign medals but his first for distinguished conduct in the field was won in the famous

Charge of the Light Brigade at Balaclava. His actions were witnessed by several officers who also survived that tragic waste of courageous lives. A contemporary account said:

> He speaks very highly of the lance, a weapon of which the Russians are very much in dread. Unfortunately for many of the brave fellows of his regiment, they had their poles shattered by the enemy's shower of grapeshot. On their coming up to the Russian guns, they were ordered to charge, when he made a point at a gunner, which took effect – the lance going through his body. He could not extricate it, as he was at a gallop.
>
> Passing through the enemy's guns, the 13th Light Dragoons and 17th Lancers were obliged to open out, when our hero came into contact with a Russian officer (a Hussar); he made for him, and the officer wheeled his horse around for the purpose of making a bolt; he, therefore, took a favourable distance on the officer's left (both at the time being at a gallop), when he delivered cut six, which instantly dismounted the officer, whose head was nearly severed from his body.
>
> At the same time his horse halted, and on dismounting, to his grief, he found that his horse had received a ball in the near shoulder. He then took a view of the Russian officer; he must have died in an instant, as the body never moved

Private John Penn with his eleven honours. (*Illustrated London News*)

after falling to the ground; he cut his pouch-belt off, and took his sword, and a clasp knife, which he wore in a belt around his waist.

Penn rejoined his comrades, who were now surrounded by Russians. He used the captured sword to cut his way through but it broke as he slashed at a seventh enemy soldier. Penn and the bloodied, tattered remnants of the Light Brigade made it back and he and his wounded horse cantered into legend. (The horse, happily, recovered after the ball was speedily removed.)

Penn saw further action at Inkerman. His superiors noted: 'He was never ill during the whole of the season, although much exposed. He was always employed on general duty.' However, he suffered sunstroke when on outpost duty at Baldar in July 1855. His condition was exacerbated by old injuries suffered when at field-drill in India three years earlier: his right collar-bone had been fractured and his lower jaw broken when a horse fell on him. He was invalided home with no fewer than eleven decorations, and joined a much-needed gallery of popular heroes. The *Illustrated London News* said that 'his honours for military services are equal to any in the British Army' and that his eventful career 'presents a noteworthy instance of devotion to a noble object'. His portrait shows a grizzled, battle-hardened veteran – hardly the sort of man you would wish to tangle with. After his fifteen minutes of fame he stepped back into the shadows of obscurity.

Not so those heroes who came from a higher and therefore more acceptable class. Those aristocrats and officers who survived their battlefield exploits went on to become fêted generals, admirals, diplomats and politicians. They received peerages, knighthoods, medals, baubles and generous life-time pensions, and won membership of an exclusive elite: their portraits hung in the National Gallery, and they enjoyed favoured places at Court, the lion's share of the spoils, public acclamation, rich wives and glamour. There is no point in railing against such gross inequalities. This was a time, after all, when just 710 people owned a quarter of England and Wales. But such disparities disguised the heroism shared by all ranks. Courage was not the exclusive preserve of the officer class. Nor were all the other traits and instincts found in war: cruelty, compassion, comradeship, betrayal, cowardice, greed, fortitude, intelligence and stupidity. The silver spoon-fed, lisping fop, his rank bought for him by money and influence, was certainly present in most Empire campaigns. But there were also talented and competent upper-class officers who shared the privations and dangers of their men.

Take the career of General Sir Redvers Henry Buller, for example. Born into the family of the Dukes of Norfolk in 1829, Buller's wealthy and privileged upbringing had nothing in common with Penn's rough childhood. He served with the 60th in China, where his massive physical strength proved a boon in negotiating the rapids during the Red River campaign of 1870. He was General Wolseley's intelligence chief during the Ashanti expedition and the subsequent Egyptian conflict, becoming Chief of Staff in the Sudan in 1884.

He commanded the Irregular Light Horse during the Zulu War in South Africa and won the Victoria Cross for rescuing Captain D'Arcy and two men at Hlobane in 1879. He served in the Transvaal War and commanded a brigade in the Sudan

'Action in the Sudan', by Captain Sir Harry S. Rawlinson. (*Illustrated London News*)

'The Aftermath at Omdurman', by H.C.S. Eppings Wright. (*Illustrated London News*)

where he was made a major-general, later being commemorated in song by Gilbert and Sullivan. Back in the Sudan he received a KCB for achieving victory against astounding odds at Abu Klea during the abortive bid to rescue General Gordon.

He was popular with his men and C.N. Robinson wrote: 'There is no stronger character in the British Army than the resolute, almost grimly resolute, absolutely independent, utterly fearless, steadfast and always vigorous commander. This big-boned, square jawed, strong-headed man was born a soldier . . .' Here there were echoes of Private Penn.

Buller was one of the greatest popular heroes of his day, but his fame was forever tarnished when he led the South African Field Force in the 1899. Much of the blame for the early shambles of the Boer War was put on his shoulders, including the disaster at Spion Kop. He was indecisive when boldness was required, foolhardy when he should have been cautious. He was a fighter rather than a strategist. Buller was subsequently recalled to duties at Aldershot and he too withdrew into obscurity – but his was a far more comfortable and well-rewarded obscurity than Private Penn's.

But both men's lives were packed with excitement and adventure in foreign lands. And the lives of such Victorians seem to have been so much more eventful than those of today's popular heroes. Those individuals who survived gruelling sea voyages, deadly diseases, starvation, exhaustion and savage foes could indeed carve out fortunes for themselves. Some, like James Brooke, could even win their own empires.

But all of this came at a fearful cost. The casualties in those forgotten wars, comrades and foes alike, were uncountable. The bleakest picture to come from those *Boy's Own* adventures is of vultures hovering over the dead and dying at Omdurman (*see* page 5). The real tragedy is that this picture could have been painted at any one of a thousand places across the globe dominated by the red of Empire in the nineteenth century.

CHAPTER ONE

The Gurkha War, 1814–16

'. . . few things look so formidable'.

In May 2000 Agansing Rai died, aged eighty, at his home, some three days' walk from Khatmandu. His death reduced to twenty-six the number of living holders of the Victoria Cross, Britain's highest military honour for valour.

Fifty-six years earlier, already a battle-hardened veteran of the Royal Gurkha Rifles, he and his comrades had faced a desperate Japanese counter-attack in Burma. Pinned down on Mortar Bluff near Imphal, Agansing Rai led his section in a charge on a machine-gun post, firing as he ran. He killed three of the four-man gun-crew. They then came under fire from a 37mm gun in the jungle. He again led a charge; this time all but three of his men were killed or wounded before they had covered half the distance. Rai's Thompson sub-machine-gun jammed and he snatched up the section's Bren; continuing the charge alone he wiped out the enemy gun-crew. He and his men, both standing and wounded, then came under intense machine-gun fire and grenades from a hidden bunker. After ordering his Bren gunner to cover him, Agansing Rai again advanced alone. Making his way along a shallow communication trench he stormed into the bunker and dispatched all four occupants with a single burst. He received his decoration from the Viceroy of India, Field Marshal Lord Wavell, in 1945.

Agansing Rai's astonishing courage typified both the reality and the legend of the Gurkha soldiers who have fought in British ranks since the second decade of the nineteenth century. For the best part of two hundred years they have been regarded as among the world's best soldiers. The mere mention of their *kukris*, the distinctive curved knife which, according to myth, must drink blood every time it is unsheathed, has sent some opponents running. Gurkhas have fought under the flags of other countries, but it is to Britain that they have traditionally owed the greatest allegiance outside their own mountain terrain. They have won admiration and respect from the officers and men who have served alongside them in Britain's colonial wars and global conflicts. They have also been held in the greatest regard in Britain, although that regard has rarely been matched in terms of pay, pensions and conditions. The respect is, by and large, mutual.

Yet it is often forgotten that before a single Gurkha served alongside a British soldier the Gurkhas fought a brief but bloody war against British military might in the foothills of the Himalayas. Like all such wars in savage places during that blood-soaked age the fighting was ferocious. Unusually, it was also marked by the honourable behaviour of both sides. It was a war with many casualties, but honour was not one of them. That was truly remarkable.

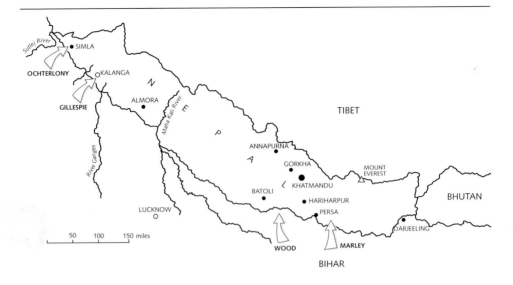

Nepal at the outbreak of the Gurkha War, 1814.

The ancient history of Nepal, a vast isolated country on the southern slopes of the Himalayas, is one of myths and legends. According to the folk tales, its central valley began as a lake which was drained by a single sword-cut wielded by the saint Manjushri. Successive dynasties traded and fought with China and the Indian moguls. Its people were always a rich ethnic mix. The Rajputs and the Aryans arrived during the wars with the Mongols, bringing with them the Hindu faith. Those tribes with Mongolian roots are generally Buddhists. In the central hills were the Brahmans and the Chetris, belonging to an ancient warrior caste. Higher in the mountains were the Magars and the Gurungs, both of fighting stock. Elsewhere were people from Tibet, including the Sherpas and the Bhutias. They were more peaceable, but tough, like all mountain dwellers.

The backbone of Nepal is the range of the Himalayas which includes Everest and many of the world's other highest mountains. Below them the central hills enjoy pleasant summers but severe winters with heavy snows above 8,000 feet, and valleys which endure torrential rain during the monsoon season. There was no wheeled traffic in the hills. The low-lying Terai region bordering India has a subtropical climate, hot in summer and extremely humid during the monsoons. The vegetation and wildlife varies dramatically according to altitude. In the valley of Khatmandu every square inch of suitable land was terraced for rice-growing during the monsoons and for wheat and vegetables during the drier months. There were, and still are, dense pine forests scattered with magnolias and wild cherry. In the uncultivated parts of the Terai were vast, impenetrable jungles teeming with deer, buffalo and wild ox, as well as elephants, tigers and leopards. In summer the hills blazed with dwarf rhododendrons, primulas and the blue poppy but the riotous colour was whited out when the winter snows came and temperatures dropped below zero. Nepal could be paradise or hell.

The Gurkhas took their name from the old city-state of Gorkha in the hills of the north-west. Its ruling family was descended from the Rajput princes of Udaipur who had been driven out of their own lands by the Muslims. The Gurkhas were both feared and admired by their neighbours. They seemed to enjoy warfare, not just for loot but also for a chance to test their own honour. A favourite proverb was 'It is better to die than to be a coward.'

They were devout Hindus who respected their kings, generals and elders. The caste system was sacrosanct. They were farmers and family men as well as fighters. Few took more than two wives and they were extremely fond of children. The birth of a son was the cause of much feasting. Divorces were permitted but a widow was not allowed to remarry. The men were square-built and sturdy, fond of sports and unafraid of hard work. Their average height was 5 foot 3 inches, although some tribes, such as the Chetri, were taller and darker. Their vices were gambling and some overenthusiasm for a grain beer called *janr*. They discouraged visitors, but Britons who managed to penetrate their borders spoke warmly of their good humour and generosity. Many saw their potential. One British officer said: 'Gurkhas are bold, enduring, frank, very independent and self-reliant; in their own country they are jealous of foreigners and self-asserting . . . though hot-tempered and easily roused, they are in general quiet, well-behaved men, and extremely amenable to discipline – from the warlike qualities of his forefathers, and the traditions handed down to him of their military prowess, he is imbued with, and cherishes, the true military spirit.' Another observer wrote: 'Their fighting qualities, whether for sturdy, unflinching courage or enduring elan, are *nulli secondus*.' A later minister, Brian Hodgson, wrote: 'In my humble opinion they are, by far, the best soldiers in India; and if they were made participators of our renown in arms, I conceive that their gallant spirit, emphatic contempt of *madherias* (plain-dwellers) and unadulterated military habit, might be relied on for fidelity . . .'

In 1742 the land-hungry Prithvi Narayan Shah reached the throne of Gorkha and fought a series of wars against the neighbouring Malla kingdoms of Khatmandu, Bhadgaon and Patan. He adopted European standards of discipline for his small but effective army which soundly defeated his strongest opponent, the Nabob of Moorshedabad. By 1768 he had subjugated the entire Valley of Nepal and declared himself king, with his capital at Khatmandu. His armies then turned east and west, conquering further principalities and defeating an ill-conceived and British-led expedition ordered by the government of Bengal. After Shah's death in 1775 his successors continued his ferocious policy of expansion, advancing as far west as the Kangra Valley in the Punjab where they were halted by the great Sikh leader Runjeet Singh. The Gurkhas then occupied Sikkim and invaded Tibet but were driven back by a Chinese counter-invasion. Such warfare and the mountainous terrain bred a nation of tough, adaptable soldiers. Their vast kingdom, skirting the northern frontier of Hindustan, was ideally placed for raids from their high strongholds into the plain regions below.

During this turbulent period relations were repeatedly strained with the East India Company, who complained of incursions into the territories under their control and protection. The Company tried to develop friendlier relations but the Nepalese kings resolutely refused to allow a British Resident in Khatmandu. They had seen for themselves how the Company used such means to extend its influence and power. The Gurkhas also pointed out, not unreasonably, that the remorseless territorial expansion of the British robbed them of the moral high ground. By the end of the eighteenth century Nepal shared an 800-mile border with the territories of John Company and the Nawab of Oudh, who was under its protection. Numerous border disputes were resolved without bloodshed, but it was Oudh that proved to be the flashpoint.

At this time Nepal's nominal king was a beardless boy and the real power lay in the hands of the Thappa family, who held the most important positions. Bheim Sein was prime minister, while his brother-in-law Umur Sing, a renowned general, commanded the army. They had long coveted the rich kingdom of Oudh to their south and in 1801 Nepal occupied its northern districts of Gorakhpur and Saran. The British protested and the Governor-General, Lord Minto, opened up protracted negotiations with Khatmandu. Bheim Sein did not believe the British were serious and in 1813 a Gurkha army swept deeper into Oudh, garrisoning the Bhutwal region. Bheim Sein told the Khatmandu court: 'The Chinese once made war on us but were reduced to seek peace. How then will the English be able to penetrate into our hills? Our hills and fastness are joined by the hand of God and are impregnable.'

The Bengal administration, now led by Lord Moira, who had succeeded Minto as Governor-General, recalled the negotiators and dispatched a strong force of troops to the disputed area. The Gurkhas, for once, meekly withdrew from the occupied lands in the face of such a show of armed might. But the British blundered. Under-estimating their opponents, and with the onset of the unhealthy rainy season almost upon them, the expedition was withdrawn. The Gurkhas immediately returned. In Bhutwal three police stations were stormed and among the dead was a British officer. Moira, later better known as Lord Hastings, sent a letter to Khatmandu accusing the young Raja of Nepal of 'wantonly' making war on the British government. A formal declaration of war was made in November 1814.

★   ★   ★

Francis Rawdon-Hastings, the first Marquis of Hastings and second Earl of Moira, had only arrived at Calcutta in October, but he was determined to tackle the Nepalese head on and to punish their 'arrogance'. Aged fifty-nine, the product of Harrow and Oxford, he was a veteran of the American War of Independence and had won a signal victory against a larger body of rebels at Hobkirk's Hill. He was known as a martinet and was publicly rebuked for the execution of the American colonel Isaac Hayne. He served as an MP for Irish seats in County Antrim and acted as the Duke of York's second in a duel. He was appointed Governor-General as an antidote to Minto's more faint-hearted administration.

Many British officials and politicians believed that the proposed campaign would be a walkover. Lord Metcalfe called it 'a mere affair with a troublesome Raja of the frontier'. Advisers to the new governor consistently under-rated the Gurkha's military prowess, concentrating on their relatively small numbers. Others were not so sure. Company civil servants could not understand the need to wage war across

A Gurkha hill-fort.

inhospitable lands for no obvious reasons of profit. Colonel Sir David Ochterlony, the military commander in the north, described the planned expedition as 'the most impolitic measure we have ever attempted'.

Hastings had available an army of 22,000 men. He and Ochterlony agreed that this force should be divided into four columns for the invasion of Nepal: Ochterlony himself was to lead 6,000 men and 16 guns to the western frontier, Generals Wood and Marley were to command the two central columns, while General Gillespie, the hero of Java, was to lead an eastern column of 3,500 men; a garrison of 2,700 men was left for the defence of the border region east of the Coosy River. Hastings was to direct overall operations from Lucknow. The Gurkhas, meanwhile, had retreated to their mountain kingdom, preferring to fight on home territory which they believed to be impregnable.

The omens for the British were poor from the start. One observer noted: 'The British troops had to advance through a rugged, unknown and almost impracticable region, full of defensive defiles. They had no experience of mountain warfare, while the Gurkhas were a very warlike people who understood the value of the mountain passes, and had occupied and fortified them.' Hastings hoped to recruit men from local tribes threatened by the Gurkhas but the advice of the political agent in Kumaon was not encouraging: '. . . for the dread entertained of the Goorkha [sic] soldiery is such, their activity, enterprise, hardiness, patience and abstinence so remarkable, that even harassing his troops cannot be relied upon.' The comforts normally enjoyed by the gentlemanly officers of the Company's army were also not conducive to the sort of rapid-marching mountain campaign which Hastings envisaged. His adjutant-general ruled: 'Two mules and two asses will be sufficient to carry a captain's baggage, with the addition of two hillmen who carry loads. Servants must be reduced; subalterns can have three, captains five. The officers must have small, light tents with low poles, eight feet high.' The baggage and the lack of porters proved to be crucial handicaps in the following campaign in one of the world's most gruelling regions. Gillespie's column faced the toughest terrain as they sweated and froze and stumbled up rocky paths towards the small fort of Kalunga a few miles north of Dehra Dun.

Major-General Sir Robert Rollo Gillespie had for forty-eight years enjoyed a life that could have come straight from *Boy's Own*. He was a free-spirited adventurer with an Irish brogue, the product of a rumbustious background. The son of a Scots-Irish family who settled in County Down, he was educated at private schools in Kensington and Newmarket but refused to go to Cambridge. Instead he joined the 3rd Irish Horse as a cornet. Three years later he contracted a 'clandestine' marriage with Annabell, a pretty Dublin girl. Soon afterwards he acted as the second to an officer friend in a duel with the brother of Sir Jonah Barrington. Both men fired twice without hitting the other, and it was proposed that the matter should end there. But an argument erupted between the two seconds and Gillespie challenged Barrington to fire across his handkerchief. Gillespie fired back and Barrington fell dead. Gillespie fled and was hidden by some of his in-laws before he and his wife escaped to Scotland. He later returned voluntarily and stood trial for wilful murder at the summer assize of 1788. The judge was hostile but the jury, which included several half-pay officers, was not and they reached a verdict of 'justifiable homicide'.

Gillespie, desperate to see active service, escaped the scandal at home by accepting a lieutenancy in the newly raised Jamaica Light Dragoons. On the way out he was shipwrecked at Madeira and suffered yellow fever when he arrived. He saw action against the French at Tiburon and was fired on while swimming ashore at Port-au-Prince with a white flag to demand the surrender of the town. His gallantry was evident at the capture of Fort Bizotten and he was wounded several times during the attack on For de l'Hopital. He was appointed adjutant-general of St Domingo to put down an insurrection there. A gang of eight men broke into his quarters, murdered his slave-boy and attacked Gillespie. He fought back with his sword, killing six, and the two survivors fled. A faulty report that the assassination attempt had succeeded reached Europe and hastened his mother's death.

After the Peace of Amiens Gillespie returned from Jamaica in command of his regiment but now faced accusations of fiddling the funds. His accuser had himself been arrested by Gillespie for sedition. The affair dragged on for two years until Gillespie was finally acquitted at a court martial in 1804. By then the cost of the proceedings, together with his 'open-handedness and misplaced trust', had left him financially ruined. The answer was to sign up for service in the 19th Light Dragoons in India. He travelled overland, disguising himself in Hamburg to escape French agents, via Greece and Baghdad. On arrival in India he was appointed commandant at Arcot. In 1806, after sepoy troops mutinied and massacred Europeans at Vellore, he rode to a fort where the British survivors were making a last stand against the mutineers. He was hauled up the battlements by a rope and commanded the defence until heavier reinforcements arrived. The following years saw him commanding the Mysore division of the Madras Army. Astonishingly, his greatest adventures were still ahead of him.

In 1811 Gillespie, now a brigadier-general, commanded the advance expedition against Dutch Java and swiftly took the city of Batavia. Although wracked with fever he continued to direct operations against the Dutch forces. The overall commander, Sir Samuel Auchmuty, said that the success of the whole enterprise was due to Gillespie's 'gallantry, energy and prompt judgement'. Gillespie was left as military commander of the island, with Stamford Raffles as the civil governor. The following year the Sultan of Palembang on Sumatra murdered the Europeans within his domain. Gillespie took a small force, deposed the sultan 'in a most summary manner' and extended British influence. On his return to Java he found that a confederation of anti-British chiefs had gathered with 100 guns and 30,000 men at a stockaded fortress at Yodhyakarta, threatening the lives of all European settlers. Gillespie promptly attacked the fort with 1,500 men and broke up the rebellion. His victory, however, was tarnished by a dispute with Stamford Raffles about the scale of military occupation. He laid charges against Raffles over the sale of lands. The issue was unresolved when Gillespie returned to India to take command of the Meerut division. His men admired both his confidence and his abilities as a sportsman. One one occasion he killed a tiger in the open on Bangalore racecourse.

★   ★   ★

Gillespie's men toiling towards Kalunga knew of his colourful past and, above all, his track record of victory. Intelligence had already revealed that the Gurkha garrison numbered barely 600 men. The battle, they felt, would be a pushover despite the cruelty of the terrain. But when they reach the approaches to the fort victory did not appear so certain. Kalunga was perched in an almost inaccessible position, surrounded by deep crevices, the snowy Himalayas providing an impressive backcloth. The attack was fixed for 31 October 1814.

Gillespie divided his force into four small columns, one to assault each face. Three of the columns would have to make long detours over difficult ground and a prearranged signal for the attack was agreed. As the four columns were getting into position the Gurkhas launched a sortie. They were repulsed but Gillespie, thinking he could follow them back into the fort, attempted to rush the defences with a dismounted party of the 8th Dragoons. The manoeuvre failed. Gillespie impatiently renewed the attack with several companies of the 53rd Foot – without waiting for the other two columns. During his desperate gamble some units appeared to panic. Gillespie, leading from the front, a sword in one hand and a pistol in the other, attempted to rally his men just 30 metres from the fort's gate. A Gurkha sharpshooter aimed at the distinctive figure, and shot him through the heart. As his body was being taken back down to Meerut, the attack collapsed.

Another attempt on 27 November met with similar failure when troops refused to storm a wide breach in the stockade. The men had been told to unload their muskets and charge with the bayonet only; they were understandably reluctant to advance, given the fearsome reputation of the Gurkhas and their *kukris* in hand-to-hand combat. The two assaults cost the British 740 casualties. The British were unused to meeting powerful opposition in such strong positions. The defeats taught them caution and the column besieging Kalunga, now commanded by Colonel Sebright Mawby, turned to their cannon and an intense bombardment was opened up. After three days the Gurkha commander Balbahadur, known to the British as Bulbudder Singh, slipped away unnoticed with the survivors of his garrison, leaving behind over 500 dead and wounded, mainly dead, piled high. Mawby said that the sight 'presented so much misery that the most obdurate heart must have bled'.

A dispatch to Calcutta said: 'The garrison is now known to have suffered most severely from the fire of the British artillery, and particularly from the shells thrown by the mortars. The place was found crowded with dead and wounded, whom the enemy was unable to carry off in his precipitous flight . . . The arduous and difficult nature of the service, the fatigues and the privations the troops had for some time undergone, and the strength of the enemy's position, demanded exemplary exertions of activity, zeal and personal bravery from the European officers . . .' The Gurkhas found alive in the rubble of Kalunga included several small children whose parents had died in the bombardment. The British took care of them and the adult wounded. Not all the Gurkhas appreciated such humanity. Mawby reported:

> To show the determined conduct of these people, the orderly Jemada to Bulbudder Sing, in attempting to escape with his Chief, was wounded and taken prisoner – finding that the wound would not put him to death, he abused

Bulbudder Singh, commander of the Gurkha defences at Kalunga. (Gurkha Museum)

both Officers and Men in the grossest terms in hopes that they would by that means shoot him – but finding that this would have no effect on their feelings – he beat his head against the Stones in the hope of putting an end to his existence – which all failing, he requested fire to warm himself, and when left by the Sepoys, he took an opportunity of throwing the whole of it on his breast – which was no sooner discovered than it was removed – he has, however, since died.

The British admired such single-mindedness. The courage of the Gurkha defenders, most of whom now lay dead, was also recognised. James Fraser, the brother of Gillespie's political agent, wrote:

The determined resolution of the small party which held this small post for more than a month, against so comparatively large a force, must surely wring admiration from every voice, especially when the horrors of the latter portion of this time are considered: the dismal spectacle of their slaughtered comrades, the sufferings of their women and children thus immured with themselves, and the hopelessness of relief, which destroyed any other motive for the obstinate defence they made, than that resulting from a high sense of duty, supported by unsubdued courage. This, a generous spirit of courtesy towards their enemy, certainly marked the character of the garrison at Kalunga, during the period of its siege.

Whatever the nature of the Ghoorkhas may have been found in other quarters, there was here no cruelty to wounded or to prisoners; no poisoned arrows were used; no wells or waters were poisoned; no rancorous spirit of revenge seemed to animate them.

The British raised a small obelisk outside the fort to honour their enemy. Its inscription read: 'They fought in their conflict like men and, in the intervals of actual conflict, showed a liberal courtesy.'

A month later another attack on a fort at Jaithak failed. British troops were halted at the first stockade, and they turned and ran as the Gurkhas counter-attacked, their *kukris* glistening. Sepoys coming up as reserves panicked when they saw the European troops in retreat and they did not stop running until they reached their base at Nahan. Gillespie's original force had by now been cut by a third and further offensive operations were halted.

The lesson of caution had perhaps been too well taken by the commanders of the two central columns. Major-General John Sullivan Wood's 4,000-strong force operating from Gorakhpur made slow progress owing to sickness and a lack of hill-porters. His intelligence and scout units were also poor and on one occasion he and his staff officers blundered to within 50 metres of an enemy stockade without realising it. After a January attack on a stockade at Jeetgarh failed, Wood wrote in dispatches about his initial success in taking a hill on the right of the redoubt: 'This party was led by a brave and cool officer, Captain Croker, who drove the enemy before them up the hill, killing a chief Sooraj Tappah; still the fire from the enemy, concealed by the trees, was kept up with great obstinacy, and the hill which rose immediately behind the work, was filled with troops, rendering the post, if it had been carried, wholly untenable; I therefore determined to stop the fruitless waste of lives, by sounding retreat.' Wood decided his force was not strong enough to advance deeper into Nepal's hill country. He reported: 'Some confusion occurred in consequence of the majority of the bearers having thrown down their loads, but the soldiers, both European and native, brought away most of the boxes of ammunition.' Wood, who appears to have exaggerated the numbers of Gurkhas facing him, also believed exaggerated reports of a Gurkha army poised to sweep down on to the plains and ordered his men on to the defensive. Or rather, as one contemporary noted, 'he did nothing'.

Meanwhile the largest column of 8,000 men under Major-General Bonnett Marley failed in its main thrust against Khatmandu. Marley crossed the Nepal border in December but, in defiance of his orders, halted the column to await further supplies. He established two outposts many miles from the main body. Unsurprisingly the Gurkhas surrounded and captured both, inflicting heavy casualties. The British lost 125 killed, 73 missing and 187 wounded. Marley tried to dodge the blame. Writing to his superiors he said that the two posts had only been taken 'after a considerable but ineffectual resistance on the part of our troops against the overwhelming numbers and superior means opposed to them'.

Dispatches from junior officers under Marley's command told their own dispiriting story. Lieutenant E. Strettell reported:

It is with the deepest regret that I have to acquaint you with the information that the left wing, 2nd battalion, 22nd regiment native infantry, was this morning attacked and compelled to retire. The enemy advanced about five-o'clock and immediately opened a very severe and well-directed fire from about twenty pieces of cannon. Captain Blackney and all the officers of the wing did their utmost endeavours to bring on our sepoys to the charge, which failed in every attempt, from the very destructive fire which opposed them.

Blackney and Lieutenant Duncan were killed.

On the fall of these two gallant officers, the sepoys became quite dispirited, and began to retire with some confusion, upon which the enemy advanced upon and destroyed our tents by fire. The village of Summunpore, in which was the commissariat, was burnt at the commencement of the action by the enemy. Finding that the detachment had suffered most severely, added to the great numbers and strength of the enemy, it was judged most prudent to retire; and as the enemy had taken possession of the road to Barra Ghurrie, we directed our course to this place. I am unable to state the exact loss of the detachment, as stragglers are coming in every moment.

Major J. Greenstreet wrote:

I am sorry to acquaint you that the post of Persa Ghurrie was this morning attacked by an overwhelming force of Goorkhas, who, I regret to say, carried their point after an hour's hard fighting which ended in the repulse of our troops there, the loss of the gun, and every kind of baggage. At break of day, when I was about to march for that post, we heard a heavy firing in that direction when I pushed on with all speed; but within three miles of the place I met a vast number of wounded, and immediately afterwards some officers, who informed me that any attempt by me to recover the fortune of the day must be unavailing . . .

Sepoys in the main camp now began to desert although reinforcements swelled Marley's force to 12,000. But the general was unnerved by wild estimates of the enemy strength. He convinced himself that he was facing some 18,000 of the best Gurkha fighters – in fact there were 8,000 at most, many of them poorly armed militia. Marley retreated to the border and sat there for a month, also doing nothing. On 10 February he appears to have broken down emotionally or mentally. Before dawn he rode out of camp without handing over command to anyone. It was a rare case of a general deserting his own army.

'Gurkha Chiefs and Soldiers', by James B. Fraser. (British Library)

Three months of campaigning in some of the world's toughest territories had left three British columns more or less where they had started. Only Ochterlony's own column in the easier countryside to the west was making slow but steady progress, aided by local tribes who had little love for the Nepalese regime. He crossed the plains from Ludiana, entered the hill country and on 1 November reached the fort of Nalagur which surrendered after thirty hours of continuous bombardment.

His limited successes, however, could not disguise the overall failure. The initial defeat at Kalunga, the death of a renowned general and hero, and the further humiliations inflicted on the Empire by mountain tribesmen caused a scandal at home. The official history of the Bengal Army said that the campaign contained 'a greater number of disastrous failures and of ill-arranged and worse-carried-out enterprises, due generally to an entire want of appreciation of the necessities of hill warfare than had ever before, or ever since, befallen the arms of the British in India'. Hastings admitted that the Gurkhas had 'intimidated our troops and our generals'. British defeats sent out the wrong message to other tribal nations bordering the Raj and the would-be rebels within them. The Sikhs of the Punjab, the Afghans and the Maratha chiefs all posed a real threat. Some alarmists forecast that Britain would lose the entire sub-continent. Lord Metcalfe, the Resident at Delhi, wrote: 'Our power in India rests upon our military superiority. It has no foundation in the affections of our subjects. It cannot derive support from the good will or the good faith of our neighbours.' He said that before the war the power of the Gurkhas was ridiculed, their forts described as contemptible, their weapons as useless. 'Yet we find that with these useless weapons in their contemptible forts they can deal out death among their assailants, and stand to their defences.' He went on:

We have met with an enemy who shows decidedly greater bravery and greater steadiness than our troops possess; and it is impossible to say what may be the end of such a reverse of the order of things. In some instances our troops, European and Native, have been repulsed by inferior numbers with sticks and stones. In others our troops have been charged by the enemy sword in hand, and driven for miles like a flock of sheep. In this war, dreadful to say, we have had numbers on our side, and skill and bravery on the side of our enemy.

Hastings, who largely agreed with Metcalfe's analysis, pledged to throw everything he could at the Gurkhas, even if that meant leaving British India's other borders dangerously exposed and their forces under-strength. By the end of January 1815 there were almost 40,000 troops facing no more than 12,000 Gurkha regular soldiers and an unknown number of militia.

★   ★   ★

As spring approached General Ochterlony provided a much-needed boost to British morale. Sir David, fifty-six and Boston-born, was the son of a gentleman who had settled in America. His service stretched back to 1777 when he had enlisted as a cadet in the Bengal army of the Company. He fought against Haider Ali, the French and the Marathas. In 1804 he commanded the successful defence of Delhi, despite weak ramparts and a shortage of ammunition. One plaudit said: 'No action of the war . . . deserves greater commendation than this brave and skilful defence of an almost untenable position.' He was known to his sepoy troops as 'Lonely-ackty'.

Ochterlony was determined not to suffer a repeat of the Kalunga disaster. He made it a rule never to directly assault Gurkha stockades, choosing instead, whenever possible, to blow them to smithereens with artillery. This involved building rough roads and bridges across the broken terrain and jagged ravines. Hundreds of coolies and porters were employed. Ochterlony wrote: 'Manual labour, strength and perseverance are our main dependencies in these Alpine regions.' He shared with his men the hardships of the campaign.

By the end of March Ochterlony, in his slow and steady fashion, had reduced and occupied all the Gurkhas forts along the route of his advance to Bilaspur. He then began a long and arduous chase of the Gurkha general Umur Sing. A fine tactician, Sing was operating a long way from his real homeland, and some of the hill tribes were hostile to his army. His main strength lay in the ability of his soldiers, fighting in a homeland of which they knew every inch, to move swiftly and with apparent ease. It was a quality envied by the British, laden as they were with heavy baggage. One officer wrote: 'These highland soldiers, who despatch their meal in half an hour, laugh at the rigour of the sepoys who cannot be in marching trim again in less than three hours.'

Ochterlony slowly advanced against a strongly fortified position near Simla, 5,000 feet up in the Himalayas, during the worst of the winter. His engineers blasted rocks and opened roads for his two 18-pounders which were hauled up by men and elephants. On 14 April he attacked Umur Singh at night and carried two

Major-General Sir David Ochterlony,
by A.W. Devis. (National Galleries of
Scotland)

strongpoints. The Gurkhas retreated to the Maloun Heights, a string of fortified hilltops, with drops of 2,000 feet on two sides. Although his position was strong, Umur Sing was effectively bottled up.

Ryla Peak was the first to fall, with little opposition. The second peak, Deothul, proved a tougher nut to crack. It was taken on 15 April only after a costly action. The British set about strengthening the captured position with further earthworks. A determined Gurkha attack of 2,000 men under Bhagtee Thapa came within a whisker of driving them out again, breaking through the British defences at several points. The Gurkhas recognised, from bitter experience, the power of the British artillery and concentrated their fire on the gun positions. After several brutally effective volleys only one artillery officer and three men were left standing. One soldier recalled: 'The Gurkhas came on with furious intrepidity, so much so that several were bayoneted or cut to pieces within our works. Umur Sing stood all the while just within musket [sic] range, with the Goorkha Colours planted beside him; while Bhagtee was everywhere inciting the men to further efforts.' The position was saved by reinforcements from Ryla Peak. The British suffered 213 casualties, the Gurkhas more than twice that. Each side's respect for the courage and fighting ability of the other increased enormously.

Meanwhile Hastings ordered two columns of irregular troops under Colonel Gardner and Captain Hearsay to march on Kumaon, a poorly organised province in the centre of the Nepalese front. The local tribes regarded the British as saviours rather than invaders and were ready to help overturn Gurkha rule. Hearsay blundered by attacking a superior force, but Gardner scored a signal success. He outmanoeuvred the Gurkhas and soon penetrated deep into their territory, threatening the province capital, Almora. He was reinforced by 2,000 regular native troops with some cannon under Colonel Jasper Nicolls, who promptly took command. After several skirmishing successes his force prepared to take the town. The Gurkha garrison was by now disheartened and, after some initial fighting, hauled up a flag of truce on 28 April. They agreed to British terms to evacuate both Almora and the entire province, and to withdraw beyond the Kali river.

The loss of Kumaon had a profound effect on Umur Sing's men, corralled along the Maloun Heights. As the news filtered through they began to desert in large numbers, some of them defecting to the British. By 10 May just 200 men were left to make a last stand in the fort of Maloun. Initially Umur Sing rebuked all those, mainly members of the royal house, who talked of appeasement. But Ochterlony's tactics of steady attrition impressed him greatly and said that the British general was the only opponent who had robbed him of the chance to give battle at the time and place of his choosing. Umur Sing was left with no choice but surrender. The British acknowledged a gallant foe and on 15 May he was allowed to march out unharmed, with his personal possessions and all the honours of war, provided he withdrew to the east of the Kali river. The British fired a royal salute at the army's principal stations. The *Annual Register* noted: 'It seems evident that the contest has been with a bold and adventurous foe, with whom the establishment of a lasting pacification is perhaps more to be desired than expected.' As a reward for his victory Ochterlony was created a baronet, and the East India Company granted him a pension of £1,000 per annum from the date of the Gurkha capitulation. The British now controlled all the mountainous country between the Kali and Sutlej rivers. Ochterlony formed the Gurkha deserters into battalions of the Company's regular army.

The proud Gurkha leaders were forced to sue for peace and an armistice was agreed. Hastings set tough terms. All the conquered territory west of the Kali should be ceded permanently to the British, along with much of the Terai region – the swampy jungle in the foothills of the Himalayas. A British Resident must also be allowed to dwell in Khatmandu. Negotiations dragged on for several months. The Gurkhas were realists and understood that the British conquests had been won fair and square. In their turn the British understood that the Gurkhas had not been subjugated, and some concessions were made on the extent of ceded territory. The main obstacle was the question of a British Resident but in November even this was agreed and a treaty was signed on 29 November and ratified by the supreme government at Calcutta on 19 December 1815.

To the astonishment of the British, the Nepal durbar refused to accept the treaty. The war was back on.

★   ★   ★

During the protracted negotiations Ochterlony was given charge of the Eastern Command. When the war resumed he was ready with an army of 20,000 men to advance on Khatmandu. He split his force into four columns. One on the right was directed towards Hariharpur, another on the left towards Ramnagar, while the two in the centre, which Ochterlony commanded personally, was to strike at the Nepalese capital. All four columns were to act cohesively and in support of each other. It seemed the British had learned some lessons from the previous campaign – as had the Gurkhas. During the lull the Gurkha commanders had fortified virtually the entire length of the Dun hills to prevent another invasion from the south.

Ochterlony began his advance at the beginning of February 1816. On the 10th he and his main force reached the entrance of the Chuviaghati Pass, having crossed the formidable Sal forest without losing a man. The enemy were entrenched behind three lines of defences, which Ochterlong decided were too strong for a frontal assault; instead he determined to turn its flank. Under cover of darkness he stripped one brigade of all their usual baggage, and during the night of the 14th led them in single file up an unguarded path. A correspondent wrote: 'They moved laboriously through deep and rocky defiles, across sombre and tangled forests, and by rugged and precipitous ascents, until the next day he reached and occupied a position in rear of the enemy's defences.' Lieutenant John Shipp of the Royal Irish Fusiliers recalled: 'Our gallant general walked every yard of this critical approach with his men, encouraging them as he went, and that sort of thing works wonders.' The Gurkhas were taken wholly by surprise by the sudden appearance of the British to their rear, complete with two elephants and guns. Uncharacteristically they panicked and hurriedly evacuated their positions, fleeing northwards without firing a shot. Ochterlony and his brigade spent four miserable days huddled on the bleak and exposed mountainside waiting for their tents and baggage trains to catch up.

The war now became a question of pursuing and wearing down the remnants of the Gurkha army. With desperation came cruelty. Lieutenant Shipp described the treatment of a prisoner taken by the Gurkhas as a spy:

> This poor creature was seized and literally cut to pieces; and it was supposed by the medical people, that he must have died a death of extreme agony, for the ground under him was dug up with his struggling under the torture which had been inflicted on him. His arms had been cut off, about halfway up from the elbow to the shoulder, after which it appeared that two deep incisions had been cut in his body just above the hips, into which the two arms had been thrust. His features were distorted in a most frightful manner . . .

The two brigades of Ochterlony's main column formed a junction on the banks of the Rapti Rover and built a strongly stockaded depot. They caught up with the enemy at Magwampur, roughly 20 miles from Khatmandu, and seized a small village to the right of the Gurkha positions. A ferocious counter-attack by 2,000 Gurkhas before the village could be fully occupied came close to giving Ochterlony his first defeat. Repeated attacks on the British positions were beaten off but the Gurkha onslaught was only crushed by a spirited charge from the 2nd Battalion of the 8th Native Infantry. Lieutenant Shipp found himself in desperate single combat with the Gurkha commander Kishnabahadur Rana, and killed him with a sabre cut to the neck, almost severing his head. Shipp recognised a noble enemy and wrote in his memoirs:

> They maintained their ground and fought manfully. I hate a runaway foe; you have no credit for beating them. Those we were dealing with were no flinchers; on the contrary, I never saw more bravery or steadiness exhibited in my life. Run they would not, and of death they seemed to have no fear, though their comrades were falling thick about them, for we were so near that every shot told . . .

The British six-pounders pulverised the Gurkhas. 'The havoc was dreadful, for they still scorned to fly,' Shipp continued. Eventually there was little left but carnage on the field.

> As long as it was light we could plainly see the last struggles of the dying. Some poor fellows could be seen raising their knees up to their chins, and then flinging them down again with all their might. Some attempted to rise, but failed in the attempt. One poor fellow I saw got on his legs, put his hand to his bleeding head, then fell, and rolled down the hill, to rise no more. This was the scene that the evening now closed upon. Believe me when I assure you that these results of war were no sights of exultation or triumph to the soldiers who witnessed them. Willingly would we one and all have extended the hand of aid to them, and dressed their gaping wounds.

The battle could not have been more decisive. The Gurkhas lost up to 800 men and all their heavy guns. Ochterlony's force lost 45 killed and 175 wounded. One report noted that the British, as on former occasions, had to contend with 'antagonists defective neither in courage nor discipline'. Ochterlony prepared to attack Magwampur itself. The following day he was joined by the left brigade which had advanced by Ramnagar with little determined opposition.

The right brigade, meantime, had been delayed by rough ground in its advance upon Hariharpur. But on 1 March the enemy positions there were successfully turned and a Gurkha attack repulsed with great loss of life. Officers once again recorded that the Gurkhas had behaved with 'desperate bravery'. Hariharpur was converted into a depot. The British were now within striking distance of Khatmandu itself. The column was about to march to join Ochterlony when envoys arrived from Khatmandu. The durbar had realised that further resistance was futile and ratified the peace treaty previously rejected. The war was over.

★   ★   ★

The Treaty of Saguili reimposed Hastings' conditions, stripped Nepal of the Terai and imposed a British Resident in Khatmandu. It was honoured by both sides. Ochterlony's biographer wrote: 'The Gurkhas, who were not only the most valiant but the most humane foes the British had encountered in India, proved also to be the most faithful to their engagement.'

Ochterlony was rewarded with a GCB, a parliamentary vote of thanks for his 'skill, valour and perseverance', and a piece of plate from the officers who had served under him. During the following year he fought successfully, and often without serious bloodshed, to suppress the Pindari tribes who had been looting and despoiling British territory. His diplomatic skills were rated as highly as his generalship and by 1822 he effectively supervised the affairs of Central India. But in 1824 he became embroiled in a succession crisis when the Raja of Jaipur died and his son, heir to the throne, was imprisoned by his nephew. Ochterlony, acting on his own responsibility, issued a proclamation urging the Jats to rally around their rightful ruler and ordered 16,000 men into the field to support the rights of the young Raja. His order was countermanded by the Governor-General, Lord Amhurst, who feared a costly campaign while the British were also fighting a war with Burma. Ochterlony resigned. He was deeply hurt, feeling that his honour was tarnished. He told friends that after nearly fifty years of active and conscientious service he felt his actions should have merited confidence from his senior. He retired to Delhi where he suffered 'agonies of the mind'. He died there just a few months later. Sixty-eight guns were fired in his honour, corresponding to his age. Shortly afterwards Ochterlony was vindicated. It later took an army of 20,000 men several months to restore the ruler of Jaipur. Senior officers reckoned that if Ochterlony's original plan had been supported it would have taken just a fortnight – and a fraction of the eventual cost.

Lord Hastings, having initiated and won the Third Mahratta War, of which the actions against the Pindari were a part, now settled down to his duties of civil administration. Despite numerous squabbles with the board of the East India Company, he supported the education of the native population, the freedom of the Press and the removal of oppressive laws. His feud with the directors continued, however, and they finally won after he blundered over a land deal. Charges of corrupt transactions, for which the evidence was profoundly suspect, were considered. Embittered at his treatment, Hastings resigned in 1821 and treated as arrant hypocrisy a vote of thanks from the Company for his zeal and ability. He was appointed Governor of Malta. There his health, already weakened both physically and mentally by service in India, began to fail and he was further injured in a fall from a horse. He died on board HMS *Revenge* in 1826, aged seventy-one.

Astonishingly, no disciplinary action was taken against Major-General Marley, the man who had deserted his own troops when he believed he was facing superior numbers. He was not even dismissed from the service but continued to hold further commands, eventually reaching the rank of full general. He died in 1842.

Sir Penderel Moon wrote: 'An unnecessary war was followed by a lasting peace. The British and the Gurkhas never fought again. Nepal remained an independent kingdom, an ally but not a vassal of the British.' For the next forty years relations between the British administration of India and Nepal amounted to frosty friendship, diplomatic indifference and occasional tensions. Those tensions were eased when the British handed back parts of the Terai to Nepal. The Khatmandu court was too busy with internal intrigue to consider further conquests to the south. Bheeim Sein Thappa, who ruled in the name of the young king, himself fell victim to lethal plotting. Chaos followed, reaching its bloody peak in the 1846 massacre of the Kot, or royal court of assembly, in which many of the most noble families were slain. Bheeim Sein's grandson, a young soldier called Jung Bahadur, seized power, became prime minister and banished the royal family. He visited England in 1850 and became a firm friend of the British.

Until Bahadur, the rulers of Nepal during this period of turmoil may have stayed aloof from the Raj, but not so the common man and soldier. The seeds of lasting friendships between fighting peoples had been sown during the bloody days of war when both sides forged a deep respect for the other. (Ochterlony privately told Lord Hastings that the Company's sepoys 'could never be brought to resist the shock of these energetic mountaineers on their own grounds'.) Part of the credit for their mutual respect must go Lieutenant Frederick Young, the thirty-year-old officer of the 13th Native Infantry who had held Gillespie as he died at Kalunga. After that siege Young was leading a party of native irregulars in the hills when they were surrounded by Gurkhas. The sepoys fled, leaving the British officers to face the enemy. The Gurkhas were amazed that the Britons did not also run and laughingly asked why they had not done so. Young replied: 'I have not come so far in order to run away. I came to stay.' According to contemporary reports, maybe romanticised, a Gurkha commander told him: 'We could serve under men like you'. Young was allowed to live and was held as an honoured prisoner. He was treated well and made friends with his captors, who taught him their language.

Young never forgot their honourable conduct or their fighting skills. During the 1815 armistice he proposed that a corps of Gurkhas should be raised to serve in John Company's army. Permission was granted and men flocked to the British colours from the surrounding hills. Some were paroled prisoners, others deserters, but most had been valiant opponents who had been astonished by the perseverance and technology of the British forces. Young said: 'I went there one man and came out three thousand.' The Khatmandu government was not happy about the defection of some of their best soldiers but there was little they could do. As the peace treaty clearly stated: 'All the troops in the service of Nepal, with the exception of those granted to the personal honour of Kagjees Ummersing and Rangor Sing, will be at liberty to enter into the services of the British Government if agreeable to themselves and the British Government choose to accept their services.'

Four local battalions of Gurkhas were raised: the 1st and 2nd Basiri, the Sirmoor and the Kumaon. The British were impressed from the start with the enthusiasm with which they trained. Within six months of its formation, Young, who commanded the Sirmoor battalion for twenty-eight years, was able to report it ready for battle. His battalion was the first to see service, in the 1817 Mahratta War. They proved their worth at the battle of Sambhar and Ochterlony expressed his satisfaction by granting the Gurkhas the honour of escorting to Delhi the 300 enemy guns captured during the campaign.

In 1824 Young led 200 of his troops against Goojar rebels and decisively beat a force four times their number at Koonja. The surviving rebels retreated into a fort which the Gurkhas took by using a felled tree as a battering ram. Over 150 rebels died in ferocious hand-to-hand fighting within the mud walls. Since that day Gurkha battalions have worn a ram's head on their regimental badges. Many more battle honours followed. After the 1825 siege of Bhurtpore the Gurkhas were praised by officers of the East Lancashire Regiment. A Gurkha soldier almost returned the compliment: 'The English are as brave as lions; they are splendid sepoys, and are very nearly equal to us.'

Over the years the original battalions were reformed into the Gurkha Rifles. More heroic service was performed in the Burma wars, against the usurper Durjan Sal and in the brutal battles with the Sikhs in the Punjab. After the bloodbath at Sobraon, which shattered Sikh power, the British commander, General Sir Hugh Gough, wrote: 'I must pause in this narrative especially to notice the determined hardihood and bravery with which our two battalions of Ghoorkas, Sirmoor and Nusserree, met the Sikhs wherever they were opposed to them. Soldiers of small stature but indomitable spirit, they vied in ardent courage in the charge with the Grenadiers of our own nation and, armed with the short weapon of their mountains, were a terror to the Sikhs throughout this great action.' Jung Bahadar sent his Gurkha armies to help the British during the Indian Mutiny. During that tragic conflict the mutineers' leader Bahadur Shah offered 10 rupees for the head of every Gurkha brought to him. The Sirmoor Battalion distinguished itself during the final assault on Delhi. On the North West Frontier Gurkhas were engaged for over fifty years in almost constant campaigning to protect the Raj from border encroachments and warring tribes. In the battle of Kandahar in 1880 the Gurkhas and the 92nd Gordon Highlanders conducted a classic bayonet charge which cemented their relationship as partners in the brigade. The Scots and Nepalese stormed a hilltop and a Gurkha stuffed his cap into one of two captured guns, signifying it was their prize. During the 1891 Manipur campaign 200 Gurkhas, whose British officers had been killed by treachery, held out in the British Residency until their ammunition ran out. Then they fixed bayonets and drew their *kukris* for a final charge, which few survived. In 1897 Gurkhas again charged alongside the Gordon Highlanders up the Dargai Heights during the Tirah campaign.

Gurkha troops continued to serve as an integral part of the Indian Army until Indian Independence in 1947. Twenty-four years earlier Britain had acknowledged Nepal's complete independence. During the First World War Gurkhas fought in Flanders, Mesopotamia and Palestine. A sizeable detachment joined the Arabs fighting the Turks under Lawrence of Arabia. At Loos the 2nd Battalion suffered so many casualties that it ceased to exist as a fighting force; General Sir James Willcocks said that the battalion had 'found its Valhalla'. At Gallipoli the 6th Gurkhas captured a key bluff, topped by a nest of machine-guns, which had previously repulsed the Royal Marines and the Royal Dublin Fusiliers.

Gurkha service during the Second World War was second to none. They were found in the thick of the fighting at Tobruk, El Alamein, Wadi Akarit, Monte Cassino and in Greece. They fought the Japanese in Malaya and Burma. Field Marshal the Lord Hardinge wrote: 'I have had experience of their skill and prowess, their courage and endurance on many a different battlefield, and I know for a fact

A Gurkha sepoy, 1816.

that they are the finest comrades in arms – happy warriors indeed.' Field-Marshal Sir William Slim said: 'Nothing looks so uniform as a Gurkha battalion, nothing looks more workmanlike and few things look so formidable.' On another occasion Slim referred to the regiment's 'magnificent reputation' for discipline and battle-worthiness. In total, the Gurkhas won twenty-six VCs, an astonishing total given their small numbers.

After Partition, some Gurkha forces were transferred to the new Indian Army and served with the United Nations in the Congo and other hotspots. Others chose to stay with the British Army as licensed mercenaries. Brigadier A.E.C. Bredin wrote:

> The Gurkha is, of course, an enthusiastic soldier, second to none in smartness and turnout, both in uniform and in mufti. For generations he has been a soldier and tends to look down on non-military people or individuals. His bravery in action has won him great renown and much esteem where the British Army has fought for the past one hundred and forty years. Though often a yeoman of some substance, he joins the Army because of tradition and for the standing it gives him.

Their meagre pay, less than a third of that of their British compatriots, fed and clothed their families in the high mountains.

Bredin, who commanded the 6th Gurkha Rifles in Malaya, wrote:

Virtually the highest pre-war standards exist in the Brigade of Gurkhas and it is a joy as well as an honour to command, or to serve with, such men; men who love being soldiers, are intensely proud of their military record and rightly regard soldiering as the most honourable and manly profession. Like their predecessors in the old British Indian Army, they are capable of fighting anywhere in the world and against any enemies.

The presence of Gurkhas in the Falkland Islands in 1982 wrecked Argentinian morale – even though they never took their *kukris* from their scabbards.

Agansing Rai's citation in 1944 concluded that 'his magnificent display of initiative, outstanding bravery and gallant leadership so inspired the rest of the company that, in spite of heavy casualties, the result of this important action was never in doubt'. These words could easily have applied to many of his comrades over the previous century.

CHAPTER TWO

The Defeat of the Borneo Pirates, 1840–9

'The miserable creatures were crushed under the paddle . . .'

A young British officer forced himself to look at the handiwork of Borneo's notorious pirates. Women captives had been slain and their bodies, abused in life, were horribly mutilated in death. Heads festooned hundreds of poles. The long-houses were stuffed with booty from across the globe.

The defeat of such a scourge was a factor in making the British adventurer Sir James Brooke the White Rajah of Sarawak. But the slaughter his campaigns entailed led to heated debates in Westminster. It was alleged that once again British military might was being used against primitive foes who were chopped up by canister shell and the paddles of the new war steamers. The question was: who were the real pirates?

★   ★   ★

Piracy was a way of life in the crowded, narrow straits of Malaysia and among the coastal tribes of Borneo. Small-scale barter in sixth-century Borneo had grown into large-scale traffic with both China and Siam by the thirteenth century. Later the South China Sea was to act as a funnel for the rich trading fleets that sailed between East and West. Peaceful and weak tribes along the coastline were easy targets for more warlike neighbours. All provided rich pickings and as powerful princedoms grew wealthy on plunder it became an almost legitimate arm of business. The island of Borneo traded in gold, diamonds, spices, pearls and rattan.

The early Hindu-Javanese people were overrun by the Malays from Singapore, and in the fifteenth century the Muslim states seized power. Sarawak, on the north coast of Borneo, became the southern province of the sultanate of Brunei. Magellan's fleet visited Brunei, whose city contained 25,000 houses. 'The King was a Mahomedan of great power,' wrote an observer, 'keeping a magnificent court, and was always attended by a numerous guard. He has ten secretaries of state, who write everything concerning his affairs on the bark of trees.' The Spanish and other early visitors from Europe agreed that the native Dyak people were peaceable and generous, while the Malay overlords were treacherous and 'piratical'.

The Portuguese tried to move in, and, according to many contemporaries, their actions created conditions for a more organised form of piracy. They disrupted the

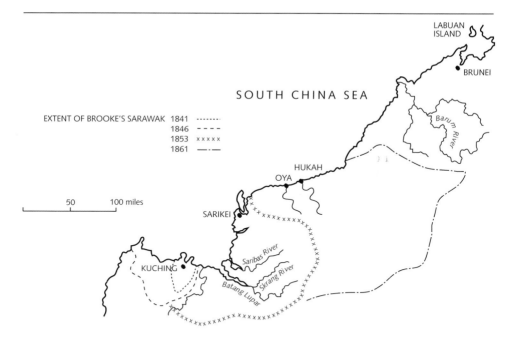

The expansion of Sarawak under Sir James Brooke.

old trade routes, created their own colonies and discouraged Chinese junks from visiting the archipelago. The Dutch and the British did much the same in Indonesia and Malacca, distorting local economies and throttling established trade. By the start of the nineteenth century the islands from the South China Sea to Australia had been cut off from trade with China for a century. As a result North Borneo saw its riches disappear and its people were forced to put piracy on a much more organised footing. The historian Owen Rutter wrote:

> The Malay potentates were driven to replenish their depleted coffers; their people sought new outlets for their frustrated energies. They were accustomed to the sea, and under the leadership of their princes they turned their ways to piracy and plunder. In course of time this guerrilla warfare by sea developed for many into a habitual mode of life, more lucrative and certainly more exciting than their former ways of peace. Piracy became looked upon as an honourable occupation . . .

The Malay and Dyak people, pirates or peaceful fishermen and traders, were skilled in river and coastal warfare. They excelled in building boats for speed and ambush. Most impressive were their *prahus* – low-slung vessels up to 70 feet long. They ranged from 'spy-*prahus*', light and sleek with a handful of paddlers and used for reconnaissance and testing defences, to war-*prahus* heavily armed with cannon and capable of carrying hundreds of fighting men. Pirate fleets could number several hundred vessels and voyages could last up to three years.

The main centres of piracy were Brunei and Sulu, a Philippine island east of Borneo with a renowned slave-market. The sultans of both either condoned piracy or turned a blind eye to it in return for their share of the loot. The chief pirate tribes were the Balagnini, the Maluku, the Sea Dyaks of the Seribas and, most feared of all, the Lanun or Illanun, known as 'the pirates of the lagoons'. They spent much of their time attacking and pillaging one another's possessions, but the mayhem also, inevitably, touched other nations. In 1838 the East India Company steamer *Diana* captured a fleet of six pirate *prahus* from Sulu after they attacked a Chinese junk and the British sloop *Wolf*. The pirates numbered 360 men, including some galley slaves wearing collars around their necks.

By then Sarawak, a country measuring about 60 by 50 miles, had for several years been embroiled in an ineffectual rebellion against the Sultan of Brunei, the nominal head of almost the entire island of Borneo. The main grievance was a system of forced trade imposed by the Sultan, Omar Ali Suffedin, on the Dyak tribesmen, who had to pay fixed and exorbitant prices for goods sold to them by their Malay overlords. The governor, a royal kinsman called Pangeran Makota, exacerbated the problem by sweating his labourers, forcing men into the mines and greedily snatching most of the profits. Unlike those in other provinces, the Sarawak tribes were forced to pay the fixed tariffs all year round. When the wretched Dyaks and the poorer classes of Malays fell into debt they were seized as slaves. Any tribes who objected were threatened with attacks from the sea pirates of Seribas and Sakarang who were in the Sultan's pay. The Sultan sent his uncle, Rajah Muda Hassim, to suppress the long-drawn-out revolt and restore order. Muda Hassim was reckoned by foreign traders to be generous and humane and, more importantly, pro-British. But he was no great general and the revolt dragged on in a desultory way. Into this volatile, if relatively bloodless, civil war sailed James Brooke, a young man who was soon to prove himself one of the greatest adventurers of the Victorian age.

★   ★   ★

The son of Thomas Brooke, a judge in the East India Company's Bengal Civil Service, James was born in 1803 in Benares and spent the first twelve years of his life in India, enjoying all the privileges and pampering attendant on the youngest son of a powerful administrator. He was expected to become a Company officer, and was sent to England to get a proper education at Norwich grammar school. He was popular, industrious and brave, and saved a fellow pupil from drowning in the River Wensum. After two years his best friend ran away to sea as a midshipman. The young James decided on a similar adventure but was caught. The school would not have him back so he was privately tutored until he returned to Bengal in 1819 and was commissioned as an ensign in the 6th Native Infantry, where he established a fine reputation for pig-sticking and big-game shooting.

He saw his first action during the First Burma War in January 1825, where he drilled a volunteer body of native cavalry. He was mentioned in dispatches for leading

James Brooke as a young man, by
Grant. (National Portrait Gallery)

a daring and successful frontal charge on enemy positions. A few days later his
courageous, if foolhardy, tactics saw him shot during the battle of Rangpur in Assam
and left for dead on the field. He was later rescued, barely alive, and was sent to
Calcutta where surgeons operated and declared he must have a long convalescence in
England. He was awarded a wound pension of £70 a year for life. Officially Brooke
was shot in the lung but rumours persisted during and after his life that he had in fact
suffered a musket ball in the genitals. According to the evidence of a serving girl in
the household where Brooke was laid up and where, a year later, the wound broke
out again: 'The slug, which had been allowed to remain in the wound, was now
extracted from his back near the spine, and afterwards kept by his mother as a relic,
under a glass case.' On the other hand, Brooke carried out a long, passionate but
platonic love affair with Angela Georgina Burdett-Coutts, one of the richest society
beauties of the day. There is a widespread belief that she proposed to him but he
politely rejected the offer 'for the best of reasons'. Indeed, he never married.

After four years he set sail back to India. His ship was delayed by storms and
numerous stop-overs and Brooke, fearing that he would not reach Bengal within the
Company's maximum five-year leave of absence, resigned his commission. He
wrote: 'I toss my cap into the air, my commission into the sea, and bid farewell to
John Company and all his evil ways. I am like a horse who has got a heavy clog off
his neck.' On the voyage back to England he visited the Straits settlements of
Penang, Malacca and Singapore, China and Sumatra. His taste for the East was well

aroused by the time he returned to his family in Bath. He conceived a vague plan to ply a schooner around the islands of the South China Sea, seeking trade, profit and, above all, adventure.

He remained at home until 1834 when, aided by his doting mother, he persuaded his ailing father to buy him the brig *Findlay* and fit out a trading expedition to the Indian archipelago. The voyage was a financial disaster, due at least in part to clashes with the ship's captain, and Brooke soon discovered that he was a commercial incompetent. He was not deterred, however. The following year Brooke's father died and he spent much of his £30,000 inheritance on buying and fitting out a 142-ton schooner, the *Royalist*. Brooke wrote in the prospectus that she was entitled to carry the white ensign, sailed fast, was armed with six 6-pounders and a number of swivel guns. Already aged thirty-three, Brooke knew he could not squander his life on chasing adventures which neither turned a profit nor made his name. He began to focus on Borneo and the opportunities it could offer. In 1838 he set off for Maluda Bay, where the British already had a toehold in Borneo. His stated purpose was to survey the coast and to observe and collect botanical specimens. After a halt at Singapore he and his crew arrived at Kuching, the chief town of Sarawak, on 15 August 1839.

Brooke was graciously received by Rajah Muda Hassim who was 'a little man, mid-aged with a plain but intelligent face'. Hassim assumed Brooke was a spy and treated him with the greatest respect. Brooke also met Governor Makota, whom he regarded as 'the cleverest man here'. Brooke set off on an expedition 100 miles upriver and fell in love with Sarawak. He wrote:

> The glorious moon rose upon our progress as we toiled slowly but cheerfully on. It was such a situation as an excitable mind might envy. The reflection that we were proceeding up a Borneon river hitherto unexplored, sailing where no European had ever sailed before; the deep solitude, the brilliant night, the dark fringe of retired jungle, the lighter foliage of the river bank, with here and there a tree flashing and shining with fireflies, nature's tiny lamps glancing and flitting in countless numbers and incredible brilliancy.

He visited huge long-houses, admired graceful women and was appalled by the grisly spectacle of captured heads dangling from the rafters. He was persuaded that the heads were mere trophies of war taken from 'bad people who deserved to die'. Brooke spent ten days living in a Dyak long-house and spent his time surveying 150 miles of coast and river shore. During another voyage to the mouth of the Morotabas river a party of Hassim's men, acting as guides, were attacked by Saribas Dyaks as they slept in their *prahu* near the shore. One of the twelve men on board was speared in the breast but survived. Brooke wrote: 'I would have given the fellows a lesson, but they came in darkness, under the shadow of the hill, and in darkness departed on our firing a gun and showing a blue light.'

After several weeks Brooke left Kuching, firing a 21-shot salute for the Rajah and receiving 42 in return. Muda Hassim said: 'Tuan Brooke, do not forget me.' It was probably a mere term of courtesy, but it lodged in Brooke's mind.

Attack on a pirate stockade. (*Illustrated London News*)

Brooke sailed on to Celebes, where he impressed the inhabitants with his riding and shooting skills. He was not well received by their rulers, however, as he had strayed into an area of Dutch influence. Brooke began to suffer badly from bouts of fever and decided to return to his more hospitable hosts in Borneo. He arrived back at Kuching in October 1840.

He discovered that the Sarawak revolt was still dragging on. Muda Hassim, impressed by the firepower on the *Royalist*, asked Brooke to help in the suppression. At first he refused, but his curiosity soon led him to the field of action. He found that Makota's army had the rebels surrounded at Sarambo. Brooke thought that the war was as good as won, but he was astounded to find that Makota's troops, a mixture of Malays, Chinese and Dyak turncoats, were reluctant to attack. It was not their way. For six days the besiegers inched forward, demolishing and rebuilding stockaded forts as they went, but consistently refused to rush the Dyak positions. Brooke surveyed the enemy through a telescope and saw barely 300 men behind simple bamboo structures. Makota had 650 men in his force, although some were poorly armed and hardly raring for a fight. Brooke wrote:

> With 300 men who would fight, nothing would have been easier than to take the detached defences of the enemy. But our allies seemed to have little idea of fighting except behind a wall; and my proposal to attack the adversary was immediately treated as an extreme of rashness amounting to insanity.

In disgust Brooke returned to Kuching and prepared to sail away. Muda Hassim begged him to stay, offering him the country of Sarawak and its government and trade if he didn't desert him. Brooke, his head reeling with ambition, returned to the front not as a friendly observer but as commander-in-chief of the Rajah's army. Makota was furious but powerless to object. Brooke selected as his second-in-command Pangeran Budruddin, one of the Rajah's brothers, who had shown signs of bravery. Brooke ordered an attack, but Makota persuaded the troops that such action was hopeless.

In frustration Brooke decided to lead his crewmen from the *Royalist* in a frontal assault. The little band was joined by just one native, Si Tundo from Mindanao. Brooke described his enthusiasm for battle: 'He danced or galloped across the field close to me, and, mixing with the enemy, was about to despatch a Hadji or priest who was prostrate before him, when one of our own people interposed and saved him by stating that he was a companion of our own.' The defenders had become accustomed to the Malay method of battle, which amounted merely to loose firing and shouted insults. The sight of a compact body of Europeans advancing on them – and the wild bloodlust of Si Tundo – threw them into a panic. The rebel line broke and they ran away. Brooke boasted: 'Our victory was complete and bloodless.'

It was the end of a four-year war. A few days later the rebel leaders sued for peace. Brooke brokered the deal and insisted that all rebel prisoners be spared. Muda Hassim began to doubt the wisdom of his promise to give Brooke the governance of

Penigran Muda Hassim, a sketch by Keppel, 1846.

Sarawak, and his doubts were exploited by Makota who had no wish to see such power handed to a foreigner. Eventually Brooke, losing patience, trained the guns of the *Royalist* on Hassim's audience chamber, and then took an armed party ashore to negotiate. Muda Hassim prudently put aside his qualms and on 24 September 1841 Brooke became Governor of Sarawak. The episode convinced Brooke that the Malay princes were untrustworthy schemers who quickly responded to force when diplomacy failed. Muda Hassim and other lords recognised a tough operator.

In the meantime a pirate fleet of eighteen *prahus* swept up the river at Kuching, 'one following the other, decorated with flags and streamers, and firing both cannon and musketry'. Their stated purpose was to pay their respects to Muda Hassim. Brooke mused: 'The sight was curious, and its interest heightened by the conviction that these friends of the moment may be enemies the next.' The rumour spread that their real purpose was to sack the *Royalist*, but they thought again after seeing her firepower. Brooke went aboard several of the large *prahus* as a guest. He quizzed the pirate chiefs about their methods of slave-trading and learnt a lot about their tactics.

The following July Brooke went to Brunei and was, again after much negotiation and delay, confirmed as the Rajah of Sarawak. He was formally installed back at Kuching on 18 August 1842. Not yet forty, Brooke now had a kingdom of his own to administer.

★   ★   ★

James Brooke, the 'white Rajah', took his work seriously. His aim was to restore a country 'beset with difficulties, ravaged by war, torn by dissension and ruined by duplicity, weakness and intrigue'. He regarded the natives as a father would unruly children, and although he believed the white race was superior he also believed that brown-skinned people should be treated as equals. His reforms were designed to bring justice and prosperity to the people, to generate a fair income for the Sultan, and ultimately to forge trading links with Britain to the benefit of all. Cynics have portrayed him as an imperialist exploiter, but Brooke himself expected only modest personal benefits. He was a dreamer who had been given the opportunity to make those dreams come true.

The first item on his agenda was to end Makota's cruel system of forced trade and exorbitant tariffs, which he replaced with a simple form of taxation in kind. He ended the enslavement of defaulters and their families. He released prisoners, women and children first, captured during raids and the rebellion. And, as Rajah, he dispensed justice from a long-room built into his house at Kuching. His zeal and fairness greatly impressed his new subjects, particularly those who had been impoverished by his predecessors. The saying – 'The son of Europe is the friend of the Dyak' – became common. His friend Spenser St John described how Brooke heard petitions even during dinner:

Often a very poor man would creep in, take up his position in the most obscure corner and there remain silent but attentive to all that passed. There he would sit till every other native had left, neither addressing Mr Brooke nor being

Brunei, *c.* 1844. A sketch by Marryat, 1848.

addressed by him, but when the coast was clear the Governor would call him to his side and gently worm his story from him. Generally it was some tale of oppression, some request for aid. None of these stories were forgotten . . .

Brooke set about educating the people of his new domain. He wrote to his mother and sisters asking for such articles as 'an electrifying machine of good power', a magic lantern, bell-ropes and old carpets. The latter the Dyaks found especially useful for making war-jackets. Brooke tried, without much initial success, to get the country's finances in order but he was hopeless at accounting. He estimated Sarawak's entire revenue as between £5,000 and £6,000, but the true figure was anyone's guess. With the crew of the *Royalist* frequently away on voyages, Brooke had only a handful of Europeans around him. He wrote in his journal: 'The time here passes monotonously, but not unpleasantly. Writing, reading, chart-making, employ my time between meals.'

During this period piracy was low on his list of priorities. More important to him were his constantly frustrated attempts to get the British government interested in the opportunities offered by a friendly land in Borneo. London, however, did not want to become embroiled in any costly enterprise which could have disastrous diplomatic consequences. Brooke seethed with frustration, dangling the carrot of supposed coal deposits in front of disinterested British eyes. Brooke was a patriot and wanted both Britain and Sarawak to gain, but he also considered making overtures to Holland and France.

A native of Borneo. (*Illustrated London News*)

Ironically, piracy on the frontiers of his land offered him a chance to involve Britain directly in his enterprise. The English Navy was charged with hunting down slavers and stamping out the slave trade around the globe. The pirates were notorious slavers: human traffic was as much the point of raids as more conventional plunder. Brooke's journals report many instances. In one village alone, on the Sanpro, twenty-two women and children were dragged away as slaves. Another common practice guaranteed to raise Christian hackles was head-hunting. Matari, a Sakarran chief seeking a treaty with Brooke, was astonished to hear him stipulate that he was not to engage in piracy by land or sea. The chief asked what he would do if any tribe entered his territory to hunt heads. Brooke replied: 'To enter their country and lay it waste.' Matari asked him again: 'You will give me, your friend, leave to steal a few heads occasionally?' 'No,' Brooke replied, according to his journal, 'you cannot take a single head; you cannot enter the country; and if you or your countrymen do, I will have a hundred Sakarran heads for every one you take here.' Brooke sent letters to the Malay sheriffs, the chiefs of tribes who practised such piracy, warning them that British seapower would be called in to take reprisals if they made further raids on territory under his control.

In fact, Brooke had no such authority but he soon found a willing ally among the Royal Navy captains who crisscrossed the seas protecting trade routes and chasing slavers. Brooke first met Captain the Honorable Henry Keppel, commander of HMS *Dido*, during a visit to Singapore. Then aged thirty-one, Keppel was the son of the 4th Earl of Albemarle and a born adventurer. The two men instantly became friends. When it was reported that a large pirate fleet was approaching north Borneo, Brooke asked his friend for help.

Keppel was eager to intervene, and so were other captains in the area. Their motives were not entirely humanitarian: an 1825 Act offered a bounty of £20 for each pirate killed or captured. The main intention of the legislation was to halt the trans-Atlantic slave trade and the law-makers had not envisaged Far Eastern slavers whose crews might number hundreds. But the law was the law and there were enough British officers ready to exploit it. Keppel, the youngest son of an aristocratic family, needed cash. His wife was an invalid and he had left England to escape the expensive temptations of racecourses and gambling dens. He was also high-spirited and energetic, and shared Brooke's love of excitement. Without any official authorisation, Keppel agreed to take his ship to Borneo and Brooke returned to Sarawak aboard the *Dido*.

The ship was immediately attacked by three marauding *prahu*s, which were easily repulsed. Brooke, who had taken to a smaller craft, fought a battle with a larger *prahu* and scattered its crew of thirty-six men. It was only a small skirmish but made a timely impression on the British officer. The pirates were a real menace, that much was clear. Keppel, like almost every other first-time visitor, was also dazzled by Sarawak. He wrote:

The scene was both novel and exciting; presented to us, just anchored in a large fresh-water river and surrounded by a densely wooded jungle, the whole surface of the water covered with canoes and boats decked out with their various-coloured silken flags, filled with natives beating their tom-toms, and playing on their wild and not unpleasant-sounding wind instruments, with the occasional discharge of firearms.

The natives were equally impressed with *Dido*: 'her mast-heads towering above the highest trees of their jungle; the loud report of her heavy two-and-thirty pounder guns, and the running aloft to furl sails, of 150 seamen in their clean white dresses and with the band playing . . .', he wrote.

Worried that pirates might attack the mail-boat due to arrive from Singapore, Keppel sent on patrol the locally built *Jolly Bachelor*, armed with a brass six-pounder, under the command of one of his lieutenants. Three *prahus* were spotted but each escaped as night fell. The British slept on board. In the small hours the lieutenant was awoken by a 'savage brandishing a *kris* and performing his war-dance on the deck in an ecstasy of delight'. The pirate believed he had single-handedly taken possession of a fine trading-boat; when he realised his mistake, he dived overboard. When dawn broke two large war-*prahus* were pressing the *Jolly Bachelor* on both sides, while another, larger, vessel waited around a point of rocks. After a 'sharp battle' one of the pirate vessels was sunk by the brass cannon and the other two were driven off. One of these was crippled and its galley-slaves quickly rebelled; they killed the remaining pirates on board and escaped upriver.

Keppel was now fully convinced of the piracy problem. Urged on by Brooke, the Rajah Muda Hassim made a formal request that the *Dido* be employed in clearing out the pirates, and Keppel readily agreed. Keppel's plan was to root out two bands of local pirates, operating from the Sarebas and Sakarran rivers, before tackling larger fleets on the high seas. Under his command were about 110 officers and men from *Dido* and about 1,000 Borneo men happy to serve under Brooke. Their transport was *Dido*'s pinnacle, two cutters and a brig, plus *Jolly Bachelor* and numerous native craft. Keppel wrote:

> The whole formed a novel, picturesque and exciting scene . . . The odd mixture of Europeans, Malays and Dyaks; the different religions, and the eager and anxious manner in which all pressed forward. The novelty of the thing was quite enough for our Jacks, after having been cooped up so long board ship, to say nothing of the chance of a broken head.

The force made slow progress, hampered by a tidal bore, and the force was slimmed down to 500 men in the fastest vessels, the rest being left to guard supplies. Around 70 miles upriver the force camped and Keppel contemplated his position: 'about to carry all the horrors of war amongst a race of savage pirates, whose country no force had ever yet dared to invade, and who for more than a century had been inflicting, with impunity, every sort of cruelty on all whom they encountered'. The force advanced with the flood-tide to Padi, the furthest inland Sarebas town, with Keppel and Brooke in the lead boat. From the crest of the bore they got their first glimpse of the enemy performing 'a most awe-inspiring war-dance' in the first fort. The river was partly blocked by a boom but Keppel steered his gig through the opening while native allies cut loose the boom's lashings, allowing the British seamen to dash ashore. They attacked the nearest fort, making no attempt at concealment in their headlong rush. The defenders panicked and fled. This pattern was repeated in all the area's stockades.

The next task was to root out the Sakarrans but before the second expedition could be launched Keppel received orders to sail to China. The captain could only obey, but promised Brooke he would return to complete the job as soon as he could.

Shortly after his departure Brooke was gratified to see another Royal Navy ship, the surveying vessel HMS *Samarang*, arrive in harbour. But her captain, the gruff Sir Edward Belcher, was not so easily captivated by the 'white Rajah'. The son of Nova Scotia colonisers, Belcher had spent thirty years at sea and had previously surveyed the coasts of west and north Africa, North and South America and the Pacific. He was able and experienced, but taciturn, bad-tempered and certainly no romantic. He was unimpressed by Brooke's assertion that Borneo was a fertile sphere of influence for British interests. Brooke offered enticements: the small island of Labuan, commanding the approaches to Brunei harbour, was, he claimed, rich in coal and would make an excellent coaling-station for the Royal Navy's new steamships. He argued that the Sultan would willingly cede it to the British in return for protection against piracy. Belcher was sceptical but agreed to go with Brooke to Brunei to see for himself. The start to their voyage was inauspicious: Belcher managed to run *Samarang* aground twice on the same reef. Eventually an impressive flotilla of seven vessels reached Brunei. Belcher refused to enter the town because of an outbreak of smallpox there and Omar Ali agreed only to a hurried conference aboard *Samarang*. The Sultan was impressed by the show of naval might, not realising that most of the ships were to follow Belcher to China, where he had been summoned in the aftermath of the Opium War. The Sultan agreed to the exchange, although somewhat warily, with Brooke's assurance that the Brunei Court wanted to see their ports open to trade and piracy suppressed. Belcher merely made notes. He glanced at two small coal outcrops on Labuan and declared them unworkable. Then he set sail for China.

Hugely disappointed, Brooke decided to approach Admiral Sir William Parker in Penang. Parker, who had heard fine things from Keppel about the 'white Rajah', pledged support for further action against the Borneo pirates. But first, Parker said, he had to deal with a similar problem in Sumatra and he invited Brooke to join him. Brooke eagerly agreed, if only to win credit with the region's foremost naval commander. The offensive against the Sumatrans was a short campaign, but bloodier than the onslaughts in which Brooke had made his name. The first town, Batu, was easily taken and burnt. But the Murdu Malays, who saw piracy as a legitimate enterprise and who were contemptuous of foreign trading rights, proved tougher. They were well armed and had recently sacked a merchant ship and massacred its crew. The fighting lasted five hours. Two Englishmen and many native allies were killed and Brooke himself was twice wounded in reckless charges. He was cheered for his bravery when he returned to his ship. Among most officers and men of the Royal Navy he had already become a hero. It was the beginning of a legend.

Travelling home via Penang Brooke met his old friend Keppel, who later recalled: 'I took the liberty of giving him a lecture on his rashness, he having quite sufficient ground for fighting over in his newly adopted country.' Keppel was more than willing to return with him to complete their earlier task, but naval business took him first to Singapore and China. In May 1844 Brooke returned alone, hitching a lift on *Harlequin*, to find Sarawak again in turmoil. Serif Sahib of neighbouring Sadong, who had opposed Brooke's reforms and whose power base lay among the supposed pirates on the Sakarran river, had taken advantage of Brooke's absence to rally opposition to the 'white Rajah'. In this he was egged on by Makota, the disgruntled former governor who had moved to his princedom. Serif Sahib had built up a large flotilla of vessels with which to raid Brooke's territory. Keppel provided Brooke's salvation from this latest threat. Late in July he arrived with *Dido* and the Company steamer *Phlegethon*. Also on board was Brooke's young nephew, Charles Johnson, a callow midshipman.

Keppel and Brooke embarked on an expedition to punish Serif Sahib and the pirates on the Sakarran. This campaign was to prove tougher than their previous adventure. Patusen, Serif Sahib's riverside stronghold, was attacked and taken, with heavy losses on both sides. The battle featured a determined and brutal charge by RN blue-jackets armed with cutlasses. Three British officers and gentlemen were killed. One of them, John Ellis, was cut in half by a cannon shot as he loaded *Jolly Batchelor*'s bow gun, just a few yards from the young Charles Johnson who was drenched in blood but unscathed. Serif Sahib, whose forces suffered much higher casualties, escaped. Brooke's Dyak allies reaped a crop of heads from their fallen enemies. Keppel recorded the celebrations: 'The whole of the late expedition was fought over again and a war-dance with the newly acquired heads of the Sakarran pirates was performed for our edification.'

The expedition moved up the Batang Lupa river. The lead spy-*prahu*, captained by Patinga Ali, was ambushed by 600 pirates in six war-boats who cut off their retreat with a fallen tree-trunk. All aboard were slaughtered, including Patinga Ali, one of Brooke's best and most loyal fighting men. That sacrifice, however, alerted the main British and Sarawakan fleet who pounded the pirate craft into blood-soaked matchwood. The fighting was the most vicious of the whole campaign. The enemy dead numbered hundreds, while Brooke's force lost 30 killed and 56 wounded. The cost was high, but in two weeks Brooke and Keppel, with their native allies, had destroyed the main pirate power base in the region.

The chase continued upriver and Makota was captured. Typically, and despite the protestations of his more war-like friends, Brooke refused to execute Sarawak's former governor. Instead he gave him a lecture and let him go. Similar treatment was given to other captured princes who agreed to keep the peace and stop attacking Sarawak. Brooke's mercy was much appreciated and it was a wise move. The 'white Rajah', by forcing pledges from other chiefs, effectively extended his own domain.

*   *   *

During this period Brooke's main concern was to create a pro-British regime in Brunei. His chief allies at court were Muda Hassim and his brother Budruddin. His main enemy was Pangeran Usop, who had been prime minister before being supplanted by Muda Hassim. Inevitably Brooke regarded all those who opposed him as the 'piratical faction', Usop included. The historian Graham Saunders wrote: 'In this there was some truth, in that their policies were inimical to those of Brooke and they included under the category of trade the exchange of goods acquired by piratical means; but their main fault in Brooke's eyes was to oppose his interests. Brooke had in fact intervened in a Brunei dynastic quarrel which had little to do with piracy.' In brief, Muda Hussim was aiming to strengthen his claim to eventually succeed the Sultan, while Usop was determined to stop him, citing his reliance on the foreigner Brooke.

Brooke, increasingly prone to fever and constantly frustrated by London's lack of interest, grew daily more irascible. He claimed the moral high ground and would not tolerate any dissent from his divisive and, some would later say, hypocritical tactics. He expressed a wish to 'change the native character'. If the British government did not support him he would halt all further negotiations and 'trust to God and my own wits'. However, Brooke's growing reputation in England was beginning to work in his favour and in February 1845 he was finally given official recognition. He was appointed Confidential Agent in Borneo to Her Majesty, with the power to act as a government agent.

Brooke interpreted this to mean he could negotiate British trade terms with Borneo and he rushed back to Brunei. The Sultan was by now 'dizzy and confused' and did not appear to understand the significance of the developments, but Muda Hassim, keen to succeed his nephew, grasped it immediately. He informed Brooke that his rival, Usop, was now in league with Serif Osman, a notorious slave trader and pirate at Maluda Bay. Brooke agreed to help flush out the 'traitors' and in August he found a new ally to help in the task.

Admiral Sir Thomas Cochrane arrived at Brunei in August with a squadron of eight ships to obtain the release of two Lascar seamen captured and sold into slavery, allegedly to Usop by Osman. Cochrane was a 69-year-old veteran of the Napoleonic Wars and a passionate advocate of steam power in warfare. He had already met Brooke, agreed with him on the private threat, and had a mandate from the Admiralty to take whatever action he saw fit. Budruddin accused Usop of holding the captured sailors and of slave dealing. Usop refused to attend a meeting with Cochrane and the admiral ordered a shot to be fired by the steamer *Vixen* through the roof of his house. Usop briefly returned fire with a heavy calibre weapon which sent a shot through *Vixen*'s rigging. The British warships bombarded the compound for 50 minutes before the 'rebels' fled. Twenty-one cannon were found in Usop's compound, which the Sultan declared were British spoils of war. Also found were European-manufactured goods, indicating the receipt of pirate booty. Brooke and Cochrane now had the excuse they needed to attack Serif Osman at Maluda Bay. This was done with the full authority of the Sultan, although he probably had little choice, given the encouragement of Muda Hassim and the presence of a powerful British armada in his harbour. Brooke, now a government official and a civilian who could not be placed in the front line, travelled with the squadron in *Vixen* but was honour-bound to stay well away from danger.

The British attack on the pirates near Maluda Bay. (*Illustrated London News*)

Cochrane commanded twenty vessels, including *Vixen, Agincourt, Vestal, Daedalus, Cruiser* and *Wolverine*, plus two smaller Company steamships, the battle-hardened *Nemesis* and *Pluto*, with a total force of around 500 men. Serif Osman was believed to command up to 1,000 fighting men and enjoyed the support of the local populace. One correspondent wrote that he would oppose any British settlement in Borneo Proper: 'It was the utmost importance that he should be expelled the island and the horde dispersed.' Another writer, justifying the attack on Serif Osman's own territory, wrote: 'This man, a half-bred Arab, had succeeded in obtaining over the poorer classes an immense influence, having employed a large capital in the most nefarious manner by investing it in boats, arms and ammunition for the purpose of the less powerful and influential tribes carrying on their only trade – a diabolical piracy.' In other words, he was a popular leader.

The fleet proceeded to Maluda Bay 'into which from many mouths debouches the water of a shallow river, the navigation of which is difficult even for boats. Upon the banks of this river the Arab chief had his settlement, and from thence his fleet could prey upon vessels in the China, the Celebes or the Sooloo seas.' Osman's settlement was well protected by a stockade with a battery of eight cannon commanding the shallow river and another of eight mounted gingalls facing inland. There were a further two batteries, one of them on a raft. The writer continued:

The defences were protected by a double boom thrown across the river, formed of enormous trees, bolted together by large iron plates on the lower part, and bound round and round by the iron cable of a vessel of considerable size, the ends of which were secured on each bank by numerous turns round many stumps of trees. It was as formidably and ingeniously contrived a boom as ever savage put together.

The intricacy and shallowness of the river prevented even the small steam vessels approaching the boom. Cochrane sent a flotilla of 25 small boats and 450 men under the command of captains Talbot and Lyster. The first day was spent trying to find the river mouth in the maze of channels and the men spent an uncomfortable night offshore until finding the right access on the morning of 19 August 1845. After pulling on the oars for 10 miles they came within sight of the town and its defences. The officers saw that a determined resistance would be made and that they were in great peril from the enemy cannon mounted just 150 yards away. 'The crew stood perfectly cool at the guns, with which eight boats were armed, ready for the commencement of hostilities.' Osman sent out an envoy under a flag of truce and invited Talbot and a small number of his men to a parley inside the fort. The captain said he would accept, provided the boom was opened but Osman insisted that he could allow only two small boats to enter. The messenger was told to say that Osman was required on board the admiral's ship and when his boat returned to the fort a 'murderous' cannonade immediately opened up. The British boats were caught in the cross-fire from the fort, a shore battery, the floating battery and the guns of pirate vessels. The very first shot killed two men and wounded three others. Leonard Gibbard, *Wolverine*'s first mate, took grapeshot in the chest and quickly died. The seamen returned fire for 50 hot minutes while *Agincourt*'s gunner lieutenant set up a rocket battery on the beach. Its missiles were then thrown into the fort with 'perfect accuracy'. A small gap was forced in the boom and the British boats passed through in single file 'under a terrifically galling fire from a 12-gun battery in the flank and a stockade of three guns in front'. As the first disciplined waves of troops landed on the shore the fort was abandoned and the shore battery was overrun. The correspondent for the *Illustrated London News* reported:

A landing being at length obtained, the slaughter commenced, and the absurdity of an irregular body of men attempting to make a stand against a corps of regular disciplined troops was here very perceptible. The infatuated beings fell like grass, their chief standing to the last on a wing of one of the principal embrasures, amid the fire of about 300 Marines, with an apparent degree of physical bravery worthy of a better cause; he received a shot at last through the neck, and was borne from his comrades from the scene of action.

The British lost 10 killed and 15 wounded. The correspondent continued:

It would be no easy task to compute the loss on the part of the enemy, but from the statements of two prisoners it was understood to have been immense, for it appeared they, who were slaves, had been employed for upward of five hours throwing dead bodies in the river. [That was the custom, to prevent the corpses falling into the hands of their enemies.] The great loss the enemy had suffered – their leaders, five of whom were dead or desperately wounded, and the remainder having fled – convinced them that victory was hopeless, and they deserted in all directions. A few of the most daring, in bringing off the last of their wounded and dead, were shot down by the marines and seamen. Spoils of every description were found; and in one hour the villages and forts for a mile up were wrapped in flames. Thirty proas [sic] were burnt and two very fine ones on the stocks, two magazines of powder, and houses filled with camphor, china ware, English manufactured goods, French prints and splendid timber were found and fired.

The chain cable on the boom was found to be from a vessel of 400 tons. In and around the stockades were found more chains, a European long-boat and two ship's bells, one of which was ornamented with grapes and vine leaves and inscribed 'Wilhelm Ludwig, Bremen.' Another observer wrote: 'Bales and boxes of European and Chinese goods, with crates of earthenware, anchors, chains, spars, etc., etc., gave abundant proof of the nature of the pursuits of the inhabitants of Maluda Bay.' Throughout the action Brooke stayed on board ship with the admiral, well out of danger and hating it. He was sick with worry for his nephew, midshipman Charles Johnston, who was with the landing parties. Again the lad emerged unscathed but plastered with the blood of comrades.

Next day boats were again sent upriver to burn the main town. A woman and her infant child were found in the smoking ruins of Osman's home. The mother had been one of his slaves and was severely wounded with a British musket ball through her elbow. Her arm was amputated by a naval surgeon, and mother and child returned with Brooke.

The magazine *Friends of China* reported:

It is to be hoped that the severe lesson they have received will for a time intimidate the pirates of Borneo; but nothing short of a European settlement, with a garrison and one or two small steam-vessels of war permanently on the coast, will effectually drive the pirates from their present haunts. Many a ship that has been reported missing has met her fate on the coast of Borneo, and the crew murdered or sold as slaves.

⋆　⋆　⋆

Meanwhile the struggle for supremacy continued in the Sultanate of Brunei. Usop tried to reassert his lost authority by force. Defeated by Budruddin, he retreated back to his own estates at Kimanis, where he was arrested and executed on the orders of Mudam Hassim and, nominally at least, the Sultan. The pro-British faction appeared to have won. The suppression of piracy, however, and the interference by foreigners only increased resentment at court. Sultan Omar Ali declared that his son, married to one of Usop's daughters, should eventually take power. Various factions intrigued and gossiped and convinced the Sultan that Muda

Hassim, previously nominated as successor, was about to launch a coup. As 1845 closed the Sultan ordered the assassination of Muda Hassim and Budruddin and their families. Budruddin was surrounded but blew himself up, along with his sister and one of his wives, rather than surrender. Muda Hassim was wounded but escaped across a river; then, all hope gone, he shot himself with a pistol. Two of Brooke's greatest allies were dead.

Brooke, hearing of the slaughter from an escaped slave, organised an expedition to avenge the deaths of his friends and to bring the Sultan to heel. In July Admiral Cochrane sailed directly to Brunei. Faced with prevarication and excuses, an armada of longboats from the warships, together with the steamer *Phlegethon*, moved threateningly upriver. Shots were fired at them at every bend and the steamship was slightly damaged. By the time they reached the city itself the Sultan was gone. So too was the entire populace, fearful of retribution. But they did find one of Muda Hassim's brothers, who was badly wounded but had escaped the massacre. The British fired the forts but sent out messengers to persuade the people to return. Most did, although the Sultan remained in hiding and an expedition into the interior failed to find him. Cochrane and the main British force then sailed away, leaving Brooke in Brunei with the steamship *Iris* and HMS *Hazard*. Eventually he persuaded the Sultan to come out of hiding, but forced him to pay penance at the graves of his murdered uncles, and to write a humiliating letter of apology to Queen Victoria. Brooke also bullied him into signing over all mining rights on the island of Labuan.

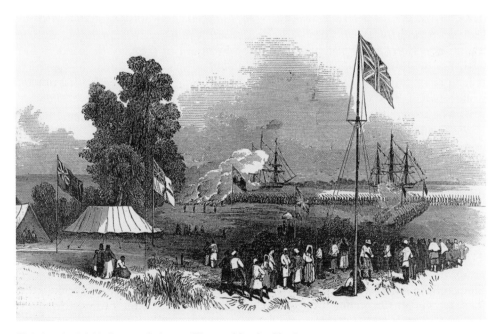

Hoisting the British flag over Labuan. (*Illustrated London News*)

This time London took notice and agreed to accept the offer. On 18 December Captain G. Rodney Mundy of *Iris*, whose guns had maintained well-aimed diplomatic pressure on the Sultan, signed a treaty under which the island became part of the British Crown. It was followed the next year by another treaty, negotiated by Brooke, which increased the stranglehold of British trade on all the Sultan's lands. It forbade 'any cessation of an island or of any settlement on the mainland in any part of [the Sultan's] dominion to any other nation, or to the subjects or citizens thereof, without the consent of Her Britannic Majesty'. Sarawak was also freed from paying tribute to Brunei. Brooke had got all he wanted and more, partly by dealing with all his opponents as if they were common pirates. Sir Spenser St John wrote:

> The tables have been strangely turned in the Eastern Archipelago. Weak, and few in number, we were (once) too happy to receive the protection and countenance of the Sultan of Borneo, of whom the buccaneers of the Sulu group seemed to have stood in awe. Now the Sultan is our humble ally and dependant, and, but for the British flag which waves in his neighbourhood, and the treaty he has concluded with us, might any hour in the twenty-four be seized in his capital by the Sulus, or any other piratical tribe, and sold like the humblest individual into slavery.

Brooke returned to England to a hero's welcome. Queen Victoria invited him to tea at Windsor Castle. She asked him how he managed to rule so many of the wild Borneans with so little force. He replied: 'I find it easier to govern thirty thousand Malays and Dyaks than to manage a dozen of Your Majesty's subjects.' It was exactly what she wanted to hear in her early imperial age – and so too did a British leadership avid for exotic tales of adventure and the inherent superiority of their island race. Brooke was knighted, given the Freedom of the City of London and awarded an honorary degree by Oxford. He returned to Borneo as British commissioner and consul-general to the entire island, and as governor of Labuan, while retaining his own title over Sarawak.

Brooke's methods, and his rewards, had their critics, particularly among the Radicals and the Liberal Opposition at Westminster. They were backed by such bodies as the Peace Society and the Aborigines' Protection Society. Brooke's overwhelming popularity thwarted their attempts to block the colonisation of Labuan. They bided their time until another expedition by the increasingly fever-ridden 'white Rajah' gave them the ammunition they needed.

★   ★   ★

The Albatross expedition, as it became known, was sparked by further outbreaks of piracy from bases on the Sarebas and Sakarran rivers, the scene of Brooke's earlier campaigns in north-west Borneo. The marauders captured two trading boats in the Rejang delta and launched an abortive assault on Serikei, which proved too well defended. Thwarted, the fleet headed for targets skirting Brooke's territory. Brooke's subsequent action was justified by Sir Spenser St John. He wrote:

During the first six months of 1849 these pirates attacked Sadong twice, as well as Susang on the Kaluka, and Serikei, Palo, Mato, Bruit and Igan. Almost all intercourse by sea ceased, as few who attempted to pass the mouths of the pirate rivers escaped unhurt. I calculated at the time that above 500 of the Sultan's subjects had been killed or taken captive between January and July 1849; and we know that one large fleet had passed the mouths of the Sarawak river to attack the subjects of the Sultan of Sambas.

St John, then a young and inexperienced officer, witnessed at first hand the aftermath of the raids. He saw piles of corpses, their heads removed. He saw the pathetic evidence of mass rape and infanticide. He was horrified.

Brooke reckoned, correctly, that the pirate forces would hug the coastline as they paddled towards undefended villages. He marshalled his own forces, with the sanction of the Sultan, to exact retribution. They were joined by a naval force under Captain Farquhar, consisting of his warship HMS *Albatross*, *Nemesis* and the steam tender *Ranee*. Their combined strength was about 3,000 men, of whom 120 were European. The pirate force was later estimated at 4,000 in 120 *prahus*. The two forces collided at Batang Marau, a sandy spit at the entrance to the Sarebas river.

On the evening of 30 July the British ships were in position to halt pirates heading for home after a raid on Palo, where they had threatened the area with destruction unless supplied with salt. Brooke and his men moved up the Kaluka river to block off one exit, while the naval men assembled at the entrance of the Sarebas. The steamer *Nemesis* took up position slightly offshore, from where she could swiftly move to wherever she was most needed. The trap was set.

As the pirate fleet approached, the British ships opened fire. The result was carnage. The British and their Malay allies had attacked at night, and the enemy boats were far away from familiar waters. The guns of *Nemesis* alone destroyed seventeen *prahus*, and in all ninety enemy boats foundered. The smaller boats, both British and native, cut in and out of the pirate flotilla as they tried, desperately and unsuccessfully, to escape out to sea. Each time their way was blocked by the warships; they were trapped by the sandy spit and the tangled coastline.

An anonymous British correspondent wrote:

It was now dark and the great danger was that of firing into each other or into our native allies. The password selected was *Rajah* and the Malays screamed this out at the top of their voices when they thought any of the Europeans were near them. Commander Farquhar, who directed the operations, was in the midst of the mêlée, giving orders and exhorting the crews of the various boats to be careful, and not to fire into each other.

Two large *prahus* were seen by the Commander escaping seaward, and the steam-tender was ordered to give chase; the nearest one, having barely escaped one of her six-pounder rockets, made for the river and met a pirate's doom – the *Nemesis*, which had been dealing death and destruction to all around her, ran her down, and the scene which took place as her crew, above sixty in number, came in contact with the paddle-wheels, beggars all description.

A large Congreve-rocket from the little steamer entered the *prahu* that had continued out to sea, and rendered her destruction complete.

The master of *Nemesis* described the whole action:

> On coming abreast of them I fired the starboard broadside with canister shot along the whole line, the nearest *prahu* being about 20 or 30 yards distant, the small-arm men at the same time keeping up a constant and important fire upon them. We then wore [sic], breaking the line and driving many *prahus* ashore in a very crippled state, where they fell an easy prey to a division of native boats under Mr Steele of Sarawak, who did good service, without interfering with our fire.
>
> We now followed five *prahus* which still pressed on for the Batang Lupar, and on coming up with them passed round each successfully, and destroyed them in detail, by keeping up a constant fire of grape shot and musketry, until they drifted past us helpless as logs, without a living being onboard, with the hope of swimming on shore, which few could possibly accomplish.
>
> The pirates had hitherto preserved good order, but now finding themselves surrounded and cut off wherever they turned, they fled indiscriminately, running their *prahus* aground in all directions, abandoning them, and taking refuge in the jungle . . .

From the first exchange of shots it was obvious that the British and their allies had won, but a rapid running fire was kept up until shortly after midnight. Farquhar then sent dispatches to Brooke, who was in the Kaluka river with his Sarawaks, away from the main action. It was dawn before the full extent of their handiwork became

A Dyak suspension bridge, by J.W. Giles, *c.* 1846. (Parker Gallery)

evident. The correspondent quoted above said it took everyone by surprise: 'At daylight the bay was one mass of wrecks – shields, spears and portions of destroyed *prahus* extended as far as the eye could reach; whilst on the sandy spit were upwards of seventy *prahus* which the natives were busy clearing of all valuables and destroying them.'

Around 400 pirates were slain for the loss of only 13 native allies killed or wounded. Captain Wallage of *Nemesis* reported gleefully:

> The pirates, having landed in a hostile country, without food or arms, will probably lose 800 or 1,000 men more before they reach their home . . . Thus, notwithstanding the smallness of the European force, and under all the disadvantages of a night attack, was fought the most decisive engagement that has ever taken place on this coast, and which (without severe loss on our side) has resulted in the annihilation of one of the most desperate piratical tribes.

A more critical writer, the Radical Richard Cobden, saw the battle of Batang Marau in a different light:

> The attacking party, without calling upon them to surrender, or in any way communicating with them, with the view of ascertaining what they wanted, fired a broadside into them of shot, balls and rockets, and the unfortunate wretches were unable to make the slightest attempt at resistance or defence. The English steam vessels of war were then driven among the boats, and the miserable creatures were crushed under the paddle wheels and annihilated by the hundreds in the most inhumane manner.

The controversy sparked a heated debate, especially when the naval officers claimed bounties on the men slain under the old system of hunting down pirates and slavers. Given the numbers of dead the total claim could exceed £30,000. Cobden claimed there was no proof that the destroyed flotilla were pirates. He described the battle as closer to the massacre of sheep or rabbits than honourable warfare: 'After this mighty feat of valour had been performed, they came to a Christian assembly and demanded twenty pounds a head for slaughtering the unhappy wretches.'

The Peace Society focused on the 'blood-money,' suggesting that thousands of innocents had been slain to claim a bogus bounty; it was no more justified, said the Society, than collecting heads. Brooke was the villain of this scenario, despite the fact that the 'white Rajah' and his staff were, as civilians, not eligible for a penny of the bounty. The payments due were later agreed by the Admiralty Court in Singapore to be £20,700, a staggering sum for the time.

A joint submission by the Peace Society and the Aborigines' Protection Society claimed there was no evidence that the attacked *prahus* were manned by pirates. It was, rather, 'a fleet waylaid on its return from a predatory excursion against some neighbouring tribes'. Brooke's allies pointed out that this was a rather strange defence. But their submission did make some pertinent points which Brooke's supporters had difficulty refuting:

According to Sir James Brooke's own shewing, four-fifths of the hands on board piratical fleets in the Eastern Seas are slaves, generally unarmed and employed at the oars, prohibited from fighting and in no case free-agents. Granting, then, the act of piracy on the part of the tribes in question, the laws of this country would treat with leniency men in this position, who could prove that they were acting under compulsion. But in the present instance a *very few* prisoners were made, whilst the slaughter was pitiless to extreme degree, the Dyaks having no firearms, but only spears and shields.

Brooke, now in Singapore, was unable to respond to such attacks in person, but he did so prodigiously by letter in tones of increasing hurt and indignation. In one he said of Batang Marau:

I was ill of the ague when the fight commenced, and during the whole night information was brought to me that a desperate struggle had taken place between the pirates and our people, and rumours were rife that we had been defeated. The morning assured us of victory. Now, will anyone state at what time the action should have been discontinued? Should all the pirates have been allowed to escape, or a half of them, or a quarter, and by what patient means is an action to be stopped at any given moment? We had one *prahu* from Sadong manned by Malays, every one of whom had lost a near relative, killed by the Sarebas during the year.

Under further attack Brooke said that there was a difference between the 30 or 40 Malay and Dyak tribes who lived in peace with each other and those of the Sarebas and Sakarran who 'constantly go to sea on piratical cruises and devastate the other countries'.

He was supported by the British officers present. One wrote:

The observer was compelled to ask himself, could destruction so great, success so complete, at least a third of this ruthless horde sent to their account, be effected in a space so brief, and with a European force so small? Had success attended the pirates our fate was certain. No more convincing instances of their inhuman disposition need be cited than the fact that the bodies of women were found on the beach on whom they had wreaked their vengeance. They were all decapitated, and the bodies gashed from shoulder to foot. These are supposed to have been captives taken by the pirates in the expedition from which they were returning.

The debates continued and Cobden, supported by Gladstone, called for an inquiry into charges that the destruction of the enemy fleet had been 'promiscuous and, to some degree, illegal'. The motion was rejected by a large majority. Lord Palmerston declared that Brooke 'retired from the investigation with untarnished character and unblemished character'. Later, with the Liberals refusing to let the matter lie, the new government of Lord Aberdeen granted a commission of inquiry. It met finally

The Rajah's bungalow at Kuching. (*Views of the Indian Archipelago*)

at Singapore but failed to find any evidence of inhumanity or illegality on Brooke's part. Rajah Brooke was too proud to call any witnesses in his own defence, but the Commissioners summoned twenty-four of their own. All testified that the Saribas were pirates and murderers. Brooke subsequently received a letter from Palmerston, fully approving 'the course which you have pursued for the suppression of the system of wholesale piracy in the seas adjoining to Borneo'.

Brooke's long war against the Borneo pirates was over and he was vindicated, at least in the eyes of the British government.

★   ★   ★

It had taken Brooke three years to clear his name. In the meantime he had established a series of forts and out-stations which, even more than the final battle, broke the power of the Sea-Dyaks and extended Brooke's Peace far up the rivers of Borneo and along the coastline.

But the 'white Rajah' was physically and emotionally drained by the time he returned to Sarawak from his 'trial'. Although vindicated he felt occasional bitterness at the aspersions levelled against him. St John wrote: 'Sir James was of a very excitable and nervous temperament. The savage attacks to which he was subjected roused his anger, and did him permanent injury. He never was again the even-tempered gay companion of former days.' He also suffered a severe bout of smallpox which left him permanently disfigured, while numerous attacks of malaria left him tired. He lost some of his fire and all personal ambition, saying that 'titles, fine clothes, penny trumpets and turtle soup' were all the same to him. He was content to administer his state, which prospered through years of peace, and to enjoy his rose garden, his library and the company of his friends. His greatest consolation was that his 'own people' remained loyal to him. Sarawak had come to peace and so too, after a while, did Brooke. St John wrote:

> This was perhaps the happiest time he ever spent. He could live in the capital or in his country cottage as he felt inclined, and he returned to a course of chess and pleasant reading. We had at this time in Sarawak the famous naturalist, traveller and philosopher Mr Alfred Wallace, who was then elaborating in his mind the theory which was simultaneously worked out by Darwin – the theory of the origin of the species; and if he could not convince us that our ugly neighbours, the orang-utans, were our ancestors, he pleased, delighted and instructed us by his clever and inexhaustible flow of talk – really good talk. The Rajah was pleased to have so clever a man with him, as it excited his mind, and brought out his brilliant ideas.

But in 1857 Chinese gold-workers from the interior launched a surprise night attack on Kuching with the intention of killing Brooke and his European entourage. Brooke's servant, Penty, wrote: 'I hurried out of my bed and met the Rajah in the passage in the dark, who at the moment took me for one of the rebels, grappled me by the throat, and was about to shoot me when he fortunately discovered it was me.' Brooke managed to escape by jumping into the river in darkness and swimming under the bows of a Chinese barge. Eighteen-year-old Harry Nicholette, recently arrived to join the Rajah's civil service, was less lucky. He was cut down as he ran towards the house. The Chinese, thinking he was Brooke, cut off his head and carried it about in triumph on the end of a pike. The attackers occupied Kuching for several days, destroying the Rajah's house and his precious library. Loyal Malays and Dyaks eventually drove them off, with heavy losses.

Brooke continued to expand Sarawak's borders by playing rival chiefs off one against another, by exploiting weaknesses in the Brunei regime, and by reaching uneasy alliances. Naturally those who opposed him were, as in earlier diplomatic exchanges, branded 'piratical'. Robert Pringle summed up Brooke's tactics: 'He used this word partly because he deeply and sincerely believed that his enemies were the wilful, lawless adversaries of free trade and good government, and partly because he hoped that public support in maritime England would be disposed to support an anti-piracy campaign.'

Brooke finally returned to England in 1863 and persuaded the British government to recognise Sarawak as an independent state. This was his lasting legacy. He died in Burrator in Devonshire in June 1868 after a series of strokes which had left him speechless and unable to move. He was sixty-five.

Sir Henry Keppel, his old friend and comrade in arms, lived much longer. He destroyed Chinese junks at Fat-shan Bay in 1857 during the Arrow War and commanded the naval brigade before Sebastopol. He became Admiral of the Fleet in 1875 and died in 1904 aged ninety-five. Admiral Cochrane took command of the

West Indies and North American naval stations, and died in 1860. Sir Edward Belcher, who had failed to support Brooke's efforts, was put in command of an ill-starred expedition to the Arctic in search of Sir John Franklin. His appointment was described by his obituarist as 'unfortunate', owing to his lack of good temper or tact. The writer concluded: 'Perhaps no officer of equal ability has ever succeeded in inspiring so much personal dislike . . .' Through the rules of seniority alone he became a non-serving admiral. He died in 1857.

Sultan Omar Ali died in 1852 and was succeeded by Pengiran Mumim. The Brunei court was still riven by factions and the new Sultan was forced to remain on friendly terms with the British as he needed their naval firepower. The battle of Batang Marau had crushed the independent pirate chiefdoms and sea-borne larceny now became a tool of the state. Brunei prospered.

Brooke was succeeded as Rajah of Sarawak by his nephew Charles Johnson. He took the name Charles Brooke and tried, with some success, to emulate his uncle's rule. The *Annual Register* reported: 'Under his firm but benevolent government, based upon the principles introduced by his illustrious relative, Sarawak, now comprising of 28,000 square miles and a population of a quarter of a million, is a flourishing settlement. Trade has expanded and agriculture is advancing . . .' He died in 1917 and was succeeded by his son Charles, who in 1941 scrapped the Rajah's absolute powers and enacted a new democratic constitution. This was halted by the three-year Japanese occupation, and liberation saw the ruined country become a British colony. It moved steadily towards self-government and in 1963 joined the formation of Malaysia.

The 'white Rajah' remains a potent symbol in the lands he controlled. Through sheer force of will and personality he created a dynasty which lasted a hundred years in an alien land. Sarawak expanded and became a nation, and, as one contemporary wrote, 'piracy and head-hunting have been rooted out'.

A new type of a pirate, equipped with a speedboat and a machine-pistol, now roams the shipping lanes of the South China Sea. Unlike their forefathers, their loot is not cinnamon, porcelain and gold, but jet fuel, computer software and aluminium ingots.

CHAPTER THREE

The Storming of Madagascar, 1845

'The queen has been amusing herself . . .'

Not all of Britain's military expeditions ended in slaughter or glory. Some ended in farce – and one such was also one of the shortest conflicts in the Empire's history. It was a joint Anglo-French operation and it concluded with the two allies brawling over a captured standard. The official foe was one of the most feared despots in history, a woman who ruled a vast island almost completely unknown to the outside world.

★   ★   ★

Queen Ranavalona loved Paris fashion and on state occasions wore elaborate dresses in the style of Marie Antoinette. She commanded well-drilled, well-armed troops and employed the latest technology to build massive palaces and fortresses. Her own quarters tinkled with the sound of tiny silver bells.

She was also a cruel despot who held on to power through terror. Her armies wiped out entire peoples in the hinterland of Madagascar and her executioners slew thousands more. She killed Christians, drove out missionaries, enslaved shipwrecked sailors and banned all foreigners apart from a favoured few whose technological skills or western goods she craved. She favoured the traditional method of interrogation that used *tanguena* poison. The Irishman James Hastie, in favour before Ranavalona took ultimate power, described the torment suffered by servants suspected of causing the illness of a princess: 'They had to prove their innocence by this ordeal, which consisted of having to swallow the poison, also bits of the skin of a black fowl, and drink many bowls of lukewarm rice water. They were considered guilty if, when vomiting, the head did not fall to the south. Only one escaped with her life, the others, after having had ears, noses, legs and arms cut off, were cast down a steep rock.' To Hastie's disgust, royal schoolchildren laughed at their suffering and threw stones at the pitiful corpses.

★   ★   ★

Madagascar is one of the world's largest islands, measuring almost 1,000 miles by 360 miles at its widest point. Its isolation, well off the south-east of Africa, resulted in a unique wildlife, with many of its species not found anywhere else in the world. There are lemurs, aye-ayes, and peculiar types of bats, tortoises, chameleons, geckos, civet cats and rodents. The people are a mixture of Africans and Indonesians who arrived by sea during several millennia. Their religion was ancestor worship, with a heavy accent on fetish symbols.

Madagascar was first spotted in 1500 by the Spanish seafarer Diego Dias, who had been blown off course. In the early 1600s Portuguese missionaries made unsuccessful attempts to convert the native tribes, and in 1642 the French won a foothold on the island's south-west tip. After little more than thirty years their garrison was massacred. For some fifty years the island's few ports were the haunt of pirates such as William Kidd and John Avery. From the 1760s the French again established settlements and in 1805 set up an agency in the main port of Tamatave. During the war with Napoleon the island was occupied by the British. A Victorian visitor noted:

Madagascar is not only immensely extensive and in parts very thickly peopled, but is also a most fertile island, offering a great variety of temperature, with some of the finest harbours and timber in the world, and the interior is remarkably healthy. It is, however, chiefly surrounded by a narrow border of swamp, owing to the sea and the mouths of the rivers being frequently on the same level, as is the case on the west coast of Africa. This swamp is most deadly, and at one season of the year Madagascar, in those parts, is almost certain death to a European.

During all that period trade in slaves and arms led to the creation of various Malagassy kingdoms. They were unified, through conquest and treaty, by the great king Andrianampoinimerina by the end of the eighteenth century. His aim, he told his son and heir, was simple: 'The sea will be the boundary of my ricefield.' That son, Radama, ruled shrewdly from 1810 to 1828. He was aided by the British Governor of Mauritius, Sir Robert Farquhar, who wanted to replace French influence on Madagascar. Radama launched a programme of education for his subjects, encouraged trade and agreed to abolish the export of slaves. In return he received an annual subsidy of arms, ammunition and uniforms along with British military instructors. Christian teaching was introduced in the capital, Antananarivo, by the London Missionary Society. Schools were established to teach the scriptures, and printing was introduced for the first time. After ten years the missionary schools had taught some 15,000 people to read; thousands of apprentices were taught the skills of ironmongery, masonry and leather-working. The capital's single printing press produced thousands of primers and copies of the New Testament. Foundries were set up to produce the necessities of both civilian and military life. The island was at last coming out of the shadows.

All that changed when Radama died, aged just thirty-six, and the crown was seized by his first wife, Ranavalona. The new queen was all-powerful, and regarded education and Christianity as threats to her supreme authority. She hated all foreigners and her declared intention was to destroy the men of all but her own

Hova tribe so that her position was truly unassailable. The women of other tribes were to be the property of her Hova soldiers. From the day of her coronation the purges began. Surrounded by Hova soldiers dressed in the uniform of the British Grenadiers, Ranavalona swore to return to the worship of idols. At the ceremony she spoke to her own sacred idols, a cornelian as big as a pigeon's egg and a green stone attached to the top of a staff, 'My predecessors have given you to me. I put my trust in you; therefore, support me.' Her anti-Christian fury was aroused when a diviner was converted and publicly destroyed his idols and charms. Schools were closed and Christian worship on the Sabbath was banned. European advisers at the court, ambassadors and artisans were assassinated. Passing a chapel and hearing the sound of hymn singing inside, the queen muttered: 'These people will not leave off until some of their heads are taken off.' All Malagassy citizens, high and low, who had been baptised were ordered to declare themselves on pain of death. Some came out, trusting the queen's justice. Others worshipped in secret. Most died anyway.

The dreaded *tanguena* poison was increasingly employed, but so were other methods which the queen herself enjoyed watching, such as flogging, spearing, boiling and sawing of spines. Common 'criminals' were simply thrown off high cliffs. Ranavalona proclaimed:

> With respect to these people who pray and read the books of the foreigners, I have admonished them several times, yet they persevere in opposing my will. Some have been put to death, others have been reduced to perpetual slavery, others fined and reduced in rank for praying and worshipping the god of the white people. But they contrive to pray in spite of all I do.

Within a month of her coronation one missionary wrote:

> The idols and diviners govern all things, as they did twenty years ago. Every superstition is renewed; the schools and divine service on the Sabbath in the native language are stopped, and I do not know when things will wear a more pleasing aspect.

In 1835, after many had died or taken prudent exile, the Christian religion was officially declared illegal. As most of the surviving missionaries had already fled, the tag of covert Christianity was a convenient way of getting rid of anyone, either individuals or whole communities, deemed to be disloyal. Then the terror really began.

People who fled Ranavalona's oppressive regime and took to the hinterland became outlaws. Every tribe or region which in any way aided them became the queen's enemies and savage retribution was exacted. In one expedition alone her Hova guards slaughtered 5,000 civilians. Furthermore her soldiers were themselves unpaid, often forced, labour, expected to live off the land. Everywhere they went they left burning, pillaged towns in their wake. Expeditions returned with anything up to 10,000 slaves, mainly widows and orphans. All shipwrecked sailors of any nation immediately became the property of the queen and were condemned to life-long slavery, although few survived long after landing on that terrible shore. Various outrages were committed against British subjects: a naval officer and seven of his men were killed, another was sold as a slave, others were falsely imprisoned. Not all these acts were ordered by the queen but the perpetrators certainly had her tacit approval. The Admiralty in London told the fleet in the region to 'watch over proceedings in Madagascar and to give prompt and effectual protection to British subjects'.

One Western observer wrote: 'The queen is constantly drunk – a clever woman, about 50. She has three or four lovers and they are said to be very desirous to keep all civilisation away.' Foreigners, especially the British whom she hated, were banned as the queen raged against the rest of the world. There were some exceptions. Ranavalona may have been brutalised by her lust for both power and blood, but she was never stupid and she understood that some alien artefacts and knowledge were worth having. Such an asset was the Frenchman Jean Laborde, the son of a blacksmith who gained special influence in the queen's court. In 1831 he took part in a bizarre and ultimately unsuccessful project to salvage treasure ships lost off Madagascar's west coast. He was himself shipwrecked and ended up on the island. When it was realised that he was a master mechanic skilled in armaments and the use of steam, he was put to work manufacturing muskets and powder for the queen's army. Ranavalona excluded him and several other Frenchmen from the general pogrom, realising that her expulsion of the British had left a technological hole in her resources. Laborde constructed an armaments factory at Mantasoa with 20,000 forced labourers supplied by the queen. It manufactured huge quantities of cannon, muskets, swords and bayonets. Connected workshops also produced porcelain, bricks, tiles, glass, cement, sealing wax, ink, dyes, rum, sulphuric acid and lightning conductors for the palaces and fine houses of Antananarivo. Laborde also constructed the queen's great wooden palace, as big as most stone cathedrals, with the central support of a single tree trunk 130 feet high. Five thousand slaves were needed to bring that trunk from the eastern forest. Over time the industrial complex at Mantasoa, with its foundries and mills, sugar refineries and silkworm nurseries, became virtually a second capital. An artificial lake was dug, gardens planted and vast stone buildings erected, with columns of pink granite. The queen and her top officials had summer houses there, and Laborde entertained them with fireworks and rockets of his own manufacture. He wrote to his brother about Ranavalona:

I'm convinced that in spite of all the crimes of which she is, so to say, the cause, she is not as wicked as is said. She is a good mother and has still other good qualities, which would astonish those who hear only of the crimes committed in her name. Unfortunately, fanaticism has made her undeniably barbarous.

Laborde's industries reduced Madagascar's reliance on foreign imports and enabled the queen to crack down on foreign traders who had used Tanatave and other ports on the east coast for generations. Most trading ships lay offshore while local agents ferried their goods ashore. For the agents it was a dangerous game, evading Malagassy embargoes and relying on the tolerance bought for them by economic necessity. Some were expelled on the queen's orders.

In May 1845 the European traders at Tanatave, of whom twelve were British and eleven French, were told that Malagassy law would in future apply to them. This included ordeal by *tanguena*, the imposition of forced labour at the queen's whim, and the penalty of life-long slavery for many transgressions. When news of their predicament filtered out, the British and French authorities were appalled. They had repeatedly objected, fruitlessly, to the treatment of their nationals who had the misfortune to be washed ashore on Madagascar. Despite such behaviour, both European nations had failed to take action, bogged down as they were by often competing diplomatic intrigue. This time something had to be done to save both British and Gallic pride.

A *Times* correspondent wrote from Port Louis: 'The Queen has been amusing herself by burning or cutting the heads off all the native Christians she had been able to lay hands on – many thousands.' The *Illustrated London News* reported that the foreign traders, mostly from Mauritius and Bourbon, were victims of the queen's edict. They were 'subject to a law which amongst other things makes them slaves, under certain contingencies'.

The Governor of Mauritius, Sir William Gomm, sent off Captain Kelly in the corvette HMS *Conway* to threaten repercussions and also to demand the release of a British shipmaster, Jacob Heppick, who had been enslaved after his barque *Marie Laure* was wrecked. The Governor of Bourbon, Admiral Bazoche, sent the men-of-war *Berceau* and *Zelee* under Commander Romain Desfosses to join the Anglo-French venture. An ultimatum produced no response. Kelly landed and met the Governor of Tamatave, Razakafidy, and other Malagassy lords. They behaved 'insolently' and told him plainly that they had imperative orders from the queen to enforce the orders against the traders. If the foreigners interfered they would be driven into the sea. Meanwhile the traders were locked up in the port's Customs House, suffering considerable intimidation. Two Frenchmen, a Spaniard, some Manila traders and a handful of Creoles from Mauritius agreed to be 'slaves of the queen'. The others, however, steadfastly refused. They were told by the Tamatave governor: 'To-morrow you must all be off or you will take your chances of losing your life during the looting.' The following day British and French longboats took off the frightened traders, who were obliged to leave behind all their possessions. M. Rautoney, for example, had to abandon 3,000 head of cattle and 16,000lb of rice. As soon as they left, their houses and warehouses were looted and torched.

Once the traders were safely aboard the warships and the French merchantman *Cosmopolite*, the two commanders held a shipboard conference and agreed, without approaching any higher authority, to bombard the town as punishment and to attack the Malagassy fort guarding its approaches the following morning. During the day the Malagassy were busy evacuating the town and carrying off the spoils. The garrison was reckoned to be 400 seasoned Hova soldiers with 600 auxiliaries.

On Sunday 15 June 1845 the three warships, lying 660 yards offshore, opened fire and their big guns wreaked much destruction in a town built largely of wood. The Customs House was completely gutted, along with 'a considerable part of the town'. That afternoon 350 men, of whom 100 were French soldiers and the rest crew members of the three vessels, crowded into fourteen boats, landed on the beach and headed for the fort 200 yards across a small plain. The landing was screened by a dense plantation. Desfosses said in his report:

> In less than 10 minutes our combatants were drawn up in battle array, with two howitzers of the *Berceau* placed on mountain carriages, in the centre of the column. The enemy confined himself, during the landing, to a few grapeshots which produced little or no effect. Captain Fiereck soon after gave the signal for the charge, and the small band rushed with incredible ardour towards the enemy, who was afraid to quit his entrenchments. The men of the *Zelee*, joined by 20 sailors and an ensign of the *Berceau*, immediately entered the low battery to the south, spiked three pieces of cannon and dismounted two others, and drove the Hova cannoneers into the principal fort, which they vainly tried to enter.

Five Frenchmen were killed storming the battery, and Ensign Berthe was run through the chest and fell on the fort's threshold. Sub-lieutenant Monod of the French Marines also fell to a spear just yards away.

The joint force soon came under sharp fire from another direction. The *Conway*'s guns soon silenced those of that battery, which was then quickly overrun and its guns spiked. Massive outworks were then stormed but the attackers soon realised that their commanders had made an enormous error in assuming that the earthen ramparts were the fort itself. Instead, they formed a screen which hid the real citadel, a solid circular structure, 30 feet high, mounted with 30 cannon and surrounded by a dry moat 30 feet wide. An observer wrote: 'It may appear incredible, but it is positively asserted that the existence of the interior fort, the keep, was not known even to the traders and people of Tamatave.'

The fort at Tamatave, sketched from the mast-head of HMS *Conway*. (*Illustrated London News*)

The French were joined by the British contingents for the main assault. Desfosses wrote: 'In the fosse which separated the two enclosures, a desperate close combat ensued in which the English and French vied with each other in ardour and courage.' The Hova defenders, 'having bravely disputed every inch of ground,' retired into their casements. The attacking force held the rim of the earth screen for 40 minutes, but the fort's guns began to take their toll.

The warships poured shot into the fort – a total of 1,500 rounds during the entire engagement – but the only damage appeared to be to the flagstaff on the upper rampart. *The Times* correspondent reported: 'It was shot through and it fell inside the circular fort; it was then put on a lance, or something of that sort, and stuck again on the wall, in a crevice of the stones. It was shot away again, and this time it fell outward, hanging down within a few feet of the bottom of the ditch, between the inner fort and the screen.' It was swiftly ripped down by Ensign Granville, and a handful of British and French sailors. There then ensued an extraordinary dispute: the British and French, under heavy fire, conducted an unseemly brawl over who should take away the enemy standard. Musket balls whistled overhead and men dropped as the brawl turned into a tug of war between uneasy allies. One correspondent wrote: 'They were about to come to cutlass-blows with one another, in the very hottest of the Malagash fire, when Lieutenant Kennedy of the *Conway*, to prevent mischief, rushed down and with his sword cut it, giving half to each party.' The French carried off that portion of the pure white standard bearing the word 'Ranavalona', while the British took the half inscribed 'Manjaka', the second part of the queen's favoured title. Moments later Kennedy attacked a gun embrasure just as the Malagassy cannon was fired. Several men were killed and he was wounded, with a large splinter through both thighs.

The Malagassy cannon thundered in a land–sea artillery duel with the foreign vessels, tearing topmasts off the *Berceau* and *Zelee*. Desfosses reported: 'The firing of the Hovas had a precision which would have surprised us, had we not been informed that their artillery was directed by a renegade Spaniard who makes a most improper use of his talents.' Most of the Malagassy balls sailed harmlessly overhead, cutting only a few ropes aboard *Conway*.

By now the attackers on the rim were increasingly exposed to fire from within the fort and to the danger of Malagassy reinforcements arriving. The howitzers were able to fire only one shot because their quick matches had become wet during the shore landing. Captain Fiereck was disabled by a wound, the men were exhausted and running low on ammunition. Desfosses reported: 'Although the complete destruction of the enemy artillery, the great object of our enterprise, was not entirely attained, the lesson we had given those barbarous spoilaters of our merchants was of a nature not to be forgotten by them.' He duly gave the order to retreat and the men scrambled back down to the beach, carrying their wounded and the captured flag with them.

The disembarkation was carried off without a hitch by early evening. Priority was given to taking off all the wounded, 43 French and 12 British. That was achieved, but the dead were left behind – 17 Frenchmen and 4 Britons. One of the latter was a captured sailor who was tortured to death and mutilated. The heads of the dead men were cut off and impaled on stakes set at intervals along the beach. The grisly sight greeted visitors for the next eight years.

A Malagassy deserter who boarded *Berceau* told Desfosses that around 200 defenders had died on the batteries and inside the fort. They included the Deputy Governor, the queen's Standard Bearer, the Director of Customs and six other chiefs. On 17 June, two days after the assault, the allies went their separate ways, and the farcical brawl over the Malagassy standard was forgotten, at least in the official dispatches. Desfosses reported:

> I have just received and returned the farewell salute of the English frigate *Conway*; at the moment of parting, as during their presence here, the officers, sailors and soldiers of both nations did not cease to give each other the most hearty proofs of high esteem and cordial sympathy.

The following day Kelly wrote to Queen Ranavalona to justify his action, referring to 'the insolence and brutal injustice of the Tamatave authorities, which demanded punishment'. His response 'would be justified by all civilised Powers, especially as all proposals to arrange amicably the questions of dispute between us have been refused. We have not declared war on the Hovas, we have merely chastised your insolent offices.' The queen replied that all the blame lay at Kelly's door as his ship had fired first. She boasted that she had defeated 'the united forces of England and France'. Her officials demanded Kelly's surrender, 'dead or alive'.

The heads on the beach enraged public opinion in Britain and France, but the queen would not countenance their removal. In a letter to Kelly she said it was 'very strange and highly impertinent' that the European powers should seek to deny she was mistress in her own country, like Queen Victoria, and to deny her the right of fixing the heads of her prisoners on lances according to the custom of her country. She said that future correspondence to her must come from Victoria alone. The Mauritian newspaper *Le Cercen* stormed: 'This is what is called talking, or rather writing, like a Queen? It remains to be seen whether the two great heads of the two greatest nations in the world will approve, or at least excuse, the logical ultra-arrogance of Her Majesty of Madagascar.'

A few months after the bombardment a young Hova official, who had been educated in Paris, ordered the heads to be taken down and buried. His reward for this humane act was that the heads were exhumed and put back on the beach – along with his own.

Ranavalona ordered the expulsion of all remaining foreign traders and halted the export of beef and rice to Mauritius and Reunion. Huge military preparations were made in anticipation of another foreign attack, including a mad scheme to encase the whole vast island behind a sea-wall, but the expected invasion never came. The French government did indeed propose a punitive expedition. It was estimated that an invasion of Madagascar would need a minimum of 30,000 men, an army three times bigger than any ever sent to sea in the Indian Ocean. It would take three months to arrive and would require 300 men-of-war, store ships and transports. The *Examiner* reported:

The first object of a judicious enterprise will be to make for the interior, so as to avoid the pestiferous marshes of the coast, and strike a blow at the capital and power of the Hovas. That capital is in the centre of the broadest part of the island, and consequently at least 200 miles from the coast, laying in a country without roads, where the thermometer is seldom under 80 degrees, and where some resistance must be expected, at least 20 marches, and the establishment of at least 20 posts to maintain the communications with the fleet. If, instead of this, the army remains on the coast, the malaria and the Hovas will do the business – decimate it in a month, and cut off nine parts out of 10 within a twelve-month.

Not surprisingly, the Chamber of Deputies vetoed the expedition. Desfosses proposed that they should send arms and ammunition to rebel chiefs in the Madagascar hinterland, both to topple the queen and to extend French control. The minister responsible wrote in the margin of his report: 'Nothing of the sort must be done.'

Likewise, the British government had no stomach or political will for an expensive military undertaking. However, pressure from beef-strapped Mauritius led to diplomatic overtures to the queen to resume trade. She said she would consider it provided the British and French paid reparations for the bombardment of Tamatave. Lord Palmerston's government had no stomach for that either, and Madagascar remained closed to British and French goods. The Americans took advantage of the situation and for years enjoyed a virtual monopoly of foreign trade there.

The chief victim of Kelly's punitive action was Mauritius, which lost more than £22,000 in commerce annually. More seriously, the embargo caused serious food shortages as the small island colony suffered from the lack of beef and rice. After several years the merchants of Mauritius clubbed together and sent Ranavalona 1,500 dollars in reparations for Tamatave, stating that 'all the people regretted the attack' and entreating the queen 'to accept it for the injury done by Captain Kelly'. She accepted, considering it payment of a fine, and the ports were opened to the smaller islands. The heads on the beach were finally taken down and buried.

The queen's domestic reign of terror continued, and in 1849 there was another purge of native Christians. Noble converts were heavily fined and reduced to the rank of a common soldier. Over a hundred were flogged and sentenced to a lifetime's hard labour in chains. Fourteen were thrown over a 200-foot precipice below the queen's palace, known as 'the place of the hurling'. Another four nobles, including a husband and his heavily pregnant wife, were granted the privilege of being burnt alive. The wife went into labour when she was tied to the stake and the infant was consumed with her in the flames. A rare European visitor, Ida Pfeiffer, wrote in her diary: 'Terror . . . The streets are resounding with cries and howling; every one is fleeing from the town as though an enemy is threatening it.'

Generally the queen's vengeance now turned inwards against her own people – suspected plotters and displaced farmers she branded as 'brigands'. When even her most loyal subjects grew weary of the spectacle of mass public executions, they were carried out at night. Britain's role in arming and training the Hova army before the queen's coronation caused much heart-searching. A former missionary, the Revd J.J. Freeman, wrote:

> Great Britain, having supplied a handful of men with weapons of destruction and taught them how to wield them more effectually, by sending a few men to drill the natives, lent herself ungraciously to the task of abetting the ruin of independence, liberty, property, homes and lives of many tens of thousands of the peaceful inhabitants of the island, who had never raised a finger against the British throne, nor against the Hovas, but who now, furnished with British weapons, could desolate whole regions of inoffensive agriculturists and glory in schemes of conquest and rapine.

Laborde eventually fell from the queen's favour and was exiled, along with several other Europeans who faced a trumped-up charge of 'having wished to establish a republic, to liberate all slaves, and to establish equality without distinction of nobles'. Laborde sailed for the Île de Bourbon, and his workmen at Mantasoa reacted with frenzy, smashing factories, workshops and machinery. He later returned and after his death was buried under a large monument at Mantasoa.

Ranavalona died, aged eighty-one, in 1861, after a reign of thirty-three blood-soaked years. Freeman estimated that one million deaths were due directly or indirectly to wars during her reign; another 100,000 people were executed or massacred, and 20,000 women and children were taken as sex-slaves for the Hova troops.

Her beloved son and heir Radama II was sickened by her excesses and proved a benign ruler. He had been born twelve months after the death of his regal father – wise courtiers ignored the discrepancy – and had been raised by French tutors under the doting eye of his mother. He reopened his kingdom to Europeans and proposed a treaty with the French. He also released those chiefs and their families who had been prisoners for all his mother's reign, allowing them to take home the bones of those who had died in captivity. He abolished trial by *tanguena* and other barbaric punishments. He even, unheard-of in royal circles, paid wages to the workmen who built new palaces and civic structures. Two years later he was murdered in his palace and his wife Rasoherina took the throne. She continued his work and treaties were signed with Britain, France and America.

French influence grew, along with trade interests which the Republic needed to protect. In 1894 the French invaded and Madagascar became a colony. There were revolts and suppression, a British occupation in 1942, after the island had declared for the Vichy regime, and Madagascar eventually achieved independence in 1960. For most of the world, however, the island's history remains largely an untold story.

CHAPTER FOUR

The First Sikh War, 1845–6

'. . . A brutal bulldog fight.'

In the rose-red dusk of 21 September 1845 at Lahore, capital of the Punjab, the four widows of Jawahir Singh walked serenely through throngs of people towards a funeral pyre. Their husband, the late Wazir, had been chopped to bits by his own army the previous day and, as was the custom of *suttee*, his wives were to join the pieces of his body to be consumed by the flames. Each was young and beautiful; they were dressed in their best finery, gold embroidered in their silk trousers, jewels studding their ears and noses. They carried silver coins to toss to the multitude.

The dignity of the occasion did not last long. Several Sikh soldiers, members of the dreaded Khalsa army, grabbed the girls and brutally ripped the gold and jewellery from their flesh, tearing nostrils, ears and cheeks, and snatched the silver from their hands. It was a despicable act, inspired not just by greed but intended to dishonour the young widows and prevent them from making their final holy offerings. The girls mounted the pyre with their faces streaming blood.

The Maharani Jindan, the dead man's sister and mother of the Punjab's eight-year-old ruler, lay prostrate before them and asked for their blessing. The four about to die gave it willingly to her, but not to the men of the Khalsa. These they cursed robustly, forecasting that their military sect would be conquered, that their wives would be made widows, and the country made desolate. *Suttees* were held to be sacred with the power of the prophecy. Shaken and enraged soldiers swung at the girls with rifle butts as the flames crackled around their robes. The women died without making another sound.

Within a few short months, their prophecy was proved correct as the Khalsa were slaughtered by the thousand in the swollen Sutlej river, at what later became known as the 'Indian Waterloo'. It marked the end of the bloodiest war the British ever fought in India and decided the history of the sub-continent for a century.

★   ★   ★

In ancient times the Punjab, the Land of the Five Rivers, was inhabited by three races, the Jats, Rajputs and Afghans. Bounded by the Himalayas and the Indus and Sutlej rivers, it straddled the main access route to India for northern invaders and thus suffered from ceaseless warfare and conquest. Its people learnt to wear their swords while ploughing their land. It was ruled successively by Afghan invaders,

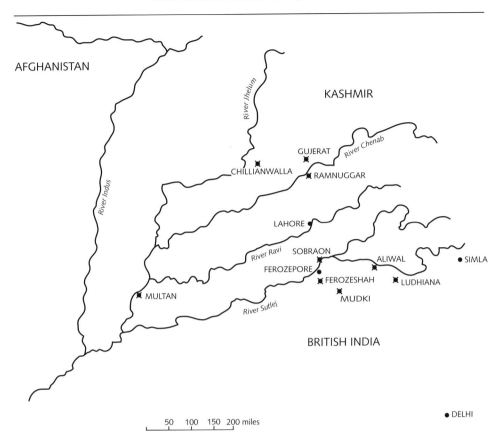

The Punjab – the 'Land of Five Rivers'.

Mongols, Turks, the Timur dynasty and the Mughal Empire. The intermingling of blood, languages and customs created a new people with their own tongue, the Punjabi. They in turn created a new faith which was to challenge and overturn the power of traditional rulers.

The founder of the Sikh religion, Baba Nanak, was born in 1469. His creed, an amalgam of Hindu and Sufi Islamic mysticisms, was based on the unity of God and the brotherhood of all men. Over successive generations the Sikh faith became transformed into a military order represented by the Khalsa, or the Pure, a religious army united against the Mughal Empire which ruled from Delhi. In the late seventeenth century the guru Gobind Raj decreed that all Sikhs should take the name Singh, meaning warrior. They must leave their hair and beards uncut, wear knee-length military trousers and a steel bangle on their right wrists, and always carry a sword. Honour could be gained in war alone. They were forbidden to molest women, drink alcohol, smoke tobacco or eat meat unless the animal was killed with a single blow. Their military prowess flourished as they beat the Mughals and the orthodox Hindus and Moslems who surrounded them. A foreigner who lived among them wrote:

All that a Sikh chief asked in these days from a follower was a horse and a matchlock. All that a follower sought was protection and permission to plunder in the name of God and the Guru under the banner of the chief. All Sikhs were theoretically equal, and he who could pierce a tree through with an arrow, or who could kill a tiger with a blow of his sword, might soon ride with followers behind him and call himself a *sirdar*. No man could consider his land, his horse or his wife secure unless he was strong enough to defend them.

James Browne, an officer in the East India Company, wrote more sympathetically: 'The Sikhs from necessity confederated tog ther, and finding that their peaceable deportment did not secure them from oppression, they took up arms to defend themselves against a tyrannical government.'

From the turmoil that followed the defeat of the Mughals emerged one man strong enough to unite the Sikhs and turn the Punjab into a nation, Runjeet Singh. Born in 1780, in his teens he led the resistance to Afghan invaders, beating two armies from the north and driving them from the capital city of Lahore. In 1801 he proclaimed himself Maharajah of the Punjab and ruled his country firmly until his death in 1837.

He was a one-eyed despot with an insatiable thirst for women and wine, and his court orgies were notorious and unashamed. He was cruel and greedy, and had little formal education. But he was a natural leader of men and no fool. He watched closely the expansion of British power to the south of his domain and the victories won by John Company's armies against all-comers. For a while he allied himself with the Marathas against the British, who were then mostly concerned with consolidating their possessions in India so they could focus on defeating the armies of Napoleon.

In 1802 Runjeet took the city of Amritsar, underlining his supreme authority. In 1803 he visited a British encampment disguised as an ordinary soldier. He observed the skill of the redcoats and sepoys as they drilled and were trained in weaponry. After concluding a humiliating treaty with the British he resolved to match them in modern firepower, ready for the day, which he knew must come, when the British Empire came knocking on his door.

He built the Khalsa into a superbly armed and killed army of 29,000 regular infantry with 192 guns, staffed with French, Italian, British, German, American and Russian instructors. British muskets were bought in their thousands and copied in Lahore's belching foundries. Runjeet's favourites were the Ghorcharas, his own irregular cavalry, which received the best arms, equipment and training. British observers were especially impressed by the Sikh Lancers, who trained by riding full pelt at tent pegs stuck in the ground, more often than not striking them with their long weapons. The heavy dragoons, clad in chainmail, were also formidable. Captain William Osborne regarded the Sikh soldiers as 'the finest material in the world for forming an army'. He, like other British visitors, was especially impressed by their drill and appearance. He recalled:

Maharajah Runjeet Singh, gouache by a Sikh artist, *c.* 1836.

I never saw so straight or beautiful a line with any troops. They were all dressed in white with black cross belts and either a red or yellow silk turban; armed with muskets and bayonets of excellent manufacture . . . The commanding officer beats and abuses the major, the major the captains, the captains the subalterns, and so on till there is nothing left for the private to beat but the drummer boys, who catch it accordingly.

Such discipline, however, could not destroy the individualism inherent in the Sikh nature, or their lust for booty. In successive wars they grew rich on the spoils won by beating the Gurkhas, the Kashmiris and the last Afghan contingents in the Punjab. And they expected to get richer fighting the British. That meant that their discipline disintegrated under their desire for battlefield looting. Runjeet understood the defect and conceded: 'The system of the British is [so] good that even if the enemy threw gold coins in the course of their flight, the soldiers would not even look at them. On the other hand, if the Khalsa soldiers saw mere corn, they would break their ranks, dash towards that and spoil the whole plan of operations.'

Runjeet prized his artillery above all and employed many foreigners in order to raise its standards to the European level. Foremost among these was Colonel Alexander Gardner. An American soldier of fortune who dressed in tartan, he became a powerful figure both in the Khalsa and the Lahore court. Two British 24-pound howitzers that had been presented to Runjeet were swiftly copied in the local foundries. Osborne witnessed a practice by the Khalsa gunners, firing at a

Sikh lancers. (*Illustrated London News*)

Sikh soldiers, sketched by an officer of the Bengal Engineers. (*Illustrated London News*)

curtain hung 200 yards away, and said their skills would have been a credit to any artillery in the world. 'At the first round of grape, the curtain was clean cut away, and their shells at eight and twelve hundred yards were thrown with a precision that is extraordinary, when the short period of time since they have known even of the existence of such a thing is taken into consideration.'

The first real test of Runjeet Singh's new army was against Kashmir, and it passed the test easily, routing its enemies and rescuing Shah Sujah, the captured former ruler of Afghanistan. The ex-captive had no choice but to award to Runjeet the fabulous Koh-i-noor, then the largest diamond in the world, as a mark of gratitude. This 105-carat gem, known as 'the mountain of light', was mined in the twelfth century in southern India and was the figurehead of the throne of the Moghul emperors. Legend said it was a gift from the sun god Surya. Each successive ruler fought to gain and retain possession of it, and it was said to be worth the value of one day's food for all the people in the world. Runjeet Singh wore it proudly on his bracelet.

In 1818 Runjeet captured Multan and the neighbouring districts and a year later annexed the whole of Kashmir. By 1823 the Khalsa had destroyed the Afghan and Pathan forces in the north-west frontier province. Runjeet controlled all the land as far as the Khyber Pass. This was the peak of Sikh power. For some years Runjeet's court at Lahore rivalled any of the royal courts of Europe. Sikh art flourished and weapons became both functional and illustrative of the artisans' finest skills. Captain Osborne described the sumptuousness of one chief, Raja Suchet Singh:

His dress was magnificent; a helmet or skull cap of bright polished steel inlaid with gold, and a deep fringe of chainmail, of the same material, reaching to his shoulders, three plumes of black heron's feathers waving on his chest, and three shawls of lilac, white and scarlet, twisted very round and tight, interlaced with one another and gathered round the edge of the helmet, a chelenk of rubies and diamonds on his forehead. Back, breastplates, and gauntlets of steel, richly embossed with gold and precious stones, worn over a rich, thick-quilted jacket of bright yellow silk, with magnificent armlets of rubies and diamonds on each arm, a shield of the polished hide of the rhinoceros, embossed and ornamented with gold, a jewelled sabre and matchlock, with his long and glossy black beard and moustaches he looked the very beau ideal of a Sikh chief.

As the Khalsa secured victory and wealth for the fledgling state, its power increased. The soldiers were commanded by the Akalis, also known as the Crocodiles, a strict sect devoted to 'misrule and plunder'. They demanded their share of political power and played a full part in court intrigue. They were hostile to the British and other faithless men, and they watched suspiciously as the British took other strategic lands in an attempt to keep their neighbour under control. The Khalsa, in their turn, cast covetous eyes across the Sutlej at the rich lands of the Raj. As long as Runjeet lived their power could be checked and channelled in useful directions, but when he died in June 1837 there was no one strong enough to replace him. He was placed on a pyre of sandalwood along with four of his eighteen wives and seven of his slave girls. Henry Princep, a Briton who admired the Sikh nation, wrote: 'Ranjit Singh has, in the formation especially of his military force, evinced the same enquiring activity, the same attention to minutiae, which characterised the first Peter of Russia.'

After his death there followed six years of turmoil and murder. Runjeet's only legitimate son, Kharak Singh, was a degenerate opium-eater. He was swiftly poisoned by his son, the eighteen-year-old Nau Nihal Singh. That young man fell from power even more quickly, and in suspicious circumstances – he was killed by a falling archway as he returned from his father's cremation. He was replaced by Shere Singh, the eldest of Runjeet's illegitimate sons, who lasted a full two years. During that time Kharak's widow, Chaund Cour, conspired against the new ruler, but was crushed to death by her own slave girls, who dropped a great stone on her while she bathed. Shere Singh could not honour his promises of greater wealth, despite his lavish expenditure on his own decadent court, and the Khalsa ran amok, sacking bazaars and killing unpopular officers. In 1843 Shere Singh was reviewing his troops when an officer shot him with a double-barrelled shotgun and stuck his head on the point of a spear. Runjeet's youngest son, the six-year-old Duleep Singh, became Maharajah of a country divided between warring factions and dominated by an uncontrollable army. When Duleep's Wazir, Hira Singh, tried to impose his authority he too was cut down by the mutinous Khalsa.

Within the Lahore Palace the power was divided between Maharani Jindan, the young mother of the nominal ruler, her lover Lal Singh, and her brother, the drunken Jawahir Singh. Together they tried to control the Khalsa in the traditional way, by bribery, by increasing its manpower to almost 80,000, and by promising

_____ ____ turns to service her each night. Jawahir Singh, who was made Wazir, was simply a drunkard. 'I sometimes feel as if I were a sort of parish constable at the door of a brothel rather than the representative of one government to another,' Broadfoot complained.

The British administration was appalled by such reports and by the succession of royal murders. The new Governor-General in British India, Sir Henry Hardinge, had initially believed that a strong, stable Sikh state could be re-established in the Punjab and would act as a solid buffer zone to protect Britain's interests. He soon realised his error, and began to build up forces at the border. This was noted by the Khalsa leaders, who also knew of Hardinge's reputation as an aggressive soldier. Sikh agents were sent to sow the seeds of mutiny among the sepoys, offering better pay and the prospect of loot to the poorly paid Company men. Few responded but the attempt caused great concern among the British officers.

Back across the Sutlej, the Khalsa grew increasingly impatient. Jawahir, terrified that he would 'die a dog's death' like his predecessor Hira Singh, offered them ever larger bribes of gold and silver, but his promises could not be kept as the treasury emptied. He promised war with the British, but the Khalsa said they would not be led by a fool. The *panchayats*, or military councils, decided to seize power themselves. On 21 September 1845 they ordered the Maharani, with her son and all the government officials, to attend the Khalsa parade outside Lahore. She agreed, telling her trembling brother that the Khalsa would not dare challenge their authority. Jawahir Singh, despite his fears, rode out with the party on an elephant, nestling the young Maharajah on his lap.

Gardner described what followed:

> An ominous salute ran along the immense line of the army – one hundred and eighty guns were fired. After the salute had died away, not a sound was heard but the trampling of the feet of the royal cavalcade. As soon as the procession reached the centre of the line one man came forward and shouted 'Stop,' and at his voice the whole procession paused. A tremor ran through the host . . .

Maharani Jindan was dragged screaming to a sumptuous tent. Her royal son was pulled from her brother's grip and handed to her. 'Meanwhile,' Gardner wrote, 'the bloody work had been done . . . A soldier had gone up the ladder placed by Jawahir

Sikh heavy artillery pulled by elephants. (*Illustrated London News*)

Singh's elephant, stabbed him with his bayonet and flung him upon the ground, where he was despatched in a moment with fifty wounds.' The Maharani, mad with grief, was allowed to crouch by his dismembered body where she screamed lamentations and pledged that every man in the Khalsa would meet a similar end.

The Khalsa leaders, shaken by her words and by those of the *suttees* at the funeral pyre, realised that they had gone too far. Two days later, when the Maharani took over the government of the country, they acknowledged her as Regent. She charmed them by appearing dressed as a near-naked dancing girl. But behind the scanty veil she embarked on a dangerous double game. The Khalsa believed that the legendary invincibility of the British Army had been dealt an irrevocable blow by the massacre by Afghans of a column retreating from Kabul, and they wanted to capitalise on that disaster. The Maharani urged caution and for a time they complied. But privately Jindan still wanted both to avenge her brother and to break the power of the Khalsa for the sake of her son's future rule. She was determined to see her own army destroyed. She delayed every military order, to give the British a chance to mass their forces, while sending Broadfoot's agents secret intelligence on the Khalsa's intentions and strength.

Hardinge responded by strengthening the British frontier defence forces to 25,000 men. They were, however, dangerously dispersed between brick barracks at Ludhiana, Ferozepore, Ambala and Meerut, 130 sweltering miles from the border. Sir Henry refused to believe intelligence reports that six Khalsa divisions totalling perhaps 60,000 men under the command of the cowardly and treacherous Tej Singh were poised to cross the Sutlej. Many British factions actively encouraged war, believing it would give them the excuse to expand British territory. Sir Henry reported:

I do not expect that the [Khalsa] troops will come as far as the banks of the Sutlej, or that any positive acts of aggression will be committed; but it is evident that the Rani and the Chiefs are for their own preservation, endeavouring to raise a storm which, when raised, they will be powerless either to direct or allay . . .

His doubts that the Sikhs meant business were proved wrong on 10 December 1845 when Sikh cavalry and skirmishers crossed the broad, muddy Sutlej at Hariki, near Ferozepore. The news provoked a shout of defiance from men of the 8th Foot, and wails from local women. The Sikh war had begun while the British were muddled and confused, and the Sikhs themselves were weakened by treachery and betrayal among their leaders.

★　　★　　★

Sir Henry Hardinge may have dithered in the run-up to the war, but there was no doubting he was a man of action. Now aged sixty, he was a veteran of the Napoleonic Wars, and had lost his left hand at Quatre Bras, two days before Waterloo. He became MP for Durham in 1820 and, under the patronage of his former commander Wellington, was Secretary of War until his appointment as Governor-General of India, where he replaced his brother-in-law Lord Ellenborough. At the War Office he was popular as a 'just, upright and considerate chief'. He was already in Umbullah when the Sikh invasion began and his first priority was to bring together his forces to face the threat.

The man in charge of those forces was Sir Hugh Gough. An old soldier born in Limerick, Gough attracted controversy throughout his career, and at sixty-six was an old warhorse whom his own soldiers affectionately called 'Tipperary Joe'. Slightly older than Hardinge, he had seen more action: he was at the surrender of the Dutch fleet at Saldanha Bay, at the capture of both Trinidad and Surinam, at the battle of Talavera, where he was severely wounded and had the first of many horses shot from under him, and at the battle of Barossa, where he led a famous charge to capture a French eagle standard. He was severely wounded at the battle of Nivelle in 1813 and spent most of his middle years on half pay, being given his first big command when he was sixty. After heroic service in the Opium War he was created a baronet and transferred to India. His command of forces in the Gwalior War was not universally praised. His critics regarded him as vainglorious to the point of incompetence. Lord Ellenborough, then Governor-General, wrote to Wellington: 'Despite his many excellent qualities, he had not the grasp of mind and the prudence essential to conduct great military operations.' That view was never shared by the men under his command who, in a brutal military age, appreciated his concern for their welfare. Private George Tookey of the 14th Light Dragoons proudly told his mother that when Gough visited him and others in hospital he treated them as if they were officers. He always led from the front, sharing the same dangers as his men. A sergeant in the Bengal Artillery wrote: 'When he was present the men looked upon success as certain, and it was not as a commander alone that he was respected, but as a kind-feeling and good-hearted old man . . .' What

General Sir Hugh Gough wearing his 'fighting coat'. (Sir Francis Grant)

confounded Gough's critics the most, as will be seen, was that he won battles, despite his perceived failings.

The plan agreed between the Governor-General and the army commander was to join up General Sir John Littler's 7,000-strong garrison at Ferozepore with the main British force at Ludhiana. Gough led the main column of 11,000 men with 42 guns while Littler waited for several days, expecting his light defences to be overrun at any moment by Sikh cavalry. But Tej Singh, the Khalsa commander, and Lal Singh, the prime minister, who held joint command, were in league with the Maharani. In a secret dispatch to Littler Lal Singh reaffirmed their friendship with the British. Major Carmichael Smyth of the Bengal Light Cavalry wrote with disgust that Tej Singh and Lal Singh, 'instead of watching for opportunities to employ the force to the best advantage, were intent only on placing their troops in such a position as might render them an easy and complete conquest to their foes'. They held back from attack and split their forces, Tej Singh investing Littler's garrison while Lal Singh went out to meet Gough's column.

Gough, the ultimate fighting general, drove his parched men by rapid marches through choking dust clouds. Incredibly, given the awful conditions and lack of both food and water, the column marched 114 miles in just five days. They reached the small village of Mudki, 18 miles south-east of Ferozepore, on 18 December, having marched 20 miles that day alone. Village shops were ordered to open to sell grain to the British, who had their first proper meal for days during the mid-afternoon. But the food had to be bolted down as the Sikhs, drawn by the smoke from the soldiers' fires, began to advance. Lal Singh commanded some 8,000 cavalry, 2,000 infantry and 22 guns. The first salvo from the Sikh guns shot a horse from under Major Henry Havelock, who was later to win glory defending Lucknow during the Indian Mutiny. Gough pushed forward his own horse artillery and cavalry across the flat terrain, dotted with sandy hillocks and thick patches of jungle. The Sikhs took advantage of whatever cover was at hand, while the British advanced in the same rigid formations that had been deployed against the French Emperor thirty years before.

The five troops of horse artillery under Brigadier Brooke galloped forward in a line towards the Sikh guns and the first part of the battle became an artillery duel at 300 yards' range. Gough reported: 'The enemy opened a very severe cannonade upon our advancing troops, which was vigorously replied to.' A young gunner tasting action for the first time recalled seeing a ventsman 'running about disembowelled,' a corporal whose hand was shattered by round-shot as he was firing his own gun, a fallen comrade shot through the eye, and another friend sitting upright in his saddle with a great hole punched through his chest. 'These sights were not pleasant,' he wrote home.

The Sikh cavalry advanced through the thick dust and smoke as the day's light began to fade, aiming to encircle both flanks. Gough saw the danger and ordered the 3rd Light Dragoons and units of the 4th Light Cavalry to stop them. The British horsemen charged with their long lances and drove into the lighter Sikh cavalry. The dragoons turned the enemy's left flank and swept down the entire line of Sikh gunners and infantry. Lieutenant John Cumming wrote: 'Oh, how I wish for a thousand more good British horse to join that whirlwind charge.' The British casualties mounted, however, as Sikh infantry hidden behind the scrub shot down horses and butchered fallen men with their swords. Sikh snipers picked off the British officers.

It was now the turn of the British infantry. With less than an hour of daylight left, twelve battalions of redcoats, mainly sepoys, marched forward. The Sikh fired disciplined volleys into their ranks while the enemy guns blasted away with grapeshot. Some sepoys began firing indiscriminately, hitting British units in the back, while others broke and ran. Lieutenant Robertson of the 31st Foot described that action as 'a regular mob, and nearly as many shots coming from behind us as in front'. Havelock, newly rehorsed, rode around them shouting 'The enemy are in front of you, not behind you.' Order was restored but the battle became a confused mêlée as darkness fell.

The Sikh gunners kept their guns 'vomiting forth at a fine rate showers of grape' while British and sepoy units lost their sense of direction in the choking, dusty gloom. Two officers carrying the colours of the 31st Foot fell and Sergeant Jones won an immediate battlefield commission by rescuing the flag. Brigadier Wheeler fell badly wounded but the divisional commander, Sir Harry Smith, led a charge into 'the very teeth of a Sikh column'. The British momentum failed again in the confusion, while Gough rode up and down yelling 'We must take those guns.' No one knew precisely where they were. Men of the 31st stumbled on one Sikh battery and took it in a rush. Others followed as the British army's five-to-one superiority in foot soldiers began to tell. But it was no easy matter as the Sikhs fought on with brave determination even when their big guns fell silent. Lieutenant Herbert Edwardes wrote: 'The last two hours of the battle were a series of dogged stands, and skirmishing retreats on the part of the Sikh troops, of sharp struggles, gun captures and recaptures, and a British pursuit over five miles of the worst ground that armies ever fought for.' Gough reported that the Sikhs,

> were driven from position after position with great slaughter and the loss of seventeen pieces of artillery; our infantry using the never-failing weapon, the bayonet, whenever the enemy stood. Night only saved them from worse disaster, for this stout conflict was maintained during an hour and a half of dim starlight, amid a cloud of dust from the sandy plain, which yet more obscured every object.

Among British soldiers unused to fighting at night, the battle became known as the 'Midnight Mudki'.

The Sikhs were driven back to their camp at Ferozeshah but were far from decisively beaten. Gough's losses were surprisingly heavy, particularly as he faced a weaker foe. Among his ranks 215 were killed and 657 wounded, many of who would not survive. Senior officers were in the thick of the fighting and their high casualty rate reflected that. Generals Sir John McCaskill and Sir Robert 'Fighting Bob' Sale, the hero of Jellalabad, were among the dead, as were Brigadiers Bolton and Wheeler. Sale's left thigh was shattered by grapeshot and McCaskill was shot through the

The death of Major Broadfoot at the battle of Mudki. (*Illustrated London News*)

chest. Major Broadfoot was hacked to pieces with spear and sword. Hardinge was highly critical of Gough's actions and reported that at Mudki 'the confusion of the attack had created a feeling that the army was not well in hand'. From then on Hardinge lost no opportunity to criticise his army commander, even though it was largely his own earlier refusal to allow Gough to deploy forces closer to the border which had made Gough's mad dash necessary.

General Sale wounded at Mudki. (*Illustrated London News*)

The British forces, half-dead with fatigue after a long march and a gruelling battle, reached their camp shortly after midnight to snatch a few hours of sleep. The bugles woke them at dawn, and they rose ready to fight another battle.

★   ★   ★

The exhausted British troops had some respite while their commanders considered tactics. They were joined by reinforcements, 3,200 men made up of the 29th Foot, the 1st European Light Infantry, and two sepoy regiments. Hardinge, the Governor-General, was eager to taste battle himself after a lapse of thirty years. Although they had been appointed lieutenant-generals on the same day, Hardinge came below Gough on the army list and he accordingly placed himself under Gough's command on the battlefield. Gough had no option but to accept him as his second-in-command, writing in dispatches 'I need hardly say with how much pleasure the offer was accepted.' Diplomacy or sarcasm? Gough must have known that to have his political superior as his military second could only cause complications at best and, at worse, confusion in the chain of command.

At 4 a.m. on 21 December, after a day's rest which enabled the Sikhs a day to strengthen their entrenchments, the British marched towards the enemy positions surrounding the small fortified village of Ferozeshah. By 11 a.m. they were ready to attack the Sikh defences which were around a mile in length and half a mile deep. Gough wanted to push on at once, while there was plenty of daylight left. Hardinge insisted on waiting until they were joined by Littler's column of 7,000 men which was marching in a sweep from Ferozepore, 13 miles distant. In a tense confrontation Gough snarled that to wait was to risk another night battle, while to move towards Littler's force would mean abandoning his wounded at Mudki. He also pointed out that the day before Hardinge had put himself under his, Gough's, command. Hardinge, who had not been impressed by Gough's pell-mell tactics at Mudki, replied: 'Then, Sir Hugh, I must exercise my civil powers as Governor-General and forbid the attack until Littler's force has come up.' Gough had no option but to comply and for several hours the general fumed as his army waited, equally impatiently.

Eventually a cloud of dust was seen and Littler's division at last took its place in the centre of the British line. Gough took personal charge of the left wing while Hardinge, who now reverted to second-in-command, took the left. Sir Harry Smith's division and a small cavalry force formed a second line. Forming up took more time and it was 3.30 p.m. before everything was in place. Already the shadows were getting longer. The bulk of the 18,000 men were to attack the Sikhs' western and southern positions, under the gaping jaws of every enemy gun.

At 4 p.m. the British moved forward as an artillery duel whistled overhead. It was an uneven fight: unaccountably, the British 18-pounders had been left behind at Mudki, while the Sikh artillery was much heavier. Captain John Cumming wrote home: 'Long before our artillery was in range, their cannon were making fearful havoc of us.' Littler, believing that only speed could save his men from the butcher's block, advanced without giving neighbouring units time to deploy. The 62nd Foot rushed towards the Sikh guns, yelling savagely. Within three minutes 17 of the 23 officers and 250 men had been cut down. Three regiments of sepoys held back; parched by the heat and dust, they went to drink from a nearby well. Gough, seeing Littler's plight, ordered a general attack to support him. Cummings recalled:

We advanced against a hailstorm of roundshot, shells, grape and musketry. The slaughter was terrible. Yet our fellows pressed nobly on with the charge, and with the bayonet alone rushed over the entrenchments and captured the guns in front of us. The Sikhs flinched not an inch, but fought till they died to a man at their guns.

A sepoy veteran, Sita Ram, said: 'This was fighting indeed. I had never seen anything like it before.' But exploding mines and ammunition boxes forced the British back and most of the survivors of Littler's division played little further part in the brutal battle, now reckoned to have been the most savage in Anglo-Indian history.

The Sikh guns kept up a continuous barrage as the British charged into the setting sun. The light infantry overran one Sikh battery, slaying every defender, but were then caught in a murderous cross-fire. All along the lines the battle degenerated into hand-to-hand combat around the Sikh guns. As one battery was taken, the British came under volley fire from the enemy infantry. A young ensign said: 'The air was so filled with fire and smoke that it seemed to be dark as night.'

Sir Walter Gilbert's division was threatened by a mass of Sikh cavalry and the battle hung on a knife-edge. A ferocious charge by the 31st Light Dragoons led by Brigadier Michael White put them to flight, but at heavy cost.

As real darkness fell, units, brigades and even divisions became intermingled in the confusion, but still the attack pressed on. To the left the red-coated lines faltered but were stiffened by General Smith's advance. Smith reported:

> I saw there was nothing for it but a charge of bayonets to restore the waning fight. I, Colonel Petit and Colonel Ryan put ourselves at the head of the 50th and most gallantly did we charge into the enemy's trenches, where such a hand-to-hand conflict followed as I have ever witnessed. The enemy was repulsed at this point, his works and cannon carried and he precipitately retreated.

Similar success was won on the right flank, as men poured over the outer breastworks and clambered over corpse-filled ditches. But the Sikhs would not accept defeat.

The battle now raged within the camp itself, along the lines of tents, outside the mud and stone defences of Ferozeshah village, every inch fiercely contested. Combatants on both sides were hit by a 'frightful roar' as a Sikh powder magazine exploded. Eighteen-year-old Ensign Percy Innes wrote later:

> The ground heaved and the men in the vicinity were blown away amongst the tents, the air being filled with fire, and a dense smoke arising, which, as it cleared away, exposed to view a horrible and appalling scene, numbers of our men having fallen frightfully burnt and mutilated, and in some instances their [ammunition] pouches ignited, causing terrible wounds, agony and loss of life.

The fire spread, casting a ruddy light on Smith's brigade as it threw itself against the heavily defended village at the camp's centre. The British line ran through the encampment and overwhelmed the Sikhs, who were hampered behind their mud walls by large numbers of richly clad horses and camels, maddened by fright. Smith pushed on past the village but his force was then encircled by Sikhs mounting a counter-attack. He formed a defensive half-circle, but his men were exhausted. Some were killed as they fell asleep, and Smith was forced to retire back into the main encampment.

Pitch darkness and fatigue forced both sides to call an uneasy halt. The British pulled back from positions hard won and settled down for a hellish night. Gough's forces held some parts of the camp while the Sikhs slipped back into others. The nights was punctuated by the crack of exploding ammunition, the screams of the wounded and dying, the sudden crackle of musketry as both sides stumbled into each other. For the British the chief priority was water. The Sikhs had laced the wells with gunpowder and corpses. Horses turned away from them with disgust but many officers and men did not, later suffering the consequences with crippling stomach cramps and vomiting. Lieutenant Robert Bellers wrote:

No one can imagine the dreadful uncertainty. A burning camp on one side of the village, mines and ammunition wagons exploding in every direction, the loud orders to extinguish the fires as the Sepoys lighted them, the volleys given should the Sikhs venture too close, the booming of the monster gun, the incessant firing of the smaller one, the continual whistling noise of the shell, grape and round shot, the bugles sounding, the drums beating, and the yelling of the enemy, together with the intense thirst, fatigue and cold, and no knowing whether the rest of the army were the conquerors or the conquered – all contributed to make this night awful in the extreme.

Hardinge spent most of the night moving among the men, trying to raise morale with heavy-handed humour, while Gough tried to bring some order into the regiments and units mixed up together. Neither man knew whether the battle was won or lost. Hardinge, despite his attempts to reassure the troops, obviously feared the worst. He sent a messenger back to Mudki with orders to destroy his private papers if they were indeed defeated. But dawn showed that they had captured most of the battlefield, along with seventy-one Sikh artillery pieces. But the enemy remained close by and the early sun reflected off thousands of bayonets. Gough immediately gave the order to attack.

Three troops of horse artillery advanced at the gallop, unlimbered and another artillery duel began, with the Sikhs answering effectively. But Gough sensed a faltering in the Sikh morale. He led the right wing and Hardinge the left in an infantry charge as a flight of rockets streaked overhead. During three hours of fighting the remaining Sikh trenches were taken, lost and re-taken. Gough wrote in dispatches:

Our infantry formed line, supported on both flanks by horse artillery, whilst a fire was opened from our centre by such of our heavy guns as remained effective. A masked battery played with great effect upon this point, dismounting our pieces and blowing up our tumbrels. Our line advanced and, unchecked by the enemy's fire, drove them rapidly out of the village and their encampment.

Lieutenant Robertson described one encounter:

We advanced very quietly upon a strong battery; they did not see us till we were right upon them, and they had only time to fire one or two rounds when we gave them a volley and charged right into them. We bayoneted a great many artillerymen and infantry who stood to the last, we also took a standard, and then charged on through the camp, polishing off all we could get at.

By lunchtime the enemy had been completely driven out of the camp and the victors were saluted by their commanders. Hardinge wrote: 'The brave men drew up in an excellent line, and cheered Gough and myself as we rode up the line, the regimental colours lowering to me as on parade.' However, the euphoria of victory did not last long. Scouts swiftly reported that another Sikh army, that of Tej Singh, was rapidly advancing on them, their fresh troops anxious to avenge their beaten comrades. For some moments even Gough's spirits fell. His men were exhausted, thirsty, hungry and almost out of ammunition. Their position seemed hopeless. As his men groaned and looked in horror at the advancing multitude, the old soldier pulled himself and his men together and prepared for another fight.

The British formed themselves into squares around Ferozeshah while the horse artillery limbered up. Troop after troop trotted out to challenge the Sikh guns. Each was either beaten back or retired when their ammunition ran out. The opposing lines of infantry, the British in red jackets, the Sikhs in blue, moved steadily towards each other. Forty Sikh guns cut bloody holes in the British ranks but the heavy guns fell silent as the Sikh cavalry skirted the plain ready to charge and sweep away their tired foe. It was 2 p.m. and the devout among the British prayed for a miracle.

The 3rd Dragoons, supported by two regiments of native cavalry, tried gamely to provide it. Led by Colonel White, they managed to lash their exhausted horses into a gallop and drove straight into the Sikh cavalry. The enemy fell back, momentarily stunned. They soon recovered from the shock, however, and their artillery again pounded the British lines. Gough spurred his horse and rode out in front of his men, aiming to draw a portion of the enemy fire. 'We, thank God, succeeded,' he later wrote, 'my gallant horse being a conspicuous mark – unheeding the thunder of a shot ploughing up the earth around him.' Such a gallant gesture momentarily put new heart in his men.

The uplift of morale was short-lived as all the surviving British and Bengal cavalry and the horse artillery suddenly wheeled around and began to canter off the battlefield towards Ferozepore, leaving the generals and the infantry alone to face the Khalsa. The cause of their abandonment, although they did not know it at the time, was an officer driven crazy by the battle. Captain Lumley, the acting Adjutant-General, had used his authority to order the artillery to retire to Ferozepore to refill their ammunition boxes and had instructed the cavalry to escort them. (Lumley, the son of a general, was later allowed to resign rather than face a court-martial.) There was nothing Gough could do, and he and his infantry stood firm, apparently facing certain massacre. The infantry's ammunition was almost exhausted and Gough told his troops to 'trust to the bayonet'.

Tej Singh's infantry began to advance to loud drum beats. Suddenly the noise of the drums was pierced by Sikh bugles sounding the retreat. In full sight of the astonished British, they turned on their heels and began to march back towards the Sutlej. Once again the Khalsa had been betrayed by their commanders when victory was within reach. Tej Singh, who always had to disguise his treachery from his army commanders, convinced them that the cavalry and artillery withdrawal was a feint and that they would attack them from the rear. The action of a madman and the response of a traitor had rescued a British army from a certain annihilation. Havelock said with awe: 'India has been saved by a miracle.'

The Sikhs did not stop until they reached the Sutlej and crossed its muddy waters. Gough had won another victory, but it was a costly one. The British suffered

2,415 casualties, of whom 694 were dead; many more would later succumb to their wounds. Gough had lost one-seventh of his entire force. A sergeant of the 16th Lancers, who arrived too late for the battle, wrote:

> On our arrival at the camp ground the stench was horrible. A great many were buried within a few yards of our tents. As soon as we had pitched our camp we walked out on the field of battle to view the place and for miles around we could see the dead lying in all directions.

Hardinge said tartly: 'Another such victory and we are undone.' Once again the casualty rate among officers was especially high and Gough took the unprecedented step of giving commissions to five sergeant-majors. He later defended his move against staff disapproval by saying: 'I scarcely had an alternative; my losses in officers were so great that it was absolutely necessary.'

Hardinge did his best to get Gough dismissed. He wrote secretly after the battle to his close friend Sir Robert Peel, the British prime minister:

> It is my duty to Her Majesty, and to you as head of the Government, to state, confidentially, that we have been in the greatest peril, and we are likely hereafter to be in great peril, if these very extensive operations are to be conducted by the Commander-in-Chief. Gough is a brave and fearless officer, an honourable man, and a fine-tempered gentleman, and an excellent leader of a brigade or a division. However, he is not the officer who ought to be entrusted with the conduct of the war in the Punjab. I cannot risk the safety of India by concealing my opinion from you. Sir Hugh Gough has no capacity for order or administration. His staff is very bad, and the state of the army is loose, disorderly and unsatisfactory.

Hardinge did not, of course, report his interference and his role in the delays which had come so close to causing a disaster. He further proposed that Sir Charles Napier should take over command of the field army. But his damning report could not overcome the fact that Gough had, again, won a victory, albeit an expensive one. The government could not justify the sacking of an officer who had won a battle. They did, however, agree in London that Hardinge should himself take overall military command. That authorisation, luckily for Gough, took a long time arriving, and by then it was too late to implement.

Gough and his men camped in a fortified position north of Ferozeshah while Hardinge went with Littler to Ferozepore. Both awaited much-needed reinforcements while the Khalsa snarled defiance on the other side of the Sutlej. The war was far from over.

★   ★   ★

The Khalsa generals did not regard themselves as defeated. They suspected betrayal and demanded reinforcements from Lahore. The Maharani, who was still in secret communication with the British, agreed to meet a deputation of 500 Khalsa leaders. She whipped them up into a frenzy, throwing one of her petticoats in their faces crying: 'Wear that, you cowards! I'll go in trousers and fight myself.' The warriors did not know it, but she was still determined to see the Khalsa, murderers of her brother, completely destroyed.

The reinforcements were provided, however, and the Khalsa established a bridgehead on the south side of the Sutlej near the ford of Sobraon, protected by their biggest guns on the far bank. A pontoon bridge was lashed into place to connect the advance force to their supply lines. The Khalsa generals also sent a force of 7,000 men and 70 guns under Runjur Singh upstream to cross the river near Ludhiana, aiming to break the British supply lines. They crossed the river and laid siege to the weakly garrisoned town, setting fire to part of the cantonment. A force under the 58-year-old General Smith was sent from Ferozepore to relieve it and deal with the menace to supplies.

Sir Harry Smith was another brave veteran of the Peninsular War who rarely dodged any opportunity for glory. The son of an Ely surgeon, he was the fifth of thirteen children. As a young officer he saw action in the disastrous expedition to Buenos Aires and the battle of Corunna and was seriously wounded near Almeida. As a major in the Light Brigade he fought at Sabugal, in the battle of Fuentes d'Onoro and the storming of Badajoz. After the latter he gave protection to a fourteen-year-old Spanish girl who had been ill-treated by the French. They married and she accompanied him for the rest of that war. More battles followed, including Vittoria, the Heights of Vera and Toulouse. Smith fought against the Americans during the 1812 war and was present at the burning of Washington and the battle of New Orleans. He witnessed Napoleon's final downfall at Waterloo. Peacetime saw him serving in Gosport, Glasgow, Belfast, Nova Scotia and Jamaica. In 1828 he was appointed army quartermaster-general in South Africa, where he and his wife gave their names respectively to the towns of Harrysmith and Ladysmith. African campaigning followed against warlike natives before Smith was sent to India. He was knighted for his distinguished service during the 1843 Gwalior campaign. One biographer wrote:

> Smith was not devoid of the self-assertion characteristic of men who fight their own way in the world and owe their successes solely to their own energies and ability; but he was popular with his colleagues and subordinates who were fascinated by his daring, energy and originality, and admired his rough and ready wit.

His men fondly recalled how he wandered through camp at night, and upon meeting a group of soldiers, would call out: 'Trumpeter, order a round of grog, and not too much water.'

On 16 January 1846 Smith set off two hours before dawn and led his brigade on a march of 26 miles to capture Dharamakot, a Sikh outpost largely garrisoned by mercenaries. A few shots from a British howitzer encouraged the defenders to hoist a white flat and Smith captured large supplies of grain. He marched on towards

Ludhiana, his baggage train of mules and elephants struggling to keep up. Parts of his force were attacked near Badowal on 21 January. Private John Pearman was in the thick of the minor but brutal skirmish as hidden Sikh guns opened up on the column. He later described how a ball hitting a comrade's head sounded like 'a band-box full of feathers flying all over us', adding, 'He was my front-rank man and his brains nearly covered me. I had to scrape it off my face, and out of my eyes, and Taf Roberts, my left-hand man, was nearly as bad.' Sikh cavalry picked off stragglers, but the column marched on.

They camped outside Ludhiana, skirmishing with the enemy and exchanging artillery fire until they were joined by Brigadier Wheeler and his brigade, who had marched at a more leisurely pace from Delhi. Smith's force was now 12,000 men with 28 field guns and 2 howitzers. They faced Runjur Singh, whose army had swelled to around 20,000 men – not the 60,000 later claimed by the British. Runjur Singh was preparing to storm Ludhiana and Smith decided to intercept him on a level, grassy plain near the small village of Aliwal. The position favoured Smith because the Sikhs, drawn up along a ridge with their backs to the river, had little room for manoeuvre.

Corporal Cowtan of the 16th wrote:

All this moment the view of the two armies was beautiful indeed – a fine, open, grassy plain, and the enemy in line out of their entrenchments ready to commence; the river in their rear, and in the distance the snowy range of the Himalayas with the sun rising over their tops.

On the bright, clear morning of 28 January Smith deployed his infantry, cavalry and artillery with textbook precision and ordered the attack.

Brigadier Godfrey's mixed brigade of sepoys, Gurkhas and the 31st Foot launched a rapid onslaught against Aliwal itself, which Smith judged to be the enemy's weakest spot and which was successfully taken. The two armies met in a general mêlée, the crystal air soon becoming befogged by the black smoke of the cannon. The British infantry charged 40 yards at a time, lying flat as the balls from disciplined Sikh volleys flew over them. The horse artillery galloped to within 200 yards of the Sikh batteries. The 16th Lancers charged past the Sikh guns, killing the gunners as they passed them, and found themselves in the centre of a large square of Khalsa soldiers. Sergeant William Gould wrote:

At them we went, the bullets flying around like hailstorm. Right in front of us was a big sergeant, Harry Newsome. He was mounted on a grey charger, and with a shout of 'Hullo boys, here goes death or commission,' forced his horse right over the front rank of kneeling men, bristling with bayonets. As Newsome dashed forward he leant over and grasped one of the enemy's standards, but fell from his horse, pierced by nineteen bayonet wounds. Into the gap made by Newsome we dashed, but they made fearful havoc among us. When we got to the other side of the square our troop had lost both lieutenants, the cornet, troop sergeant-major, and two sergeants. I was the only sergeant left.

The 16th Lancers breaking the Khalsa square at the battle of Aliwal. (National Army Museum)

Another lancer wrote:

> Our brave fellows fell very thickly here, and every man whose horse was killed was to a certainty slain also, for the moment those savages saw any one on the ground they rushed at him and never ceased hacking at them, till they had literally severed them to pieces with their *tulwars*, which were like razors. All of us that escaped owed our lives, under God, to our horses, for no one escaped which once came to the ground.

Corporal Cowtan was in the thick of the same action:

> Sergeant Brown was riding next to me and cleaving everyone down with his sword when his horse was shot under him, and before he reached the ground he received no less than a dozen sabre cuts which, of course, killed him. The killed and wounded in my squadron alone was 42, and after the first charge self-preservation was the great thing, and the love of life made us look sharp, and their great numbers required our vigilance. Our lances seemed to paralyse them altogether, and you may be sure we did not give them time to recover themselves.

General Smith asked where the officers of C Troop were. 'All down,' was the reply. The 16th Lancers lost more than a third of its strength in the action, suffering 'most severely, much more so than in any battle in the Peninsula or at Waterloo', one officer told his wife.

The 53rd Regiment came under deadly fire from a strong Sikh force hidden below the lip of a ravine, but a flanking charge by the 30th Native Infantry saved the Britons from destruction. The Sikhs, hemmed in and blasted at close range by the British horse artillery, began to stampede towards the river ford beyond their camp. The battle became a rout as the Sikhs scrambled for the boats or splashed through water churned into mud by the British howitzers. Sikh gunners deployed to cover the fleeing Khalsa were cut down before they could fire twice.

General Smith vividly described the scene in his dispatch:

> The battle was won, our troops advancing with the most perfect order. The enemy, completely hemmed in, were flying from our fire, and precipitating themselves in disordered masses into the ford and boats, in the utmost confusion and consternation. Our eight-inch howitzers soon began to play upon their votes, when the debris of the Sikh army appeared upon the opposite and high bank of the river, flying in every direction, although a sort of line was attempted to countenance their retreat, until all our guns commenced a furious cannonade, when they quickly receded.

The Sikhs left behind 2,000 dead, 60 guns, and all their baggage and ammunition trains and stores of grain. It was the first complete victory of the war and Smith made sure his superiors knew it. He wrote:

I have gained one of the most glorious battles ever fought in India. A stand-up gentlemanlike battle, a mixing of all arms and laying-on, carrying everything before us by weight of attack and combinations, all hands at work from one end of the field to the other. Never was victory more complete, and never was one fought under more happy circumstances, literally with the pomp of a field day; and right well did all behave.

Thackery later wrote of Smith's dispatch: 'A noble deed was never told in nobler language.' The Duke of Wellington, in a House of Lords debate, said: 'I never read an account of any affair in which an officer has shown himself more capable than this officer did of commanding troops in the field.' When news of Smith's victory reached Gough he became 'frantic with joy', leapt from his horse and gave three cheers for the 'gallant gentlemen' of Aliwal.

The Sikhs saw the bloated bodies of their comrades floating downstream to the entrenched positions at Sobraon. Tej Singh was all for reaching terms with the British, but his generals were not. They strengthened their defences, believing that the enemy would be destroyed in the inevitable assault on their earthworks. Tej Singh concentrated less on orchestrating the defences than on supervising the construction of his own private shelter. Shaped like a beehive, it was built to the peculiar specifications of Brahmin astrologer: the inner circumference was thirteen-and-a-half times Tej Singh's waist measurement, while the walls were the thickness of 333 long grains of rice laid end to end. Tej Singh spent much of the time before the battle praying inside it. Characteristically, Gough wanted to make an immediate assault on the heavily defended Sikh position in a bend of the river. Again Hardinge over-ruled him and the British waited for reinforcements and, most crucially, for the arrival of heavier guns. (In Gough's defence, the heavy artillery had been delayed because Hardinge had earlier decreed that they were not necessary.) Eventually, the artillery train arrived and Gough's army, now grown to 20,000 men, prepared to face the Sikh army of around 30,000 men with 70 guns, some of them on the other side of the Sutlej. Henry Lawrence, the new political agent, received from the treacherous Lal Singh a rough sketch of the Sikh trenches at Sobraon. The fortifications had been designed by Colonel Hurbon, a Spanish officer who served with the Khalsa. The date for the attack was set for 10 February. Three days of heavy rainfall before that turned the normally sluggish Sutlej into a boiling torrent, straining the tethers of the pontoon bridge that offered the bulk of the Khalsa an escape route.

Dawn was obscured by a dense fog, but when the sun finally broke through, the entire line of British artillery – thirty heavy howitzers and five 18-pounders – opened up a bombardment on the three lines of Sikh defences forming a semi-circle. An observer said it raised such a noise ' no thunder was ever equal to'. Trooper Bancroft of the Bengal Horse Artillery saw a body of Sikh cavalry charge his battery:

We immediately gave them a salvo of rockets, followed by single doses; the hissing noise of the long destructive shafts and the shells bursting unerringly

Major-General Sir Harry Smith.

among them suddenly threw their ranks into the utmost confusion and they were driven back in a whirlwind of defeat, leaving hundreds slain upon the field.

The Sikh batteries returned the fire and the combined detonations of over a hundred guns were the heaviest combination yet heard in India. After two hours British ammunition began to run low. Gough was told that only four rounds per gun were left and famously replied: 'Thank God, then I'll be at them with the bayonet.'

In his dispatch Gough recorded how the infantry and horse artillery moved forward, each supporting the other, until they were within 300 yards of the heaviest Sikh batteries. 'Notwithstanding the regularity and coolness, and scientific character of this assault,' he wrote, 'so hot was the fire of the cannon, musketry and *zumboorucks* kept up by the Khalsa troops, that it seemed for some moments impossible that the entrenchments could be won under it. . . .'

The 10th Foot led the advance on the Sikh right, and went forward into terrible Sikh fire of musket-ball and grapeshot. They pressed on despite heavy casualties and took the first line of Sikh trenches with the bayonet. The divisional commander, Sir Robert Dick, was slain in fierce close-quarter combat. But attempts by Generals Gilbert and Smith to draw the enemy's fire by a feint attack on the left failed, and the Sikh infantry counter-attacked. Firing steady volleys they forced the 10th backwards, step by step, from the hard-won trenches. Meanwhile, on the Sikhs' extreme left the British tried desperately to scramble up steep ramparts, only to be repulsed by muskets and slashing *tulwars*. At one point, Gough, seeing his men throw themselves at the defences, exclaimed: 'Good God, they'll be annihilated.' As the tide of battle ebbed and flowed the British were enraged to see the Sikhs, in intervals in the mayhem, hacking to pieces their wounded comrades left lying below the earthworks.

The British attacked again with renewed frenzy, while the Gurkhas 'used their *kukris* with unaccountable zeal among the Sikhs'. In some areas the British scaled the defences by climbing on one another's shoulders. Sergeant Bernard McCabe planted his regimental colours high on the ramparts as a rallying point. Smith, as always leading from the front and not shy of recalling the fact, wrote:

> I carried the works by dint of English pluck, although the natives corps stuck close to me, and when I got in, such hand-to-hand work I never witnessed. For twenty-five minutes I could barely hold my own. Mixed together, swords and targets against bayonets, and fire on both sides. We are at it against four times our numbers, sometimes receding, sometimes advancing. The old 31st and 50th laid on like devils . . . a brutal bulldog fight.

Gough wrote:

> The battle raged with inconceivable fury from left to right. The Sikhs, even when at particular points their entrenchments were mastered with the bayonet, strove to regain them by the fiercest conflict, sword in hand.

A Sikh gunner, Hookhum Singh, later wrote of the eerie silence with which the British attacked, without shouting or firing, but appearing 'as evil spirits bent on our destruction'. The British paused to take breath and then,

> with a shout such as only angry demons could give and which is still ringing in my ears, they made a rush for our guns, led by their colonel. They leapt into the deep ditch or moat in our front, soon filling it, and then swarmed up the opposite side on the shoulders of their comrades, dashed for the guns, which were still bravely defended by a strong body of our infantry. But who could withstand such fierce demons, with those awful bayonets, which they preferred to their guns – for not a shot did they fire the whole time – and then, with a ringing cheer, which was heard for miles, they announced their victory.

All across the front line the British broke through but the Sikhs, with their backs to the river, fought on and the battle was far from won. Engineers blew a small gap in the ramparts on the enemy right, where they were lowest, and Gough ordered in the cavalry under General Sir Joseph Thackwell. The 3rd Light Dragoons trotted through the gap in single file but were halted by a surviving Sikh battery. The blue-jacketed dragoons, helped by the Bengal Light Cavalry, soon rallied and cut down the gunners.

Still the Khalsa fought on, contesting every inch of ground within their encampment. Their treacherous commander, Tej Singh, had fled the field early in the battle, but there were other generals determined to die with their men. Thackwell commented: 'They never ran.' The veteran general Sham Singh Attariwala, who had spent forty years fighting in the Khalsa, was the centre of one last-ditch resistance. A British officer wrote:

> He repeatedly rallied his shattered ranks, and at last fell a martyr on a heap of his slain countrymen. Others might be seen on their ramparts amid a shower of balls, waving defiance with their swords . . . The parapets were sprinkled with blood from end to end; the trenches were filled with the dead or the dying.

Horse artillery was drawn up to fire at point-blank range. At last, their leaders dead or fled, the Sikh resistance crumbled into a rout. Thousands rushed for the head of the pontoon bridge. The press of men, jumbled together in a bottleneck, made an easy target. Those who could crowded on to the 400-yard bridge, already weakened by the floodwaters and by the accidental unmooring of a boat at its centre. Rumours later abounded that Tej Singh deliberately sabotaged the bridge to ensure the complete destruction of the Khalsa, but that does not square with eyewitness accounts of its collapse under sheer weight of numbers. The Governor-General's son, Arthur Hardinge, described the outcome:

> I saw the bridge at that moment overcrowded with guns, horses and soldiers of all arms, swaying to and fro, till at last with a crash it disappeared in the running waters, carrying with it all those who had vainly hoped to reach the opposite shore. The river seemed alive with a struggling mass of men. The artillery, now brought down to the water's edge, completed the slaughter. Few escaped; none, it may be said, surrendered.

Gough later wrote:

> Policy precluded me publicly recording my sentiments on the splendid gallantry or the acts of heroism displayed by the Sikh army. I could have wept to have witnessed the fearful slaughter of so devoted a body of men.

These fine Christian sentiments, expressed much later, did not mean he called a halt to the fearful slaughter. Heavy guns and muskets continued firing into the river until was a red stew. A civilian observer, Robert Cust, said: 'The stream was choked with the dead and the dying – the sandbanks were covered with bodies floating leisurely down. It was an awful scene, a fearful carnage.' A sepoy, Sita Ram, described watching men choking the river, their long black hair streaming in the white water, scrabbling hold of each other in their panic, until the teeming mass sank, 'to rise no more alive'. No mercy was shown. The men were prompted by the fresh memories of wounded comrades butchered below the Sikh parapets. Gough later said of the Sikhs:

Their awful slaughter, confusion and dismay were such as would have excited
compassion in the hearts of their generous conquerors, if the Khalsa troops had
not, in the early part of the action, sullied their gallantry by slaughtering and
barbarously mangling every wounded soldier whom, in the vicissitudes of
attack, the fortune of war left at their mercy.

Gough also knew that only the complete annihilation of the Khalsa would bring the
war to an end. And the battle – later dubbed the Indian Waterloo – had been costly.
By noon the British forces had lost 320 dead and 2,063 wounded, many of whom
would not survive. The Khalsa losses were estimated at 10,000 dead, perhaps most
of them killed in the last doomed attempt to cross the river. The Maharani's revenge
was complete.

★   ★   ★

The bloodbath at Sobraon crushed Khalsa resistance. It was perhaps the most
decisive battle fought by the British in India, and it ended any real threat to the Raj
for a century. The war, one of the shortest on record, lasted just fifty-four days, in
which time four major battles were fought to bloody effect. The Duke of Wellington
wrote to Gough:

> Great operations have been planned and undertaken and successfully carried
> into execution under your command, glorious battles have been fought and
> victories gained, and the war has been brought to a termination by the
> destruction of the army of the enemy . . . and peace has been dictated to the
> enemy upon terms equally honourable to the Army and to the Nation.

Gough lost no time in crossing the Sutlej to pursue the beaten foe. The first units
crossed by the early evening of the day of the battle. Most of his forces followed
within two days and occupied Kasur, 30 miles from Lahore. On 15 February
Hardinge there met Rajah Gulab Singh who had been authorised by the Lahore
Durbar to negotiate the peace. Gulab Singh was an acceptable envoy because he
and his Dogra Hindu troops had remained broadly neutral during the conflict. He
was a canny operator and persuaded Hardinge not to annexe the Punjab.
Although the Khalsa had been beaten, there were still as many as 35,000 Sikh
soldiers between Lahore and Amritsar, with others at Peshawar and Multan. The
Sikhs agreed that the British should control both banks of the Sutlej and take the
rich and fertile Jullundar Doab lands between the river and the seas. British
territory effectively advanced 100 miles. In addition, the Sikhs were to pay a war
indemnity of £1,500,000, to allow Sir Henry Lawrence to be stationed in their
capital as Resident, and to reduce their army to a maximum of 20,000 infantry
and 12,000 cavalry. These may have been the best terms a defeated side could
hope to gain from the victors, but the main winner proved to be Gulab Singh.
Faced with a shortage of riches in Lahore to cover the war indemnity, the Sikh
administration handed over instead the hill territories which included Kashmir

and Hazara. These the wily Gulab bought from the British for the knock-down price of £750,000.

Hardinge and Gough, with their staff and escorted by four cavalry regiments, entered Lahore on elephants as a band played 'See the Conquering Hero Comes'. Sikh salutes were fired and the beasts threatened to stampede but were quickly calmed down. They were greeted by Maharajah Duleep Singh, described by one officer as 'a child of an intelligent and not unpleasing appearance', his still glamorous mother and Gulab. Hardinge agreed that the treacherous Lal Singh should be appointed vizier or chief minister, while the equally treasonable Tej Singh should be commander-in-chief of the much-reduced Khalsa. They were to be protected at home from their ungrateful followers by a British force which would remain in Lahore until the end of the year. British officers and officials would effectively administer the outlying regions. Lieutenant Herbert Edwardes told Bannu tribesmen:

> You shall have the best laws that an enlightened people can frame for you; but they will be administered by a Sikh governor. He cannot oppress you, for the English will be over him. You shall be justly ruled, but you shall be free no more.

The treaty of Lahore was ratified on 9 March. Included in the small print was the gift of the Kho-i-noor diamond, the 'mountain of light', to Queen Victoria.

Gough was raised to the peerage by his grateful queen, while the Governor-General became Viscount Hardinge of Lahore and Durham, with a lifetime's pension of £3,000 from the British government and a further pension of £5,000 from the East India Company. Hardinge assured Victoria that there was no native power left anywhere in India capable of again taking on the British Army. The contemporary historian W.L. McGregor wrote: 'The battle of Sobraon may be justly termed the Waterloo of India; it was the last, and one of the most hardest contested; like that great and ever memorable engagement, it completely broke the power of the foe.' But Joseph Cunningham countered that the Sikhs' strength 'is not to be estimated by their tens of thousands, but by the unity and energy of religious fervour and warlike temperament. They will care much, and they will endure much . . .'

Certainly many in the remaining Khalsa were convinced they had only been defeated by treachery. They were probably right, and Hardinge's assurances to the queen were all too soon to be proved disastrously wrong.

CHAPTER FIVE

The Second Sikh War, 1848–9

'Every gun was turned on them . . .'

In the grounds of the Royal Chelsea Hospital stands a stone obelisk that bears the names of 238 officers and men of the 24th Foot, a regiment that later knew greater fame as the South Wales Borderers. These men fell at an unremembered battle in the Punjab, charging massed cannon head on, cold steel against heavy artillery.

Unlike the Charge of the Light Brigade little more than five years later, there was no Lord Tennyson to immortalise the 24th Foot in verse. Unlike the mad charge at Balaclava, in which 113 died, they did not enjoy the glamour associated with dashing cavalrymen. Their's was a bloodier affair – almost half the regiment were casualties – but their exploits barely registered in the public consciousness then, and are entirely forgotten now.

What the two incidents have in common, apart from breathtaking courage, is that both were the result of a monumental blunder. The 24th at Chilianwalla were ordered to take the Sikh cannon by the bayonet, without a shot being fired. It was, as their own general later admitted, 'an act of madness'.

★   ★   ★

For some time after the slaughter of the Khalsa at Sobraon the British and Sikhs cohabited uneasily, and their forces cooperated in suppressing minor frontier uprisings. British officers and officials accompanied an expedition led by General Shere Singh to deal with the Sikh Governor of Kashmir, who had refused to surrender his authority to Gulab Singh. The recalcitrant governor gave up without a fight and Gulab entered Kashmir city as its ruler in November 1846. Such military alliances were frequently strained, however, not least by the intrigues of the Maharani Jindan and her allies in Lahore. The Sikh generals knew they had been betrayed by their leaders in the first war. Their pride was hurt and they did not believe in the notion, accepted elsewhere, of British invincibility. Thousands of discharged and unpaid Khalsa soldiers roamed the countryside, spoiling for a fight and looking for plunder.

In addition, Sikh sensibilities were gravely upset when the British took guardianship of the young Maharajah Duleep Singh. The queen-mother was furious at being sidelined. Always a libertine, she began to approach British officers with offers of marriage, convinced that such a union would advance her cause. She was wrong and Sir Henry Lawrence, the British Resident in Lahore, ruled that she was a malign influence on her son. A plot to kill Lawrence, in which the Maharani was said to be involved, offered an ideal pretext to get rid of her. To the delight of some Sikh generals and courtiers, but to the consternation of many others, she was banished to a distant fortress at Sheikapur. She wrote to Lawrence:

You have been very cruel to me. You have snatched my son from me. For ten months I kept him in my womb. Then I brought him up with great difficulty. Without my fault you have separated my son from me. You could have kept me in prison. You could have dismissed my men. You could have turned out my maidservants. You could have treated me in any other way you liked. But you should not have separated my son from me. In the name of the God you worship, and in the name of the king whose salt you eat, restore my son to me. I cannot bear the pain of this separation. Instead of this you put me to death.

The Punjab was simmering like a cooking pot, but Lord Hardinge appears to have been oblivious to the unrest. The Afghan and Sikh wars had left British India with massive debts. Determined to balance the books, Hardinge decided to reduce the Indian Army by 50,000 men. He was convinced that peace was secure and when he returned home in 1847 he forecast that 'it would not be necessary to fire a gun in India for seven years to come'. He was replaced by 35-year-old Lord Dalhousie as Governor-General of India. Dalhousie was a product of the aristocracy, Harrow and Oxford. He was a natural politician and attracted the attention of Wellington and Peel when he entered the Lords after his father's death. He was an active member of the General Assembly of the Church of Scotland, and in 1845 succeeded Gladstone as vice-President of the Board of Trade. He was known as a tireless worker, the first in and last out of his office daily. Although a Tory, he owed his new job to the new Whig administration of Lord John Russell. When he reached Calcutta a leading Anglo-Indian newspaper declared that the new governor had 'arrived at a time when the last obstacle to the final pacification of India has been removed, when the only remaining army which could have caused alarm has been dissolved and the peace of the country rests upon the firmest and most permanent basis'. Events quickly persuaded Dalhousie to ignore such rosy sentiments.

The flashpoint came in the province of Multan, lying between the left bank of the Indus and the right bank of the Sutlej. Multan had been conquered by Runjeet Singh only after many ferocious battles. In April 1848 the governor, a Hindu called Diwan Mulraj, resigned after expressing dissatisfaction with the new regime and the presence of the British. After negotiations with the Lahore Durbar it was agreed that Sirdar Khan Singh should replace him. The new man travelled to Multan city with a small escort. He was accompanied by two British representatives, 26-year-old Patrick Alexander Vans Agnew, a Bengal civil servant and assistant to Lawrence, and Lieutenant W.A. Anderson of the Bombay Fusiliers. They entered the city without incident and officiated at the formal transfer of power to Khan Singh. But on the following day, 18 April, Mulraj's supporters revolted and attacked the two Britons. Desperately wounded, they were carried with Khan Singh to a small fort outside the city which swiftly came under fire from Multan's parapets. Three days

Troops marching in India. (*Illustrated London News*)

later Mulraj's troops attacked the fort and its Sikh defenders, members of the initial escort, immediately opened the gates and let in the assailants. Lieutenant Anderson could not move from his cot but Agnew tried to fight. A battle-scarred veteran, Goodhur Singh, cut off his head with three blows. Anderson was hacked to death where he lay. Both bodies were dragged outside, mutilated and left in the courtyard. Mulraj always claimed that the fort had not been attacked on his authority, but the murders left him no option but to declare open revolt. A Sikh commander fastened on to him one of his own war bracelets. Mulraj sent the fiery cross of revolt around the countryside, the signal to rise up against the British who 'are treating the Maharajah and our proper rulers as prisoners'. All across the land disenchanted Sikhs and Muslims answered the call.

Sir Frederick Currie, standing in for Dalhousie, then on leave in Europe, ordered a Sikh army under Shere Singh to suppress the rebellion. He wrote: 'The fort at Multan is very strong and full of heavy cannon of large calibre. This cannot be taken possession of by direct attack. Except the Multan garrison, Mulraj has not many troops, and only five or six field guns. He is very unpopular both with the army and the people.' But before Shere Singh's force could march, more independent action was already being taken. The main instigator was an extraordinary young officer and poet, Lieutenant Herbert Edwardes of the Bengal Native Infantry. Aged twenty-nine, from Shropshire, slender and multi-lingual,

Edwardes did not look like a fighting soldier. When he arrived at Calcutta in 1841 an observer described him as 'slight and delicate-looking, with fully formed features and an expression of bright intelligence; not given to the active amusements by which most young men of his class and nation are wont to speed the hours, but abounding in mental accomplishments and resource'. His language skills in Urdu, Hindi and Persian made him a natural interpreter and he served on Gough's staff at the battles of Mudki and Sobraon. Before the revolt erupted, Lawrence, who had spotted his talents early on, put him in charge of a small force engaged, ironically, in collecting land taxes for Mulraj in outlying districts. On hearing of the murders and the rebellion, Edwardes began putting together a native army. He occupied the trading city of Leia, where he enlisted mercenaries, both to strengthen his own tiny force and to prevent them going over to the enemy. Without funds and no outside aid, this remarkable young man raised a levy of 3,000 Pathan fighters with the promise of a mere 15 rupees a week and all the plunder they could carry. He said: 'War is their trade and also their pastime.' He also persuaded the Nawab of neighbouring Bahawalpur to send him troops. On 18 May a contingent of his men left at Leia were charged by 400 Multan horsemen. The attackers were beaten off, leaving behind them ten light field guns.

As Edwardes set off for Multan his force was swelled by 4,000 men under Colonel Van Courtlandt, the commander of the British garrison at Dhera Ismael Khan; this new force included three mixed Sikh regiments, 1,500 irregular horse, 8 guns and 20 swivel pieces. Together they easily beat off a determined attack by Sikh rebels. The native levies, Edwardes noted, 'fought bravely and showed no disposition to fraternise with the rebels'.

Mulraj moved out of Multan to prevent the British gaining further reinforcements. His men attacked Edwardes when his force was split by the Indus river near Soojabad. Edwardes, who had barely seen any action in his short life, was confident of success. He later wrote: I doubted only for a moment – one of those long moments to which some angel seems to hold a microscope and show millions of things within it. It came and went between the stirrup and the saddle.' After several grim hours' fighting on a baking-hot, waterless plain, the outcome was still in the balance until two of Van Courtlandt's troops of horse artillery were able to ride to the rescue. Edwardes wrote:

Oh, the thankfulness of that moment! The relief, the weight removed, the elastic bound of the heart's main-spring into its place after being pressed down for seven protracted hours of waiting for a reinforcement that might never come! Now all is clear. Our chance is nearly as good as theirs, and who asks more?

Van Courtlandt's gun-crews unlimbered and opened up a close-quarter duel with the Sikh cannon. The range was so close that both sides fired grapeshot rather than shot at each other's crews. Edwardes wrote:

For the first time and the last in my short experience of war, did I see hostile artillery firing grape into each other . . . General Courtlandt's artillery were well trained and steady, and their aim was true. Two guns were quickly silenced and the rest seemed slackening and firing wide. A happy charge might carry all. I gave the order to Soobhan Khan's regiment to attack, and away they went, Soobhan Khan himself, a stout, heavy soldier, leading them on, and leaping over bushes like a boy. Before they could reach the battery . . . a cluster of half a dozen horsemen dashed out from the trees behind me, and passing the regiment threw themselves on the enemy's guns. Their leader received a ball full in his face, and fell over the cannon's mouth . . . The regiment followed, and carried at the point of the bayonet the only gun which awaited their assault. Another gun lay dismounted on the ground.

Dispatches reported: 'After an obstinate conflict the enemy gave way and fled, leaving behind them six guns and all their baggage and stores.' The Sikhs lost around 500 men dead or mortally wounded on the field. British casualties were some 300 killed and wounded.

Mulraj fell back on Multan and Edwardes pursued him there. But the lieutenant's force, even with Van Courtlandt's reinforcements, was not strong enough to mount a proper siege. Mulraj, after some savage skirmishing, withdrew his whole force behind the city walls. Edwardes remained outside, however, waiting for Lahore to send a proper army under Major-General William Whish to complete the job. Edwardes was a hero and Sir Henry Lawrence, now back from his European travels, said, 'since the days of Clive no man has done as him'. Another accolade said: 'Young, alone, untrained in military science and unversed in active war, he had organised victory and rolled back rebellion.' Now, however, it was the turn of a veteran.

Whish was, at sixty-one, relatively old but he was an experienced artilleryman. The Essex-born son of a vicar, he had served in India since 1804 and later commanded the rocket troop of horse artillery in the Pindari and Maratha campaigns. He was mentioned in dispatches for his part in the 1826 capture of Bhartpur and was promoted for distinguished service in the field. Early in 1848, after a long furlough in England, he took command of the Punjab Division at Lahore. Whish arrived at Multan with an 8,000-strong field force made up of the 10th Regiment, a troop of horse artillery, the 7th Irregular Horse and other troops. They were swiftly joined by a column from Ferozepore, including a train of heavy guns, bringing the total army assembled outside Multan's thick walls to about 28,000, of whom 6,000 were British. The Sikh troops in the army were commanded by Shere Singh.

After several days of skirmishing and sharp firing, Whish decided to launch a general attack on the city's outworks on 12 September. At daybreak around 2,500 troops under Brigadier Harvey marched against a group of defenders deeply dug in around a garden and hamlet near the city walls. The British took one trench but were forced out of a second by a shower of shot, bullets and arrows. They took their revenge on the defenders of a small, enclosed courtyard. One eyewitness told the *Dehli Gazette*: 'The men, both European and native, mounted the walls, determined that not a soul should escape. Certainly the massacre that took place within – enclosed on all sides by loop-holed walls and entrenched all round – was something awful to one who had never been in service before.'

Shere Singh with his bodyguard and troops. (*Illustrated London News*)

The correspondent, an unnamed officer, went on to give a graphic account of the close-quarter fighting and the losses it entailed:

At this entrenchment Lieutenant Cubitt of the 49th Regiment Native Infantry, was shot by a wounded man. After being sent up to camp he survived only about seven hours. Poor fellow! He will be a sad loss to his regiment, for a better soldier never breathed . . . After setting fire to this entrenchment in several places we returned to the one we had first taken, and this we were obliged to get scaling ladders to take, as it was so strong. No sooner were the scaling ladders up than Colonel Pattoun was the first to ascend, and down he jumped, right amongst the enemy within, when, as a matter of course, he was instantly cut to pieces; for these fellows, immediately you attempt to close with them, draw their *tulwars*, and they know how to use them too . . . Here too fell Lieutenant Taylor, Quartermaster of Her Majesty's 32nd Foot, and Major Montizambert of Her Majesty's 10th Foot . . . But not a man [of the Sikh defenders] escaped, for the doors were burst open, and an attack from above and below made; every man within these walls fell a victim to the bayonet . . .

The following day the Multanese troops launched a desperate sally against Lieutenant Edwardes' camp but they were repelled. Edwardes counter-attacked and captured an important breastwork. It looked as if Whish could swiftly wear down the defences, but any such hopes were shattered by the next dawn.

Shere Singh, who had never been a lusty campaigner against the rebels, defected to Mulraj with 5,000 men and 10 cannon. The British should have seen it coming as his father, Chuttar Singh, Governor of Hazarch, had joined another 'mutiny' in north-west Punjab. Newspapers in Delhi stormed that such treachery 'proved the folly of placing any reliance upon the fidelity of the Sikhs'.

Shere Singh's defection, forced on him by the changing allegiances of both his family and his men, meant that Mulraj's force now totalled 15,000 men and up to 80 guns. Whish had 20,000 men and 44 guns – nowhere near enough to sustain a siege against strong defences. He had no choice but to lift the siege of Multan and retire his army to a defendable position a few miles away at Tibi to await reinforcements.

Shere Singh, in the meantime, issued a statement accusing the British of tyranny and violence against the Maharani and the Sikh people. He called on all the people of the region, Sikh, Muslim and Hindu, to join together in a holy crusade against the oppressors. Fearful that many more sepoys and native mercenaries would answer that call, Edwardes promised his own men that if they stayed loyal and fought against the rebels they would be taken on as regular soldiers for the lifetime of the Indian government. They agreed, but Shere Singh's call to arms spread elsewhere across the Punjab. At Peshawar and Lahore government troops mutinied and attacked the Residency with shot and grape. Troops in the Bunnoo district, near the Afghan border, also rose and killed both the Muslim governor and Colonel John Holmes, a British soldier of fortune. Several thousand Khalsa troops, pensioned off under the Treaty of Lahore, retrieved their arms and swarmed to Shere Singh's banner.

The *Annual Register* reported:

What had at first been considered as an isolated act of contumacy on the part of Mulraj assumed now a more serious aspect, and it became evident that we should have to engage in another struggle with the whole of the fierce soldiery of the Sikhs, whose spirit was no-ways disheartened by their former collision with British troops.

A minor revolt had now escalated into the Second Sikh War.

★   ★   ★

For several weeks there was little skirmishing as the two opposing armies gathered strength. Early in October Shere Singh left Multan with his force and headed north-west along the line of the Chenab, the central of the Punjab's Five Rivers. His father, Chuttar Singh, marched south to join him. They met near Ramnuggar, and there Shere Singh took overall command of a Sikh army numbering no fewer than 30,000 men.

Meanwhile Dalhousie announced: 'Unwarned by precedent, uninfluenced by example, the Sikh nation have called for war, and on my word, sirs, they shall have it.' A large force was to gather at Ferozepore under the commander-in-chief, Lord

Gough. More troops were sent from Bombay until the numbers had swelled to one cavalry and three infantry divisions. Any attempts at a diplomatic solution were thwarted by British outrage at what they considered Sikh treachery and desertion. Dalhousie gave Gough full discretion to punish the offenders but financial considerations were always at the forefront of his mind. He wrote at the end of July: 'Where I am to find the money to pay for this, God above only knows.' By then, however, Dalhousie had decided that the only satisfactory outcome would be the complete annexation of the Punjab. That he later confirmed in a letter to Sir John Hobhouse, President of the Board of Control: 'There no longer remains any alternative for the British Government. The die is cast.' He brushed aside complaints at home that the war was a cynical attempt to steal the kingdom of the boy Maharajah. He described the lad as 'a brag begotten of a Bhistie – and no more the child of old Runjeet than Queen Victoria'. And he told the directors of the East India Company that a successful outcome would greatly increase revenue because 'the defection of so many chiefs will be followed by extensive confiscation'.

Gough took command of his army on 21 November. His arrival was not welcomed by all, as men remembered the massive casualties he suffered during the First Sikh War. Engineering officer Richard Baird Smith warned that 'our success will be gained by the blood of the officers and men and will owe nought to the genius of the Chief'.

Gough immediately set off for Shere Singh's positions at Ramnuggar on the east bank of the Chenab. At 2 a.m. on the 22nd orders were issued for a strong force of cavalry and infantry to parade silently and in marching order in front of the British camp. They moved forward in darkness and assembled at the river. The strength of Shere Singh's forces, both on the opposite bank and on an island in midstream, quickly became apparent. Some Sikh troops left on the west bank were quickly driven across the river fords by the 3rd Dragoons and the 8th Light Cavalry. An officer in the Bengal Horse Artillery wrote home:

The Sikhs had placed their guns in masked batteries; and, as you might suppose, the sudden discharge took our people by surprise; nevertheless they went on, seeing a great number of the enemy beyond the nullah. The ground was very heavy and sandy: a large portion of our cavalry got into a quicksand, and the horses, being somewhat exhausted by the march over heavy ground, were not able to extricate themselves as soon as they might have done. The enemy's infantry were, in the meantime, behind large sand hillocks, and steadily firing into our men, as well as from the large Sikh guns on the other side of the river.

The Horse Artillery pushed on slowly and painfully, and opened up a duel with enemy batteries on the far bank. They soon found that their 6-pounders were ill-matched against the heavier guns facing them, and they were forced to pull back. Seeing that, Shere Singh ordered more than 3,000 of his cavalry across the stream, which had shrunk during the dry season, under cover of his guns. Gough now made a serious blunder. He seems to have been unaware of the poor nature of the terrain –

The charge of the 14th Dragoons at Ramnuggar. (*Illustrated London News*)

or perhaps he let his impetuous nature get the better of him. He ordered the 14th Dragoons, under Lieutenant-Colonel William Havelock, and the 5th Light Cavalry to attack the larger Sikh body. The British troopers managed to drive the Sikhs back and then charged down the sandy river bank after them. Here, however, they were exposed to a murderous fire from the Sikh batteries. Men and horses were scythed down by the well-trained and experienced Sikh gunners. The 5th had charged blindly into a trap laid by the cunning Shere Singh. The Sikh cavalry now turned and wreaked more havoc. Colonel Alexander tried to rally the troopers but his sword arm was shattered by a cannon ball, which then careered on its way, killing a quartermaster-sergeant and striking a lieutenant on the foot. Alexander fell, and the Sikh swordsmen who rushed to hack at him were beaten off by Sergeant-Major Mallet. Alexander survived but the arm was later 'removed from the socket'. Captain Scudamore took a sabre cut across the face, Lieutenant Macmahon was shot in the head, and Lieutenant Chetwynd was punched in the side by a spent cannon ball. Sergeant Todd's head was cleanly taken off by a round-shot. The *aide-de-camp*, Lieutenant Hardinge, was shot through the shoulder.

Colonel William Havelock, a Peninsular War veteran and the brother of the more renowned Henry, fell dead during a second charge on the Sikh positions. An observer said that Havelock was last seen in the thick of the enemy, 'his left arm half severed from his body, and dealing frantic blows with his sword'. His second-in-command, Colonel King, reformed the line for a third charge. After that proved unsuccessful the British cavalry commander, General C.R. Cureton galloped up with orders from Gough that they should retire. Within moments of uttering the words two matchlock balls hit him in the throat and head and he too fell dead. The squadron was withdrawn. Gough had succeeded in clearing the west bank of the river but the main Sikh positions were untouched. And, as one report put it, 'we had

The death of General Cureton at Ramnuggar. (*Illustrated London News*)

to mourn the loss of many brave soldiers, whose lives were lost in a useless and unmeaning combat'.

Twenty-one officers and men were first posted as dead, although the eventual death toll must have been higher given that there were 55 wounded and 9 listed as missing. Over a hundred horses were lost. The high casualty rate among his senior officers shocked Gough.

For a week the two armies sat facing each other across the muddy waters. At the end of November Gough ordered Major-General Sir John Thackwell to march a strong body of troops upriver so that he might cross and attack the Sikhs from the rear while Gough himself led a frontal assault. Shere Singh was too canny a tactician to be outmanoeuvred. Instead of sitting still, he moved forward to meet Thackwell's force. The British troops crossed the river in pitch darkness on the night of 1 December. Captain Lawrence Archer recalled:

In the mazes of small channels and pools of water, which chequered the loose sands, many a regiment lost its way, while the increasing darkness added to the general confusion, and the knowledge of abounding quicksands produced a sense of insecurity. It is hard to say what might have befallen the force, had the enemy only taken the trouble to guard this ford, or form an ambuscade.

The following morning Thackwell's force came under heavy bombardment at Sadullapur. Gough ordered an answering fire on the Sikh batteries facing him but a mix-up over orders delayed Thackwell's gunners from following suit. In addition, unknown to Gough, his gunners were pounding largely empty entrenchments. Heartened by this the Sikhs threw themselves on Thackwell's detached column. The Sikh attack was further encouraged when Thackwell made a tactical retreat to better positions 200 yards back. The Sikhs cried: 'The English are running.' The position was extremely hazardous until the British gunners under Lieutenant-Colonel C. Grant at last began pouring shot and grape into the enemy. After two hours of heavy shelling the Sikh guns were silenced and the Sikhs withdrew to their original positions after suffering heavy losses. But by then the British combatants were so exhausted that Gough decided to postpone the general attack until the next day.

During the night Shere Singh withdrew his entire army. Sikh sources point to a tactical and highly disciplined retreat; the British claimed they left 'in great disorder'. Either way, Shere Singh had not been defeated. Senior British officers, however, believed that the war was virtually over. Lancers and dragoons immediately crossed the Chenab, and were followed over in the next few weeks by Gough and the rest of the British forces.

★   ★   ★

While Gough was engaged around the Chenab, General Whish, reinforced by Bombay troops, was resuming his siege of Multan 230 miles to the south-west. The city was home to 80,000 people and it was a rich centre of trade. The *Bombay Times* wrote of it:

> Never perhaps in India have such depots existed of merchandise and arms. Her opium, indigo, salt, sulphur, every known drug are heaped in endless profusion – ancient granaries in the bowels of the earth disclose huge hoards of wheat and rice; here bale on bale of silks and shawls; there some mammoth chest discovering glittering scabbards and gold gems, there tiers of copper canisters crammed with gold coin . . .

Such riches were not going to save it. But the citadel's strong walls, through which eighty cannon poked their black barrels, might.

Whish's force now consisted of 32,000 men, of whom 15,000 were British; the remainder consisted of loyal native units and Indian allies. Whish could also deploy 150 cannon and mortars. On 27 December Whish ordered a general attack in four columns and the defenders were forced to abandon the suburbs, allowing the British artillery to close within 500 yards of the main fortress walls. On the 28th a general cannonade and bombardment opened up and on the 29th the British heavy guns were pulverising the walls at a range of just 80 yards. Corporal John Ryder wrote in his diary:

> Salvo after salvo went thundering into the town, both shot and shell, and must have committed awful destruction . . . killing men, women and children. We got more guns into play during the night, and approached much nearer the walls.

A battery manned by European sailors besieging Multan. (*Illustrated London News*)

Two breaches were commenced in them, one at the Delhi Gate and the other more to the left. A great many prisoners were taken in trying to make their escape from the town; but numbers were women and children. They were treated well.

An officer noted with the callous humour of the time: 'Great damage was caused in the town by our shot and shell practice.' In the fort a granary and several small magazines were set on fire. There was a bigger bang to come on the morning of the 30th. Another eyewitness wrote home:

Yesterday I saw one of the most awful and grand sights I am ever likely to witness; the whole of Mulraj's principal magazine, which he has been five years collecting, was blown up by one of our shells. The shock two miles off knocked bottles off the tables, and the report was terrific . . . At first we felt a slight shock, like that of an earthquake, and then, a second or two afterwards, such a tremendous and prolonged report, that it was like an awful clap of thunder. I hardly know what to liken it to – it was so inconceivably grand; then a mass of dust rose to the very clouds, yet so perfectly distinct was its outline, and it was so dense and thick, that nobody at first could tell what it was. It looked like an immense solid brown tree, suddenly grown up to the skies, and then it gradually expanded and slowly sailed away.

Sikh prisoners told the besiegers that the fort's magazine had contained 16,000lb of powder, and as many as 800 men blew up with it. But although the fort's main buildings, barrack houses and temples were destroyed, its battlements were

Huzzarehs firing with juzafels. (*Illustrated London News*)

untouched because of the upward thrust of the explosion. The city, where most of the Sikh defenders were, was also largely undamaged. For several minutes after the explosion there was silence, which was broken by Sikh gunners in the citadel who, once they had recovered from the shock, redoubled their fire with furious disdain. Mulraj sent word to Whish the next day that he still had enough powder and shot to hold out for a year. He urged the British to 'do their worst' and said that he would never surrender as long as there was a single Sikh standing.

The cannonade continued for two more days, and more breaches were made in the Delhi and Bohur gates. On the last day of 1848 the Sikhs made a sortie from the south-west gate and attacked the division commanded by Edwardes, who had been promoted major for his earlier gallantry. The Sikhs were driven back with heavy losses and Whish ordered a two-pronged attack on the city, by-passing the fort, two days later. The first storming parties were repulsed in the narrow breaches by defenders hurling not just gunfire but also boulders, broken furniture and wooden beams. Three companies of the 1st Bombay Fusiliers under Captain Leith, a giant of a man, followed. An officer noted:

Up we charged and the moment we arrived at the top we were saluted with a volley of Sikh matchlock balls, which, wonderful to relate, all went clear over our heads, except one which struck poor Leith in the shoulder. The enemy had made a large stockade, which we scrambled over somehow (I am sure I cannot recollect how, for it looked a horrible place afterwards), and there stood about a thousand of the enemy with their swords drawn. We gave a volley and a thundering cheer, and charged them with the bayonet. Poor Leith had his left hand cut off through the wrist by a sword. The enemy could not stand a charge with British steel, and fell back; we followed them closely.

The Bombay column fought its way through the outer defences and the first colours were planted in Multan by a sergeant-major of the Company's Fusiliers.

More troops poured into the narrow streets, to be met with fire from the windows and house-tops, and the siege became a house-to-house battle with no quarter given. Corporal Ryder, in his famously graphic diary, wrote:

We broke open the doors with the butt ends of our muskets, and blew off the locks, when not one of those within was left alive: everyone being killed on the spot. They were despatched wholesale. One place was fought very hard for by the enemy. This was a Hindu mosque [sic], occupied by a brave officer and a number of determined men. They had a colour, a very handsome one. They were attacked by a party of our men, who took the colour and killed nearly all the men. We were confined for room: our muskets with bayonets fixed we found rather awkward, as we had not room to turn them about. A man by the name of McGuire, a corporal, was attacked by the officer bearing the colour: he came sword in hand, and the corporal not being loaded at the time (for he had just fired) had quite as much as he could do to defend himself. However, he

The 1st Bombay European Fusiliers storming a breach at the Kooni Boorj, Multan. (*Illustrated London News*)

parried off the cuts of the swords until he had a chance, when he made a thrust and gave the officer the bayonet, and at the same time, received a cut from the sword upon his left arm. They closed upon each other, and grappled each other by the throat; when the corporal gave him the foot and threw him upon the floor. The corporal then took his opponent's sword and cut off his head, and brought the colour away as his prize.

The murderous fighting did not spare women and children who were fatally intermingled with their menfolk in the narrow streets. Ryder was haunted by their 'wild terrified screams . . . the cries of the affrighted children as they clung around their mothers'.

Before sunset on 2 January 1849 the city was in British hands but the slaughter continued. Whish ordered his British and sepoy troops to herd the city's inhabitants into the main squares. Ryder wrote:

some of this work was attended with horrible brutality by our men. In several instances, on breaking into the retreats of these unfortunate creatures, a volley of shots was fired amongst them as they were huddled together in a corner. All shared the same fate. One of my fellow-corporals, who never was worthy of the jacket he wore, was guilty of cold-blooded murder. He shot a poor, grey-headed old man while he was begging that he would spare and not hurt his wife and daughters; nor take away the little property they possessed, consisting of a few paltry rings upon their fingers and in their ears. This fellow pulled the rings off in a most brutal manner. I learned that several of our men were guilty of murder. Our native soldiers were much worse, and more brutish; but they were more to be excused, as they were natives.

Ryder also reported several cases of rape, including that of a young girl in front of her mother by a man of the 3rd company of his own regiment. 'Had I been upon the spot at that time,' Ryder wrote, 'I would have shot him dead.' Ryder's frank account contradicted the official reports. Dr John Dunlop, surgeon of the 32nd Foot, said: 'The soldiery were glad to extract from the town whatever enjoyment it afforded. Few excesses were, however, committed.'

The citadel still held out. Within its scorched but strong walls Mulraj surrounded himself with his finest soldiers. For two full weeks the fort was constantly bombarded while engineers dug trenches ever closer. Sappers, too, had been busy and on the 18th three mines were exploded, hurling masonry into the ditch. A further shaft was driven under the walls, while 24-pounders and 8-inch howitzers battered at close range against the defences. Live shells buried themselves in the mud and brickwork of the main citadel and 'exploded like mines, tearing vast masses away with them'.

Mulraj sent out several messages saying he would concede provided his life was guaranteed. Whish insisted on unconditional surrender and on the morning of the 22nd, as British columns were preparing for the final assault, Mulraj gave in. A contemporary account said:

First appeared about 200 miserable wretches who seemed broken and dispirited; then followed about 350 hard, trained, stern, and stalwart-looking men; they had defended the fort to the last, and only abandoned it when it was untenable. They looked as if they would have fought to death in the breaches, if such had been the will of their chief. They brought camels, and horses, and large bundles of things along with them. These, together with their arms, were placed in charge of the prize agents as they passed. At last came Mulraj, and his brethen and chiefs . . . He was gorgeously attired in silks and splendid arms, and rode a magnificent Arab steed, with a rich saddle-cloth of scarlet, which bore no marks of suffering or privation. No small curiosity was experienced to discover the appearance of one who had maintained a defence obstinate and protracted beyond any related in the annals of modern warfare. He but little exceeds the middle size; is powerfully but elegantly formed; his keen, dark, piercing, restless eyes surveyed at a glance everything around. He neither wore the face of defiance or dejection, but moved along under the general gaze as one conscious of having barely done his duty, and aware of being the object of universal regard.

Ryder's account of the fall of Multan was less flowery and much more direct:

Heaven only can tell what were the sufferings of those poor creatures after the siege commenced. And no-one can tell how many were killed. No respect was paid to nobility of blood, innocence of youth or to the tears of beauty. Mountains of dead lay in every part of the town, and heaps of human ashes in every square, where the bodies had been burnt as they were killed. Some were only half consumed. Many had been gnawed and pulled to pieces by dogs; and arms, legs, heads and other parts lay in every place. The town swarmed with millions of flies.

Soldiers broke into Mulraj's treasury and found a hoard of gold and silver coins and bars; the quantity was so vast that it took three days to weigh and count it and pack it into ammunition wagons. The prize agents reckoned its worth at nearly £3 million sterling. Not all the treasure was officially counted. Soldiers who got there first filled their pockets to spend in the grog shops. Ryder reported: 'The money was so plentiful that the men would not carry copper; and some of the men who had got the most would not carry silver!'

Mulraj was sent a prisoner to be put on trial for his life and the revolt in his region was extinguished. But the real war had still to be won. Leaving a strong garrison at Multan, Whish ordered an immediate march northwards to join Gough's grand army facing Shere Singh.

★   ★   ★

While Whish was on the march, Gough was already in hot pursuit of his Sikh enemy. The proud old general was clearly stung by Dalhousie's jibes about his lack of success so far. He noted in his diary: 'Heard from Governor-General that he would be glad if I gained a victory.' His determination to counter such snide remarks, coupled with his own instincts for frontal assaults, contributed to the near-disaster that followed.

At noon on 13 January 1849 Gough's army approached Chillianwalla, a small village on the left bank of the River Jhelum roughly 85 miles from Lahore. His 12,000 men had been on the march for three days. Spies told him that Shere Singh's army of between 32,000 and 40,000 men, with 62 guns, were encamped around nearby settlements and along a low range of hills intersected with ravines. They were hidden from the British view by thick jungle and the broken terrain. Gough reported that the nature of the country was 'excessively difficult and ill-adapted to the advance of a regular army'. Gough's scouts cautiously probed the area, and the following morning his army advanced in equally tentative fashion. Gough detoured to the right, partly to distract the enemy's attention but mainly to get as clear as he could of the embracing jungle 'on which it would appear that the enemy mainly relied'. A strong picket of Sikh cavalry and infantry was driven off a mound just outside the village. From this vantage point Gough was shocked to see the entire Sikh army drawn up in battle order. The enemy, having moved from their positions either overnight or earlier that morning, occupied the ground in front of him which 'though not a dense, was still a very difficult jungle'. By now it was past noon and

British light dragoons engaging the enemy at Chillianwalla. (Victoria & Albert Museum)

Gough sensibly held back while scouts tested the enemy flanks. He intended to make camp for the night and leave the fight to the following day.

However, just as engineers and the quartermaster were preparing the camp, a troop of Sikh horse artillery advanced and blasted the skirmish line in front of the village. The heavier British guns were unlimbered and opened up an artillery duel. Their fire was instantly returned by the whole of the enemy's field artillery. The British commander decided to attack at once. Defending his actions later, Gough said that the cannonade had exposed the positions of the Sikh guns, which until then had been well hidden. He added: 'It was now evident that the enemy intended to fight, and would probably advance his guns so as to reach the encampment during the night.' Other officers, however, believed that Gough had been stung into foolhardy action by the Sikh horse artillery attack.

While the guns blasted each other for more than an hour, Gough drew up his battle lines. Sir Walter Gilbert's division was on the right, flanked by Brigadier Pope's brigade of cavalry, strengthened by the 14th Light Dragoons. Brigadier-General Colin Campbell's division formed the left, flanked by Brigadier White's cavalry brigade and three troops of horse artillery. The 24th Foot, flanked by the 25th and 45th Native Infantry, were in the centre, under orders to take the Sikh guns directly in front of them.

To the footsore and weary infantry it seemed madness from the start. The *Annual Register* later commented:

> Such was the order of the attack; but the question now arises, was it prudent under the circumstances to make the attack at all? The troops were wearied with their march, the day was almost spent, and there was no time to make proper arrangements so as to avoid unnecessary loss of life. The truth seems to be that Lord Gough was irritated by the fire from the horse artillery of the Sikhs, and suddenly changing his plan of waiting, he resolved to chastise their presumption on the spot. If such be the fact, the Commander-in-Chief was certainly, in this instance, more brave than discreet, and his indiscretion cost us dear. No sufficient reconnaissance was made of the ground that lay between our troops and the enemy, and it was not known in what part of his line his chief strength lay.

The 24th Foot, a regiment that had been battle-hardened in the Napoleonic Wars forty or more years before, had taken no part in the First Sikh War and had arrived in India only six months earlier. The regiment was nearly at full strength, with 31 officers and 1,065 men. It had a reputation for both courage and ill-luck.

At around 3 p.m. they began their advance, under Brigadier Mountain, through thick scrub and jungle, picking up speed as the foliage cleared. In front of them was a wide open space commanded by twenty Sikh guns. The enemy gunners barely needed to take aim before opening up. Round shot and grapeshot mowed down officers and men in their dozens, the cannon being no respecters of rank. They moved steadily forward, but the order to charge was given when they were still too far from the Sikh positions. Gough reported: 'This unhappy mistake led to the

Europeans outstripping the native corps, which could not keep pace, and arriving completely blown at a belt of thicker jungle, where they got into some confusion.' Astonishingly, the 24th were given orders that muskets should not be fired and only the bayonet used against the enemy. The blame for the disaster later fell on Brigadier Pennicuick, who had given an over-literal interpretation of Gough's orders that the guns should be taken by the bayonet point.

A young officer noted that his men, with their colours unfurled, made a 'good target' for the Sikh gunners. The 24th rushed blindly forward. Captain Thackwell wrote: 'It fell to the lot of this gallant regiment to experience an atmosphere solely compounded of fire, grape and roundshot.' They were mown down, gaping holes appearing in the advancing redcoat ranks as the Sikh gunners in their yellow turbans battled to maintain their ceaseless barrage. Lieutenant Andrew Macpherson recalled:

> One charge of grapeshot took away an entire section and for a moment I was alone and unhurt. On we went, the goal is almost won, the ground clears, the pace quickens . . . the bayonets come down for the charge. My men's pieces were loaded but not a shot was fired, with a wild, choking hurrah we stormed the guns and the battery is won.

The fight which began when the bloodied remnants of the 24th reached the Sikh guns was close-quarter and savage, with the blade the main weapon used. Half-blinded by smoke, deafened by blast and pumped up with adrenaline, men grappled in a stabbing, slashing, cursing mêlée. Major Paynter was shot through the lungs; his horse carried him to safety but he later died. Lieutenant Lloyd Williams suffered twenty-three sword and lance wounds and a fractured skull, and his left hand was severed. Astonishingly, he survived. Pennicuick did not, nor did his seventeen-year-old son, an ensign who fell across his father's body during his first taste of action. The queen's colours were lost in the confusion, but not the regimental colours. The Sikh batteries were taken and several guns spiked. General Campbell reported in dispatches: 'This single regiment actually broke the enemy's line and took large numbers of the enemy's guns to their front without a shot being fired or a musket being taken from the shoulder.'

As soon as the central Sikh guns were silenced the 24th came under flanking fire from other cannon, with musket fire from almost all sides. They were forced to retreat 'in good order and with determined bravery' over the bodies of their fallen comrades. One report of the action said:

> The Sikhs no sooner saw they were deprived of the use of their guns than they renewed such a fire with musketry, not only on the flank, but in the rear of the brigade, that common prudence dictated a retreat, and it was effected with the same determination that had distinguished the three brigades throughout.

Virtually every correspondent described the charge, unsupported by artillery or cavalry, and caught in a vicious cross-fire, as 'magnificent'. Charles Napier wrote: 'Their conduct has never been surpassed by British soldiers on a field of battle.'

The King's Own Light Dragoons charging the Sikh cavalry at Chillianwala. (National Army Museum)

It was a victory of sorts, as some enemy guns were spiked, but it was a costly one. By the end of the day the regiment had lost nearly half its men, with 515 casualties, including 238 dead. Of its 29 officers, 13 were killed and 10 wounded. The dead officers were laid out on their polished mess table later that night.

Elsewhere other men were either distinguishing or disgracing themselves. Gilbert's brigade marched through thick jungle to confront a large body of Sikh infantry, which easily outflanked them. Two companies of the 2nd European Regiment wheeled up and charged, but found themselves quickly surrounded. They immediately faced right-about, fired and charged, the rear rank to the front. Horse artillery was effectively deployed to help them beat off the enemy. Lieutenant D.A. Sandford of the 2nd Bengal Europeans described another infantry charge on the British right:

The men bounded forwards like angry bulldogs, pouring in a murderous fire. The enemy's bullets whizzed above our heads; the very air seemed teeming with them; man after man was struck down, and rolled in the dust. But a passing glance was all that we could give them. And onward he went, bearing on their line with a steadiness which nothing could resist. They fired a last volley, and then turned and fled, leaving the ground covered with dead and wounded. Pursuit in a jungle like that was useless, where we could not see twenty yards before us . . .

Later, when Sandford's unit was itself surrounded, the horse artillery blasted them an escape route in the enemy's ranks. He recalled:

Every gun was turned on them, the men working as coolly as on parade; and a salvo was poured in that sent horse and man head over heels, in heaps. The fire was fearful; the atmosphere seemed alive with balls. I can only compare it to a storm of hail. They sang above my head and ears so thick that I felt that if I put out my hand it would be taken off.

On the extreme left a dashing cavalry charge led by Brigadier White was successful. And the 61st Foot captured several guns, much ammunition and an elephant. Their officer said that his men 'saw game ahead and I couldn't hold them in'. Such successes were almost thrown away by the performance of the cavalry under Brigadier Pope.

Pope was a distinguished veteran of the East India Company army but he was now old, infirm and almost blind. He was a known ditherer and had only a shaky grasp of command. Gough, who rarely had a bad word to say about any officers under his command, said that Pope was unfit for the responsibilities to which his seniority entitled him. Pope's men had little confidence in him and their doubts were swiftly confirmed. Pope's cavalry division was made up of the 14th Light Dragoons, the 9th Lancers and two regiments of native cavalry. They were ordered to move against a large body of enemy horsemen, variously estimated at between 1,000 and 5,000 men. Pope had difficulty in getting his men faced in the right direction and his orders were confused and conflicting. Finally he halted them to give himself time to think. Suddenly, some Sikh cavalry appeared in front of them and Pope, by now thoroughly confused, ordered 'Threes about' instead of giving the signal to charge. The troopers obediently wheeled about and galloped away. Only a body of the 9th Lancers were rallied by screaming officers. The rest rode straight through the British artillery lines in a compact mass, upsetting four cannon and several wagons. Leaving a trail of wreckage, they continued to a field hospital and were only halted by the Revd W. Whiting, who was attending the wounded. The panicky troopers told him that the battle was lost. Whiting said that he was a man of God but he would shoot any trooper who continued to retreat. Gough, tongue in cheek, later proposed that Whiting be made a brevet-bishop.

The Sikh cavalry, meantime, took advantage of the mayhem and followed the troopers into the now-chaotic British artillery lines, a mass of thrashing horses and upturned limbers. They cut down seventy-three gunners who had, by the flight of their own cavalry through their ranks, been deprived of the means of defending themselves. A cannonade of grapeshot halted the Sikh advance but they carried off four guns, two of which were later recovered.

The battle dragged on inconclusively until eight that night. Under cover of darkness the Sikhs withdrew, taking most of their guns (including several previously captured by the British), five stands of regimental colours, and several British guns. According to British reports the Sikhs 'in their night excursions to recover their guns, killed many of our wounded, and stripped and plundered all the bodies within their reach'.

After possibly the hardest battle the British ever fought in India, Gough rode along the lines, bareheaded in the pouring rain, and was cheered everywhere by his bloody and exhausted men. But there was precious little cheering when news of the 'victory' reached London.

The British had remained masters of the battlefield and Gough naturally claimed a resounding success, which was 'complete as to the total overthrow of the enemy', estimating Sikh casualties at up to 8,000. But the cost shocked his masters at home. The losses, including those incurred by the ill-advised charge of the 24th,were 26 European officers and 731 men killed, 104 missing, 66 officers and 1,585 men wounded. Nearly 1,000 of the losses were British rather than native troops and the public at home were unused to such slaughter of their own boys during Indian campaigns. Gough, previously seen as a hero for his 'up and at 'em' tactics was now roundly condemned by all, from Queen Victoria to the tavern tactician. Dalhousie regarded Gough as a relic who was overly fond of the bayonet and ignorant of the sciences of modern warfare. The Governor-General wrote: 'If he again fights an incomplete action with terrible carnage as before, you must expect to hear of my taking a strong step: he shall not remain in command of that army in the field.' Such threats were soon exceeded by the outcry in London. The *Illustrated London News* stormed: 'Though masters of the field, our laurels are drenched with blood, and it is the universal opinion that two more such victories would be virtual ruin.' The post mortem focused on Gough's initial decision to attack without a proper reconnaissance. The same periodical published an explanation which was widely accepted:

The old chief had merely given an order to change ground, and it was not his intention to have attacked the Sikhs until the next day, but they seem to have enticed him on; they allowed their advanced posts to be driven in, and then opened a heavy fire, which put him into a passion, and he swore that he would drive them from the face of the earth. Several people advised him not to fight them until the next day, but he would listen to no one, and even said he would put any officer under arrest who presumed to suggest anything to him.

The *Annual Register* reported:

The news was received in England with a burst of sorrow and, we must add, indignation. Want of due caution on the part of the General was patent on the face of the accounts of the engagement, and it was felt that it ought not to have been hazarded, nor so great a waste of life so wantonly incurred. There was no need to test the courage of the soldiers who had been engaged in this campaign against the Sikhs, and the duty of the Commander-in-Chief was to effect the overthrow of the enemy by superior strategic skill, rather than by dashing exploits of personal valour and hand-to-hand conflicts with the sabre and the bayonet. The consequence was an almost unanimous demand for the recall of Lord Gough and the appointment of a general who would carry on the war in a more scientific and less desperate fashion.

Within 48 hours of the dispatches being received the government agreed to replace Gough with Sir Charles Napier, the conqueror of Sind, who was then in England.

The queen wrote: 'The news from India is very distressing, and makes one very anxious, but Sir Charles Napier is instantly to be sent out to supersede Lord Gough, and he is so well versed in Indian tactics that we may look with safety to the future *after* his arrival.'

Napier was appointed Commander-in-Chief of the Forces and Member Extraordinary of the Council of India, and set sail from England towards the end of March to take charge of the campaign. By the time he arrived events had turned Gough back into a hero and the war was over.

★   ★   ★

After the bloody 'victory' of Chillianwalla, Gough sensibly decided to wait until he was reinforced by General Whish's army. Dalhousie, the severest critic of Gough's previous foolhardiness, now rebuked him for the delay. In a letter to Sir John Hobhouse he wrote:

> I regret to say that every man in the army – generals of divisions – officers, Europeans and sepoys – have totally lost confidence in their leader – loudly proclaim it themselves, and report it in their letters to their friends. It is with pain that I state my opinion that I can no longer feel any confidence that the army is safe from disaster in the hands of the present C-in-C, and add that there is not a man in India who does not share that feeling with me.

On 12 February Shere Singh and his father Chuttar Singh deployed a cavalry screen while their army struck their tents and retreated to Gujerat near the Chenab river. Their force, strengthened by 1,500 Afghan cavalry sent by Dost Mohammed, now numbered up to 60,000, with 59 guns. When Whish joined him, after securing several fords across the Chenab, Gough had 24,000 men under his command, and set off to pursue the enemy. Gough's scouts reported on the Sikh position:

> It was found to be immensely strong, and consisted of a double line of entrenchments, in front of which they had planted large bushes in every direction, so as to mask themselves, and to prevent the movement of cavalry. Their camp had been pitched upon the slope of a hill, with a battery in the midst of broken ground. Close to this battery was a deep and rugged ravine with a narrow bridge. To the rear of this natural fortress was a perpendicular wall of rock.

The camp encircled the small town and the Sikh army was drawn up between it and the dry bed of a small river. Despite the strength of the enemy positions and their numerical supremacy, Gough, knowing his career was finished unless he could win a quick victory, decided to attack. On 21 February 1849 he fought his 'last and best battle'.

A half-hearted Sikh cavalry attack was repelled on the flanks and at 7.30 a.m. Gough ordered his army to advance against the Sikh centre. The enemy artillery opened fire at long range, thereby exposing their positions in the scrub. Gough halted his infantry and brought forward his own cannon. The general wrote in his dispatches:

> The cannonade now opened upon the enemy was the most magnificent I ever witnessed, and as terrible in its effects. The Sikh guns were served with their accustomed rapidity, and the enemy well and resolutely maintained his position; but the terrific force of our fire obliged them, after an obstinate resistance, to fall back.

Gough then ordered a general advance under cover of his cannon. A large body of Sikh infantry concealed in the small village of Burra Kalra was taken 'with great slaughter' by the 3rd Brigade under Brigadier Penny, a mixed force of the 2nd Europeans and the 31st and 70th regiments of native infantry. Lieutenant Sandford wrote:

> The round-shot flew about us, and ploughed up the ground in all directions. Five or six men were knocked down in as many seconds . . . A company from each regiment in the brigade was sent up to the front to support the troop of horse-artillery attached to us; and, poor fellows, they suffered dreadfully, being brought in one after another wounded – some with legs shot off, some cut in half, some torn with grape – scarcely half of our rifle company was left. All this time, the fire was very hot on us, carrying off three men at a time, shells bursting over us, or burying themselves in front, scattering the earth in our faces.

At the same time a 'very spirited and successful' move was made against troops in another hamlet, Chota Kalra, by the 10th Foot under Lieutenant-Colonel Franks. This proved to be the toughest engagement of the battle. The Sikhs fired through loopholes in the village walls and in 30 minutes killed or wounded ninety-four attackers. Light artillery blasted the defences from yards away and an infantry charge reached the walls, but the Sikhs fought on with fanatical stubbornness. Once again the rifle butt and bayonet were used against sword and spear in house-to-house fighting which left the flagstones slippery with blood. Gough reported:

> The heavy artillery continued to advance with extraordinary celerity, taking up successive forward positions, driving the enemy from those they had retired to, whilst the rapid advance and beautiful fire of the Horse Artillery and light field-batteries, which I strengthened by bringing to the front the two reserve troops . . . broke the ranks of the enemy at all points. The whole Infantry line now rapidly advanced and drove the enemy before it; the *nulla* was cleared, several villages stormed, the guns that were in position carried, the camp captured and the enemy routed in every direction.

Campbell's division pursued them on the east flank, and the Bombay column on the west. Gough's report continued:

The retreat of the Sikh army thus hotly pressed, soon became a perfect flight, all arms dispersing over the country, rapidly pursued by our troops for a distance of 12 miles, their track strewn with the wounded, their arms and military equipment, which they threw away to conceal that they were soldiers.

His victory was genuine and complete, as Gough underlined in his gleeful report to Dalhousie: 'A result, my lord, glorious indeed for the ever-victorious army of India.' The Sikh army had been routed with heavy losses, leaving behind fifty-seven guns. It was the end of the Khalsa. Given the scale of the battle Gough's casualties were astonishingly light: 96 killed and 682 wounded, of whom many were saved by the use of anaesthetics for the first time on a British battlefield. One commentator sniffed, however, 'The success of the operation at Gujerat renders it more painful to contemplate the sacrifice of life at Chillianwalla.'

The following morning Major-General Sir Walter Gilbert, with 15,000 men, set off in pursuit of the demoralised remnants of Shere Singh's army. It became a simple chase through rain-drenched ravines and across swollen rivers. The revolt had effectively been crushed. On the 24th Major Lawrence crossed the Jhelum river and opened communications with Shere Singh. Four days later Gilbert's main force crossed the torrent with extreme difficulty. Shere Singh retreated further, his army now reduced to 10,000 men and 10 guns. But on 6 March Major and Mrs Lawrence, who had been held captive by the Sikhs, arrived in Gilbert's camp and announced that Shere Singh was ready to lay down his arms. Two days later the Rajah himself arrived and was told that only unconditional surrender was acceptable. He returned to consult with his father and other chiefs while the British advanced steadily. At Rawalpindi on the 11th he again crossed the British line, this time with his Sirdars and the guns captured at Chillianwalla. An observer noted:

Shere Singh then returned again to the remnant of his army, to prepare it for the surrender that was to take place the following day. This humiliating act occupied some time, and it was not until the 14th that the whole of the Sikh officers and soldiers had delivered up their arms. Each man as he passed received one rupee to provide him with the means of subsistence until he reached his home, and they were all allowed to retain their horses.

General Campbell was impressed by the dignity of one old Khalsa soldier who put down his musket, saluted and cried out: 'Today Runjeet Singh is dead.' The British campaign medal later struck showed Sikhs laying down their arms in front of a mounted general in a cocked hat.

After witnessing the surrender, Dalhousie gloated in a letter to Queen Victoria: 'Your Majesty may well imagine the pride with which British officers looked on such a scene, and witnessed this absolute subjection and humiliation of so powerful an enemy.'

Gilbert then set off after the fleeing Afghan cavalry, under Akram Khan, hoping to cut them off before the crossed the Indus. He just failed, reaching the river just as

The Sikh cavalry surrendering their arms at Rawalpindi, 11 March 1849. (*Illustrated London News*)

the Afghans were destroying the bridge of boats they had used to cross. A few desultory shots from light Afghan cannon marked the end of the Second Sikh War.

★   ★   ★

The revolt and subsequent war offered the excuse to annexe the Punjab to British India, which is precisely what the Governor-General had intended all along. A proclamation issued by Dalhousie on 29 March referred to the first war and the clemency then shown by the British government. It went on:

> The Sikh people and their chiefs have grossly and faithlessly violated the promises by which they were bound. Of their annual tribute no portion whatever has at any time been paid, and large loans advanced to them by the Government of India have never been repaid. The control of the British government, to which they voluntarily submitted themselves, has been resisted by arms. Peace has been cast aside. British officers have been murdered when acting for the State; others engaged in the like employment have been treacherously thrown into captivity. Finally, the army of the state and the whole Sikh people, joined by many of the Sirdars in the Punjab who signed the

treaties, and led by a member of the Regency itself, have risen in arms against us, and have waged a fierce and bloody war for the proclaimed purpose of destroying the British and their power.

On 2 April the Punjab officially became a British province under a three-man administrative board, which was replaced by a commissioner four years later. The process of conquest which Clive had begun was now complete: Britain possessed the whole of India. Gough told his men: 'That which Alexander attempted, the British army have accomplished.'

British troops were stationed within the Punjab's borders. Former Khalsa soldiers were recruited into the new Punjab Frontier Force and from then on Sikhs provided some of the finest fighters in the British Army. They proved invaluably loyal during the Indian Mutiny. All sirdars and chiefs who had waged war on Britain saw their property confiscated. All strongholds and forts not occupied by British troops were destroyed. Those few chiefs who had not joined the revolt retained both property and rank. The young Majarajah Duleep Singh and his mother the Maharani Jindan were to be exiled. Freedom of religion was guaranteed and the British government forbade 'any man to intervene with others in the observance of such forms and customs as their respective religions may either enjoin or permit'.

Mulraj was put on trial before a special military commission consisting of four British and two native officers and a colonel of the Sikh army. He was charged with the murder of Vans Agnew and Anderson; he was an accessory before the fact in that he had instigated the attack, and an accessory after the fact in that he had rewarded the actual killers. He asked Edwardes to speak for him but the gallant major refused, saying afterwards: 'I believed him guilty, and would not defend him; I had hunted him with an army in the field and had no wish to follow him into the dock.' Instead a British advocate, Captain Hamilton, spoke for him with 'great zeal and ability' and the trial lasted fourteen days. Mulraj was found guilty and sentenced to death, although the sentence was later commuted to life imprisonment after the tribunal judged him 'the victim of circumstances'. He was banished. No mention was made of his looted fortune.

His citadel at Multan, which had resisted so much British artillery pounding, was almost entirely washed away the following August when the Chenab and Jhelum rivers breached their banks. The waters of the swollen rivers entered the ditches of the fort and ate away at its walls of sun-baked brick. Within hours the walls of the scarp and counterscarp slipped down 'like shaken sand' as the brickwork melted into slime. Over the next few days the enormous dome of the Bahwul Huk fell with a tremendous crash and other large buildings followed. Eventually the whole citadel resembled 'a mere island of mud amidst the expanse of water'. A British observer wrote in a private letter: 'Mooltan [sic] seems this season to be the victim alternately of fire and water – of the British Artillery and the Naiads. What Whish was so long in effecting, and then performed but imperfectly, the waters of the Chenab have accomplished noiselessly and without difficulty.'

Lord Gough, who had come so close to disgrace, returned home a hero. He had fought in more battles than any other living soldier and Gujerat had, thankfully, topped the lot. During a House of Lords debate no less a general than the Duke of Wellington praised him. Skimming over earlier 'untoward accidents which it was impossible to avoid', the duke described the overall campaign as 'brilliant in the extreme'. Sir Robert Peel said that he had never doubted that the campaign would 'rebound to the honour of Lord Gough'. Sir J.W. Hogg said that a more complete victory than Gujerat had never been fought. Gough was created a viscount and given a pension of £2,000 for his own lifetime and for that of his next two heirs. *Punch*, which had previously labelled him an 'incompetent octogenarian' now lauded him as a 'gallant veteran'. Gough, despite the accolades, resented the criticism of his generalship at Chillianwalla and other battles in the earlier war. He wrote: 'Thanks to a gracious God for not only covering my head in the day of battle, but for granting me a victory, not only over my Enemies, but over my country.' The East India Company voted him thanks and a further pension, and the City of London gave him its freedom. He saw no more active service but became a full general in 1854 when he was appointed colonel-in-chief of the 60th Royal Rifles. The following year he became colonel of the Royal Horse Guards after the death of Lord Raglan. In 1862 he became a field marshal. Sir Charles Napier, on taking up his Indian appointment, wrote of him: 'Everyone who knows Lord Gough must love the brave old warrior, who is all honour and nobleness of heart. Were his military genius as great as his heart, the Duke [of Wellington] would be nowhere by comparison.' His wife Frances, by whom he had a son and four daughters, died in 1863. He followed her at St Helens, his County Dublin seat, in 1869, aged eighty-nine.

Whish received the thanks of the court of directors of the East India Company and both Houses of Parliament. He was promoted a knight commander of the Order of the Bath and took command of the army's Bengal Division as a lieutenant-general. He died at London's Claridge's Hotel in 1853, aged sixty-five, leaving two sons, both soldiers.

Edwardes returned to England in 1850 and found himself lionised. He was knighted, showered with further honours and publicly entertained in London and Liverpool. The East India Company struck for him a unique gold medal, the mould of which was afterwards destroyed. This was the high water mark of his career. Long and worthy political service followed in frontier stations, where he deftly used his diplomatic skills to avert crisis after crisis. During a long trip back to England he was invited to stand as MP for Glasgow but declined. He died following a serious attack of pleurisy late in 1868. His mural tablet is in Westminster Abbey and his first district posting in the Punjab was named, by the Sikhs themselves, Edwardesabad.

Dalhousie ruled India for eight years and extended its boundaries even more after the annexation of the Punjab. His real legacy to India derived from his role as a reformer and moderniser – his projects included a railway, telegraph networks, a postal service and the development of irrigation and roadworks. He died in 1860 at Dalhousie Castle. His predecessor as Governor-General, Lord Hardinge, was blamed for many of the logistical failures of the Crimean War but that did not prevent him being raised to the rank of field marshal in 1855. He was stricken with paralysis while attending the queen and died, aged seventy-one, in 1856.

The conquest and annexation of the Punjab brought riches to many men of differing ranks. Sergeant John Pearman received a bounty of £3 16s after Gujerat. Private Perry, who had saved his regimental colours at Chillianwalla, was promoted to corporal and received a Good Conduct Medal. General Campbell, the son of a Glasgow carpenter, was knighted. After a distinguished career he ended his life as a field marshal, the Lord Clyde and a hero of the Indian Mutiny.

But the biggest prize went to Queen Victoria herself. Dalhousie was at last able to present her with the fabled 'mountain of light'. The Koh-i-noor diamond was a token of submission from the defeated Sikhs. Dalhousie reasoned that its removal from India would snuff out any lingering Sikh hopes of resistance. A British officer described the scene when it was taken from its imported Chubb safe in the grand palace at Lahore: 'I wish you could have seen the vast quantities of gold and silver, the jewels yet to be valued – and the Koh-i-noor, far beyond what I had imagined.' Shah Shuja, whose wife had included it among her jewels, said that whoever owned it would enjoy good fortune and victory over all enemies. However, the stone's history had been bloody, and those who took it wrongfully were cursed. Nadir Shah, who seized it after the 1739 sacking of Delhi, was murdered as he slept in his tent. Runjeet Singh may have escaped the curse but his successors did not (see Chapter 4). The curse appears to have stayed with the diamond: the ship which transported it to Britain barely survived a storm and its crew were ravaged by cholera. Within a month of Queen Victoria receiving it she was attacked twice, first by a deranged would-be assassin who fired a pistol at her, and then by a retired junior officer who swung at her with a walking stick. She never again wore the diamond. In 1854 it was poorly cut down by an incompetent artisan to 106 carats, little more than half its original size. It graced several royal crowns after Victoria and was last worn by the Queen Elizabeth the Queen Mother at her coronation in 1937. Some would even claim that the curse has continued down the House of Windsor line. It is currently on display among the other crown jewels in the Tower of London. In May 2000 the Indian government asked for it back. Kuldip Nayar, the MP who tabled the relevant motion said: 'The Koh-i-noor is so much part of India – so much part of our history, our psyche, our honour. It is one of the symbols of India. When you talk to any Indian about the Koh-i-noor, it stirs up a lot of emotion.'

The strangest story of all to come out of the Sikh wars concerns the fate of the child Maharajah, Duleep Singh. The ten-year-old signed away his kingdom under pressure from Dalhousie. He abdicated, gave up all his rights, titles and claims to sovereignty and was placed in the care of his guardian, a Bengal Army surgeon called Dr John Login. All his wealth was sold off as indemnity. In return he was to receive a life-time pension of £50,000 a year, which was admittedly a massive fortune. He was also obliged to leave his homeland, but could choose his destination. Under advice from Login he chose England. His long Sikh hair was cut, and the boy and the doctor took first-class cabins on the next available P&O steamer. Duleep travelled in his fine clothes, taking with him a casket of jewels and a favourite hawk.

He was warmly welcomed by Queen Victoria, who insisted that everything should be done 'to render the position of this interesting and peculiarly good and amiable

Prince as agreeable as possible'. Victoria praised his 'pretty, graceful and dignified manner'. She was, however, clearly embarrassed about wearing the Koh-i-noor, and sensitive to any charge of receiving stolen goods. The boy tried to put her mind at rest, saying that it gave him great pleasure to hand over such a magnificent gift.

Duleep settled on the Elveden estate near Thetford, purchased with money from the British government, and under Login's tutelage grew to like his new country. He became a Christian and practised with Purdey shotguns until he was reckoned the fourth-best shot in England. His mansion was conventional on the outside, but its interior was transformed into a Mughal palace filled with parrots. Apes played in the kitchen garden and kangaroos hopped across the manicured lawns. Duleep built up his 17,000-acre estate into one of the most sought-after venues in the country among the shooting gentry. Hunting parties would slaughter up to 3,000 birds in a single day. He kept a string of mistresses and was a frequent guest in London's most fashionable salons. As a thoroughly Anglicised young gentleman he was granted permission by the government to meet his mother and, after thirteen years apart, their reunion took place in Calcutta early in 1861. Jindan wept with emotion and vowed that she would never be separated from her son again. She was allowed to return to England with him, a betel-chewing curiosity, an old lady dressed in crinoline and dripping pearls. She told him all the tales of his ancestors and the way his inheritance had been stolen. In 1863 she died, followed two months later by

Duleep Singh, deposed Maharajah and English country gentleman, by G.G. Rejlander. (*Illustrated London News*)

Login, who had become Duleep's much-loved surrogate father. He married the seventeen-year-old daughter of a German missionary and sired three sons and three daughters, several of whom became Queen Victoria's godchildren. The names he chose for his children speaks volumes about the royal connection: Victor Albert, Frederick Victor, Bamba Sofia, Catherine, Sophia Alexandra and Albert Edward. He was a local magistrate, squire, Conservative, gentleman of leisure, a portly figure of the Establishment.

But a mixture of Jindan's words and growing money concerns set his mind into turmoil. Elveden was hugely expensive to run and Duleep also incurred heavy gambling debts. His bank, Coutts, sent him warning letters. These he simply sent on to the India Office, with copies to the queen. Ministers, fearful of a scandal if the bank foreclosed, reached an agreement whereby his debts were cleared provided that on his death Elveden would be sold to repay the loan and to provide pensions for his family. Despite such generous terms, Duleep grew ever more resentful and fired off numerous letters to the queen complaining of the lost power and wealth of his dynasty. When that did not work he turned to intrigue. He fantasised about winning back his lost kingdom, influenced by the words of the guru Gobind Singh who prophesied that a man with his name would 'drive his elephant throughout the world'.

Such fantasies made him easy prey for con-men and spies. He embarked on convoluted plans involving the agents of Irish nationalists, Bismarck and the Tsar. Duleep was kept under constant surveillance and some officials feared that he could become an active participant in the Great Game then being played out on north-west frontier between Britain and Russia. Queen Victoria was so concerned that she wrote to him about,

> extraordinary reports of your intending to transfer your allegiance to Russia! I cannot believe this of you who have always professed such loyalty and devotion towards me, who you know have always been your true friend and who I may say took a maternal interest in you from the time when, now 32 years ago, you came to England as a beautiful and charming Boy!

She need not have worried. Hardened schemers regarded him as a comic figure and all his intrigue came to nothing.

The flames of Sikh nationalism were fanned, however, in 1886 when Duleep became a Sikh again in a ceremony conducted in the Punjab. The British government was by then so relaxed about him that they allowed him to go. By now he was regarded as more of an embarrassment than a threat to the British Empire. He travelled to Paris, where he became involved with notorious anti-British factions. He made his way to Russia in 1887, taking a train across Europe with his teenage mistress and a number of dogs wearing embroidered jackets, and announced that he could 'guarantee an easy conquest of India'. The Tsar was initially impressed but the scheme foundered when it emerged that Duleep's chief of staff was a Foreign Office spy, and when his main political backer died. The plot quickly fell apart and he returned to France after less than a year. His first wife died and in 1889 he married Ada Wetherill, the twenty-year-old daughter of a London gas-fitter. They had two daughters, named Pauline and Ada. From France Duleep wrote to Queen Victoria, demanding the return of the Koh-i-noor which he intend to sell to fund an Indian revolt. His letter, like many others written during his middle age, was signed 'Implacable Foe of the British Government'. Soon afterwards, his dreams shattered by more experience of the cruel world outside his pampered normality, he wrote again, this time begging Victoria's forgiveness. He said: 'I feel that in fighting against your country I have been fighting against God. I would return to England were I assured of your free pardon.'

In 1893 Duleep Singh, the last Maharajah of the Punjab, died of a seizure in Paris. He was just fifty-five. By the end he had returned to the Christian faith. His body was taken by his son Frederick in an oak coffin from France to a funeral in St Andrew's church next to his Elveden estate. A wreath sent from Balmoral said simply: 'From Queen Victoria.' His grave in the churchyard remains a place of pilgrimage for Sikhs.

In 1947 India gained independence and the Punjab was divided as part of a tragic ethnic carve-up. Lahore, the Sikh capital, was included in the new Pakistan, while the Sikh holy city of Amritsar was part of the new India. Millions of Sikhs became displaced and homeless refugees.

In July 1999 Victoria's descendant, Charles, the Prince of Wales, unveiled an equestrian statute of Duleep at Thetford. Commissioned by a Sikh Trust, its inscription reads, in part, 'Even today the Sikh nation aspires to regain its sovereignty.'

CHAPTER SIX

Eureka Stockade, Australia, 1854

'A riot becoming a revolution.'

James Scobie, a Scots gold-digger who was going through an unlucky patch on his claim, spent the afternoon and evening drinking and jawing with his countryman Jimmy Martin in the Star Hotel in the mining township of Ballarat. Apart from bawdy jokes at the expense of the 'gold lace' gentlemen who presumed to exercise their authority in the Victoria goldfields, their behaviour was good-natured, if loud. Eventually the landlord grew tired of their singing 'Fanny, My Queen from Top to Toe' and threw them out. They found someone to sell them another bottle of grog and sat under a tree until midnight, talking weepily about the mists and mountains of home. Their drink gone, they stumbled towards their claims but stopped at the only light showing, the Eureka Hotel.

Behind the barred doors, enjoying some late-night drinking of their own, were hotel-keeper James Bentley, an ex-Norfolk Island convict notorious for cheating miners, for running a rough house and for bribing officials, his young wife Catherine, several guests and one of the recipients of Bentley's backhanders, the police magistrate John D'Ewes. The two Scots diggers banged loudly on the door, demanding service, and a lamp was somehow broken. Bentley called them 'drunken scum' but did nothing more. The magistrate urged him to do something about the disturbance, threatening him with the loss of his licence. What followed remains unclear.

The two diggers, thwarted, apparently set off home. Martin later recalled only the sound of several pairs of running feet in the moments before he was attacked; beaten senseless in the dark, he was left all night in a ditch. His mate was less fortunate. James Scobie was kicked to death by heavy boots. It was a grubby, senseless death, but one that was far from unique on the rough edges of the civilised world. It was, however, to have enormous and tragic consequences, fanning the flames of rebellious republicanism and creating a legend which still remains sharp and pertinent in modern-day Australia.

★   ★   ★

On 12 February 1851 Edward Hargraves, sifting gravel in Lewes Pond Creek near Bathhurst, found the fleck of yellow he was looking for. He told his companion:

'There it is . . . I shall be a baronet, you shall be knighted, and my old horse will be stuffed and put in a glass case and sent to the British Museum.'

His luck swiftly ran out but gold fever swept southern Australia. Extensive goldfields were found in New South Wales and Victoria. The goldfields changed the social structure of a continent still being colonised and better known as a dumping-ground for convicts than as a land of fabulous wealth. Men flocked to the fields where, it was said, nuggets could be had for the simple energy it took to bend down and pick them up. They came from all across the continent – stockmen, bushrangers, farmers and merchants; refined gentlemen sifted dirt alongside Irish, Scots and German immigrants; ex-convicts rubbed shoulders with their former gaolers. As word spread, they came from further afield: miners from the Californian goldfields, revolutionaries from strife-torn Europe, Sikhs and Chinese, the already wealthy, greedy for more, and the dispossessed. The population of Victoria swelled from 75,000 in 1850 to almost 290,000 four years later. A sparsely populated but prosperous land of sheep ranchers changed almost overnight to a boom zone where money was swiftly earned – and just as speedily spent. With the diggers came the profiteers, exploiters, entrepreneurs, grogshop owners, suppliers and criminals. Many indeed got rich quick, but all too often saw their new wealth taken from them; others squandered it at the Melbourne races, in ornate city saloons and on equally painted ladies. No matter, there was always more where that came from.

The boom time was heady indeed. Manning Clark wrote:

The diggers lived in a constant state of excitement which found outlets in all kinds of emotional extravaganzas. In their professions of loyalty to Her Majesty they were profuse; in their account of their feeling for each other they were excessive; in their account of their feelings for their enemies they were bloody, murderous and extreme. When a strike was made the fields rang with enthusiastic huzzas. The eager cry went up, 'There's a speck.' A gleam of wild delight shone in the eyes of the successful; a terrible despair darkened the eyes of the men who had missed out.

Gold there was in abundance, but little was found on the surface. It had to be dug for with spade and pickaxe, often in vertical shafts 160 feet deep. By 1854, when Victoria overtook New South Wales in population, the number of miners in the Victorian goldfields was almost three times that of two years earlier – but the amount of gold taken had fallen to half the 1852 total of £12 million. Big business could afford heavy machinery to pulverise rock and rape the ground, and thus took an ever-bigger share. Increasingly, the ordinary diggers lived a subsistence life, scrabbling for gold dust under mountains of grit. It was too hard for most of the 'gentlemen', who left the fields to the desperate and dispossessed from Ireland and Scotland and other places which had exiled their 'trouble-makers'. There were Chartists and Reformers, Fenians and Republicans, even the occasional anarchist. Most were simply men desperate to build a new life for themselves and their families.

As the population of largely landless men grew, so did the avarice of corrupt officials and police officers. The government saw a need to raise more revenue to build roads, schools, sanitation works and public buildings. In the last three months of 1851 the Victoria diggers brought in £374,000, yet none of that money went into government coffers. The government's answer was 'that bloody licence fee', the hated poll tax.

Victoria had become a colony in July 1851, and a digger's licence of £1 a month was imposed. It was a crippling amount for those struggling diggers who had sunk all their savings into their shafts with little return. Furthermore, such men had no representation on the fledgling Legislative Council, no vote, no say in how their money was spent. Unrest spread through the goldfields, fanned by the arrogance of the gold lace and the brutish tactics of the police – the hated 'traps' – sent to collect the tax. Public meetings were held, licences burnt, threats of civil insurrection issued. At Bendigo and Ballarat placards bore the slogan 'No chains for free Englishmen'. At View Point 12,000 diggers protested with red ribbons tied to their hats. Pistols were discharged. There was the occasional riot and crazy rumours spread of a German – or American, or French – brigade formed to rush to assist the diggers. The government saw the hand of agitators everywhere.

The man presiding over this powderkeg was simply not up to the job. Governor Charles Joseph La Trobe, a scholarly clergyman's son, briefly suspended the licence fee and was accused of giving in to ruffians and malcontents. Newspapers branded him an 'imbecile'. During his tenure Victoria's deficit approached £2 million and the capital, Melbourne, remained a foul-smelling sink. His announcement of impending retirement, following the early death of his wife, was widely greeted with relief.

His replacement, who arrived in June 1854, was charged with raising revenue and crushing discontent. A Royal Navy veteran from Suffolk, Captain Sir Charles Hotham was expected to instill quarterdeck discipline and make the new colony solvent. He did not want the job – he would have preferred to sail with his naval comrades to glory in the Crimean War – but accepted it out of his strongly defined sense of duty. After the usual civic receptions he embarked on a tour of the goldfields. He appeared initially sympathetic and the diggers cheered him as their champion. He soon disillusioned them. He was appalled by the threats of insurrection and was uncomfortable with the hearty familiarity of diggers he regarded as his inferiors. He prepared to exercise the firm hand of authority. He was encouraged to do so by the Resident Gold Commissioner, Robert Rede, another well-educated, impeccably dressed gentleman from an old Suffolk family. Rede was convinced that the goldfield unrest had nothing to do with the licence fee, but was stirred up by European revolutionaries who wanted nothing less than the overthrow of the established order. He regarded the Irish as the worst, a 'drunken, shiftless, violent race'. He believed they needed to be taught a harsh lesson and he hoped that the troublemakers would go one step too far so that the lesson could be vigorously enforced at the point of a bayonet.

One outcome was the notorious 'digger-hunts'. 'Traps' were empowered to demand production of the licence at any time, anywhere. Failure to provide it resulted in a £5 fine – half of which the arresting officer could pocket himself – and a stay in a stinking blockhouse or chained to a log. No excuse was permitted, even if the licence had simply been left in a tent or with another official. Hotham, to Rede's

Sir Charles Hotham, by W.A.
Hirschmann. (Mitchell Library, Sydney)

delight, ordered sweeps at least twice a week to catch tax-dodgers. The operations
were conducted like fox hunts. Armed 'traps' rode down diggers for sport. Men
toiling 160 feet underground were expected to haul themselves back up to produce
their licences for the entertainment of a smirking policeman. Even when the licences
were produced the men could be left broiling in the sun for several hours until the
paper was scrutinised. Independently minded, proud and hard-working men
seethed as much over the indignity of the digger-hunts as over the fee itself. Others
believed that only those with the hearts of slaves paid up.

A select committee inquiry found plenty of evidence that the diggers were being
treated badly. Doctor Owens reported: 'The main objection of the diggers is to the
mode of collecting the licence fee, since this is managed with so much offensiveness
as to make the diggers appear like a criminal class, and digging like a crime.' George
Purchase told the inquiry: 'The police are unpopular because of the power they
have, and which they exercise frequently, of going into a man's tent and rifling and
turning over his property to find grog, just whenever they please.'

Resentment was running highest in the Ballarat Basin, where Rede's writ was
most enthusiastically enforced. It only needed one spark to trigger turmoil. The
murder of James Scobie provided it.

★ ★ ★

The inquest into Scobie's death convened the next Monday and, to the astonishment of the onlookers, returned an open verdict. Bentley and his murderous friends were to escape justice. The resentment of the diggers boiled over. Here was proof positive that they were treated like vermin, liable to be killed at will by cronies of the ruling class. When nine of the jurors at the inquest had a change of heart, claiming they had been misdirected by the coroner, a court of inquiry was set up. John D'Ewes, a witness to the incident – possibly even its instigator – and well-known as a taker of bribes, sat on the board which decided by two to one that no charges should be laid against Bentley and his associates. It was a blatant fix, and fury spread through Ballarat and its outlying diggings.

On 17 October a meeting was convened outside the Eureka Hotel to discuss the 'unholy compact' between magistrates and crooked publicans. The mood was ugly as 5,000 diggers milled around outside while a terrified Bentley hid inside, drinking brandy. Rede dispatched a file of troopers under Sergeant-Major Robert Milne, a well-known bully, to ride through the crowd to support a line of policemen guarding the hotel. There were fiery speeches but order was kept, despite the provocation, by Peter Lalor, a quiet Irishman who was rapidly emerging as a leader of the diggers. His brother James was a hot-headed journalist who had been killed during an attack on a Tipperary police station during the 1849 Young Ireland uprisings. A trained engineer, who had worked on the Melbourne–Geelong railway before heading for the goldfields, Lalor was the son of a Home Rule supporter and landowner. But Lalor was no revolutionary and wanted little more than to work his claim to raise the cash he needed to buy a farm for himself and his planned bride. He believed that the rule of law would eventually redress wrongs. Lalor proposed that the meeting should

Peter Lalor. (The Government Printer, Melbourne)

pledge to 'use all lawful means to have the case brought before other, and more competent, authorities'. That proposal was carried, along with demands for a reward for the prosecution of Scobie's killers, and the meeting was then formally closed.

And that could have been it. But a hot wind was blowing, nerves were frayed, emotions aroused, and flasks of grog passed around. No one knows who started the violence. Some claimed that it was a trooper who sneered that the subscriptions would be used for drink, others that a drunken digger, Henry Westerby, called on his mates to pull Bentley out of his refuge. The cry went up: 'We'll smoke the bugger out.' Either way, the wood and tar paper hotel was soon blazing and Bentley, having been bundled out of the back door by a policeman, was soon riding for his life towards the army camp on the edge of the township.

Commissioner Rede watched the mob go wild, smashing everything which the flames did not consume. He was powerless to intervene as the official who had come ready to read a copy of the Riot Act dropped the document in panic. Troopers and police also stood impotently by. Rede, though horrified by the display of mob rule, later said that he was pleased that the diggers had now 'gone too far'. Rede reported the outrage in person to the governor in Melbourne the following day. Newspaper editorials expressed horror, and the capital's good burghers and property-owners demanded firm action. It was music to Rede's ears. Two diggers, Thomas Fletcher and Andrew McIntyre, were arrested virtually at random and were held at the Ballarat Camp. Later a hung-over Henry Westerby, who could barely remember the torching of the Eureka Hotel, was also picked up. They were to stand trial as an example to the rest.

Things did not go all Rede's way, however. Police Commissioner Charles McMahon said openly that the whole affair was Bentley's fault. It also began to dawn on the Melbourne administration that an open trial would involve evidence from the magistrate D'Ewes which might expose the level of official corruption. And then Attorney-General William Foster Stawell examined the evidence and concluded that Bentley and his associates should themselves stand trial. Sir Charles Hotham reluctantly agreed to hold an inquiry into the series of events but stipulated that the inquiry report would be for his eyes only. The results smelled so strongly of official corruption that Hotham was forced to conclude that some appeasement was necessary. D'Ewes was sacked as a magistrate and Sergeant-Major Milne was arrested for taking bribes. The governor agreed that Bentley and two associates should stand trial for manslaughter and cheers rang out across the goldfields when they were convicted and sentenced to three years' hard labour on the roads.

Again, the crisis could have been settled at this point. But the diggers had challenged authority and won a partial victory. They had become better organised under the committee elected to fight Scobie's case. Three of their comrades were also facing trial for riot and tumult at the Eureka Hotel. And the 'damned licence' was still there, despite Hotham's promise of a wider-ranging commission of inquiry into goldfield grievances. On the other side, the governor, Rede, the gold lace and the military were seething that crimes of insubordination to proper authority had gone unpunished. The downhill slide towards tragedy picked up pace again.

Troops arriving at the government camp at Ballarat, 1854, by S.D.S. Huyghue. (Ballarat Fine Art Gallery)

Feelings were inflamed when the rumour spread that the authorities were about to introduce 'Government by artillery' in the goldfields, enforcing the tax with cannon as well as bayonet, truncheon and chain. Another mass meeting at Ballarat on 11 November declared that taxation without representation was tyranny. That meeting passed off peaceably as diggers gathered with their wives and families in their Sunday best and voted for the Ballarat Reform League. But fury reasserted itself when the diggers learned that their three comrades had been sentenced to terms in Melbourne gaol – six months for Westerby, four for Fletcher and three for McIntyre.

By now several leaders had emerged among the unkempt diggers and they formed the backbone of the new Ballarat Reform League. Lalor, a civilising influence at every meeting, still believed there could be a peaceful resolution. He remembered the terrible injustices he had witnessed as a boy in Ireland and regarded himself as a true democrat rather than a republican or communist. 'If a democrat means opposition to a tyrannical press, a tyrannical people, or a tyrannical government,' he said, 'then I have been, I am still, and will ever remain a democrat.' George Black, the editor of the *Gold Diggers Advocate*, also wanted justice without further bloodshed and believed it was just possible. So, too, did John Basson Humffray, a curly-haired Chapel man with a fine tenor voice from Newton in Montgomeryshire, who hated the thought of taking another's life. Humffray, who articled as a solicitor, before succumbing to the lure of gold, was a Chartist with a lawyer's faith in legal channels.

More hot-headed were the balding Scots Radical Thomas Kennedy, a friend of the murdered Scobie, and Rafaello Carboni, a red-bearded Italian from Ursino who once trained for the priesthood. Instead, he had become a clerk, then a soldier, being wounded three times in the service of the Young Italy movement, and later a language teacher in London. After emigration to Australia he had been a shepherd and lived for a time among the aborigines. He regarded British rule as akin to the Austrian oppression of his own home country. He was an exotic character and popular among the diggers. The same could not be said of Friedrich Vern, a bombastic Prussian who bought his way into the diggers' committee by promising a £100 loan, and then tried to dominate meetings with his boasts of unlikely military exploits in the service of red republicanism. Carboni, whose martial record was proven, detested him.

The men of the Ballarat Reform League shared common aims but had different agendas. All of them alarmed the Melbourne administration. Henry Seekamp, editor of the *Ballarat Times*, fed their paranoia when he wrote that the League was,

> not more or less than the germ of Australian independence. The die is cast, and fate has cast upon the movement its indelible signature. No power on earth can restrain the united might and headlong strides for freedom of the people in this country.

Black, Humffray and Kennedy comprised a delegation sent to see Governor Hotham in Melbourne on 27 November in one last attempt at conciliation. He greeted them stiffly and without offering any concessions beyond his earlier promise of a long-term Commission into goldfield conditions. The three jailed diggers would remain inside, the licence would be enforced, the digger hunts would continue. Hotham treated them 'with disdain' but by then it was probably too late anyway.

While they were still negotiating, a detachment of the 40th Regiment marched from Geelong to Ballarat to reinforce Rede's garrison. The miners greeted them first with foul oaths and ridicule, then with sticks and stones. Several soldiers were hurt in a vicious brawl around the baggage cart, and a drummer boy was shot in the leg during the confusion, most probably by a digger. A squadron of mounted police was also attacked with cudgels. The diggers, convinced that the iron might of the British Empire had been sent to crush them, fired weapons into the air all night. The soldiers and policemen, nursing their bruises and lost dignity, vowed bloody vengeance.

On 29 November another monster meeting was held on Bakery Hill, just outside the town. Here, the diggers unveiled their new, home-made standard, the Southern Cross, the work of Charles Ross. Friedrich Vern urged all those present to burn their hated licences. The next time the 'traps' came they would stand or fall together. One man set fire to his licence and threw it on the ground. One by one others followed suit until there was a bonfire blazing in the hot still air. A grog seller did good business with his black bottle. The chairman of the meeting, the normally placid Irishman Timothy Hayes, asked the company: 'Are you ready to die?' They replied with loud cries of affirmation and pistol shots.

All this was reported back to Commissioner Rede, who had a network of informers. He called a council of war with the senior army officers in Ballarat Camp and convinced them that only a show of force would prevent an armed rebellion. It was announced that the following morning there would be another licence hunt. At 10 a.m. Rede, backed by mounted police with swords drawn and foot soldiers with bayonets fixed, set out for the diggings. There was immediate trouble. A maddened crowd of about 70 diggers hurled stones and broken bottles.

Dozens of individual brawls broke out and above the bedlam Rede could be heard reading the Riot Act. Eight miners were surrounded and taken prisoner. Shots were fired by both sides, but not yet at each other. Some order was restored on both sides too, but by now it was too late. The die was truly cast. Diggers fell into line two abreast, and marched together towards that part of the diggings known as Eureka. Rumours spread that diggers had been butchered and that cannon were on the way. The call 'To arms' rang through the Ballarat Basin. 'This is madness,' Peter Lalor thought, and later recorded the same sentiment in his diary.

★　★　★

By 5 that afternoon 500 diggers had gathered on Bakery Hill below the Southern Cross, fluttering from a makeshift flagstaff. They were light-headed with excitement, pride, drink or fear, or any combination of the above. Each recorded his name and knelt below the flag to swear 'to stand truly by each other, and fight to defend our rights and liberties'. They elected Lalor their commander-in-chief, much to Vern's chagrin; he petulantly refused the Irishman's offer of second in command. Lalor, who abhorred violence, knew that they must prepare for the inevitable military onslaught. He said: 'I tell you, gentlemen, if once I pledge my hand to the diggers, I will neither defile it with treachery, nor render it contemptible with cowardice.'

The night passed in confused preparations for the oncoming storm. One last attempt was made at conciliation. George Black and Carboni went to the government camp under a flag of truce to submit their demands one last time to Rede. The commissioner would offer them nothing and objected strongly to the word 'demand'. The two-man delegation returned by starlight to Eureka.

Rede decided to play a waiting game. The diggers, he contemptuously reckoned, would disperse in the morning when their hangovers cleared. If not, reinforcements were on their way from Melbourne, armed, he had been assured, with field guns and howitzers. In the meantime the perimeter fence of the camp was strengthened with logs and bales. The 12th and 40th Foot were on stand-to, their pouches bulging with extra ammunition for their modern Minie rifles. Spies were sent into the enemy camp and Rede surmised that order would be swiftly imposed and the ring-leaders quickly and suitably dealt with. The morning light proved Rede wrong. Dawn showed that the number of diggers had swelled from 500 to 800, as mates came from across the goldfields. Throughout the first two days of December the diggers built their own stockade on high ground above the Eureka claim. Moreover, Rede soon received word that the promised heavy artillery had not left Melbourne.

The Eureka Stockade was poorly constructed from wooden pit-props known as slabs, branches and logs. It enclosed an acre of ground, and included John

Diamond's store, Lalor's own hut and a smithy run by the German John Hafele. Shallow diggings outside the barricade were transformed into useful rifle pits. The stockade commanded the main road to Melbourne, but it could not have withstood cannon fire for a minute. Inside, Vern, wearing a long and cumbersome sword on his belt, drilled hobnail-booted diggers in Prussian style. The blacksmith produced a steady supply of pike-heads to be attached to shafts. The hill resembled a disturbed ants' nest.

On the first afternoon Thomas Kennedy, who had missed the previous day's mayhem, arrived with almost 300 new recruits from Creswick. Lalor's pleasant surprise turned to dismay when he realised the new men were armed only with pitchforks, and expected to be supplied with guns, beef stew and copious amounts of whiskey. Lalor could offer them only water after their long hot march. The commander-in-chief gloomily surveyed the crowded stockade and its outlying huts and realised that he could barely feed and house his own men, never mind the newcomers. He need not have worried. By the following morning most of the Creswick mob, realising there was no free grog, had drifted away, muttering that they would not fight with empty stomachs and clear heads.

That same Friday afternoon Governor Hotham, sweating in his airless Melbourne office, finally received the news that Major-General Sir Robert Nickle was on the march for Ballarat. His force consisted of the rest of the 12th and 40th Foot, naval detachments from HMS *Electra* and HMS *Fantome*, and heavy artillery which would shatter the Eureka stockade and all those within it. The governor had already sent Rede ambiguous orders to 'act with temper, caution and judgement, but to enforce the law'. He added that 'a Riot was rapidly growing into a Revolution'. Rede decided to wait for Nickle.

Early on Saturday morning the church made a half-hearted bid to stop a bloodbath. Ballarat's idealistic young priest, Father Smythe, was abandoned by his bishop and walked into the stockade alone to address his congregation. He told them:

> I know you are preparing to do battle in what you believe to be a just cause, but I implore you to count the cost. There are seven or eight hundred men under arms within the Camp. I know for a fact that more are on their way. You are not well-armed or well-trained. Although your hearts may be pure, you cannot fight cannon with pikes.

Looking individual diggers in the eye he went on: 'I ask you to give thought to your womenfolk and children. Don't deprive them of husbands and fathers. Don't reap a harvest of tears, my sons. Bring them instead to Mass tomorrow and let us all pray together for salvation.' At that, a man in the front rank threw down his pike and walked away. The ranks disintegrated as others followed him, to the catcalls of former comrades and the curses of Vern. Most, however, stayed.

That afternoon, tired of meaningless drill, many of the defenders drifted between stockade and home. As night approached it became clear that more of them, nagged by wives or tempted by the normal Saturday night pub session, were not coming back. However, at 4 p.m. the tide was turned when James McGill arrived with 200 men of his Independent Californian Rangers Revolver Brigade, marching stoutly uphill in riding breeches and slouch-hats, wearing pistols and long knives on their belts. McGill was a mysterious figure who recruited fellow Americans to spread the Republican movement across the goldfields. Some suspected he was an *agent provocateur* or a double-agent. The diggers cheered their new comrades from across the ocean and clapped them on the back. Their reputation for deadly pistol-fighting matched the drill and discipline of the redcoats. McGill also brought Lalor the long-feared news that General Nickle was on his way with two field guns and two howitzers. The confident American offered to intercept Nickle's column and destroy the artillery in a guerrilla strike. Lalor gave the enterprise his blessing and all but twenty of the Americans marched off again. Later it was said that McGill had been warned by American envoys that he and his men would pay dearly if their intervention sparked a diplomatic crisis with Britain. Whatever the truth, McGill never found Nickle's column and never returned to the stockade.

More diggers, convinced that the British would not attack on the Sabbath, set off for the hotels and their other usual Saturday night drinking haunts. There they spouted whiskey breath and fine words about how they would slay the oppressors. Lalor sent seventy men away on some ill-conceived errand. By midnight there were barely 150 diggers left within the stockade, although many more intended to return the following day once they had slept off the effects of their binge.

Intelligence to that effect was passed to Commissioner Rede by an American spy, Doctor Charles Kenworthy, who had visited the stockade on the pretext of offering medical help. He reported:

> A more disorganised gang I never did see. Some of them presenting broomsticks to a Prussian who keeps falling over his sword. Others out looting. Lalor is more like a schoolmaster whose pupils like and respect him for his honesty and high purpose but who also like to get up to mischief behind his back. And that stockade of theirs – why, it wouldn't keep out a prairie dog.

Kenworthy also boasted to Rede that it was he who had persuaded McGill and his men to leave.

The soldiers and policemen in the camp were eager to take revenge for their earlier humiliations. To the delight of their senior officers, Captains Pasley, Thomas and Wise, Rede decided on a gamble. He would not wait for Nickle but would strike before dawn while the rebels were depleted, at their weakest and asleep, possibly intoxicated. He argued that it would mean a swift end to the deadlock and would reduce the heavy casualties which were certain to be incurred once Nickle's artillery arrived. The officers also would win greater credit for themselves if the rebellion was crushed before their commander-in-chief arrived.

A plan of action was devised by lamplight, and the force of 276 men was given an hour's notice early on Sunday 3 December. The storming party was to be led by Captain Henry Wise, with forty picked men of the 12th and 40th, and twenty-four foot police. They were to be flanked by 70 mounted police on the right and

'The battle of the Eureka Stockade', by Thaddeus Welch and Izett Watson. (Engraving from the La Trobe Collection, State Library of Victoria)

30 mounted infantry on the left. The remainder of the attacking force would be held to the south as a reserve. Their route was not along the main road, as the rebels expected, because the noise of marching boots would be sure to give them away. Instead it was to be a circuitous slog through heavy bush, converging on the stockade at first light. Captain Thomas, the most senior officer, said: 'A dawn assault, sir, should be highly effective, catching most of the beggars fast asleep but giving us enough light to see by.' Rede replied: 'Then let us take a glass together, gentlemen, and drink to your success.'

The approach went as planned. Captain Wise, twenty-six years old, popular with his men, and raring for his first real taste of action, was sure that the enemy would hear the snap and crack of dry leaves and twigs as they neared the stockades. He was right, but the noise was twice regarded as a false alarm by those digger watchmen who remained awake. More splashings and whinnies were heard and ignored as the mounted police and soldiers crossed a small creek.

Dawn's red light shone on the buckles and blades of the government force as the men lined up to attack. Captain Thomas gave the order: 'Pass the word. Advance.' A line of redcoats, bayonets fixed, walked steadily towards the stockade, with Captain Wise and Lieutenant Paul out in front. Inside the defences Lalor was woken by a sudden crackle of fire and the shout: 'Stand to. Stand to. Redcoats.' On the west side of the stockade the diggers and some of the remaining Americans opened up a ragged but well-directed fire. Mounted redcoats were seen pouring out of the bush on one side, while a solid mass of blue-coated troopers emerged from the other. Carboni, who had been sleeping in his tent outside the stockade, heard an English voice cry: 'Steady men. A volley when you hear the bugle.'

At 200 yards Wise's infantry dressed into two lines, one kneeling, the other standing, and let rip the volley as the boy bugler sounded his horn. The Minie rifle was accurate up to 300 yards and the infantry were well-practised. The effect on those diggers who, bleary-eyed, had reached the stockade's parapet was devastating. Carboni later described how every head that was showing when the volley crashed was gone an instant later. The bullets tore through the spindly defences into the muscle, bone and guts of men. Lalor, who had stood on the parapet to urge on his men, fell with wounds in his shoulder, arm and sides. A high proportion of the overall casualties were suffered in that first, terrible blast. Vern, the Prussian braggart, was among the first to run. Others followed but many more stood firm while the remaining Americans kept a cool fire with their Colts from the rifle-pits. Patrick Curtain, who had tried to shoot Vern when he saw him run, rallied his band of pike-men, their blades newly gleaming from the forge.

Captain Wise ran full-pelt up the hill, roaring his head off as his men struggled to keep up with him. On each flank the cavalry and mounted police reached their ends of the stockade. But, 100 yards short of his target, Wise was hit in the knee. He struggled to rise but was shot again in the other leg. The official dispatch noted: 'Wounded in two places at the head of his men, as he lay on his back he cheered them on to the attack.' The stricken officer told Sergeant Hagerty: 'Keep going! At 'em, the 40th!'

His men did just that, their bloodlust high. Several soldiers fell in that last charge, but they were swiftly avenged by their comrades as infantry and horsemen swept over the flimsy defences. The long, unwieldy shafts of Curtain's pike-men were hopeless against disciplined bayonet-thrusts and sabre-cuts. The result was, inevitably, a bloodbath. A pike-man shot in both legs swept his weapon around like the hands of a clock until he was shot in the head. An American, shot in one leg, was seen hopping on the other, firing his Colt until the chambers were empty and he was cut down. John Hafele, the blacksmith and pike-maker, suffered a sabre slash which took off the top of his skull. Another German, the talented chess-player and lemonade-seller Edward Thonen, was shot full in the mouth. Some diggers who tried to escape into the bush were in turn run down. Police and military men stabbed and shot indiscriminately, and set fire to everything that might burn. Several wounded diggers took refuge in John Diamond's store but it was set ablaze. Carboni wrote: 'The howling and yelling was horrible. The wounded are now burnt to death; those who had laid down their arms, and taken refuge within the tents, were kicked like brutes and made prisoners.' Diamond was shot down as he tried to escape the flames. Two diggers, who had slept unawares in a drunken coma throughout the mayhem, were consumed by fire when their tent was torched.

Charles Ross was cut to pieces as he tried to defend the Southern Cross, the flag which he had so lovingly designed himself. Trooper John King from County Mayo climbed the flagstaff and hauled down the standard. Cheering soldiers stabbed it with bayonets, and trampled it into the dirt. The soldiers threatened to murder every prisoner but Captain Pasley ordered that any man who did so should be shot. Captain Thomas ordered the firing to cease. The blood-lust ebbed away and his men obeyed. The entire battle had taken just 15 minutes. A contemporary report said:

After burning all the tents within the enclosure, and in the immediate vicinity, the troops returned to camp, and carts were sent out for the dead and wounded. The latter thus obtained immediate medical aid. They were covered in blood and mostly shot in the breast. Among the arms taken in the fight were pikes of a rude construction, made on the spot and furnished with a sort of hooked knife to cut the bridles of the cavalry.

Throughout the engagement Peter Lalor lay semi-conscious under a pile of slabs and cut turf outside the stockade. His arm shattered, he was hidden by a digger called Ashburner. Carboni, who had taken no part in the fighting, tried to rescue some papers from a burning tent, but was stopped by a trooper who shot his cabbage-tree hat off his head. He became a meek captive, shocked by the speed with which his dreams had been destroyed.

Twenty-four insurgents died in the brief battle. At least ten were from Ireland, with two each from England, Scotland, Germany and Canada. Several names went unrecorded, including the real name of a man known on the goldfields as Happy Jack. The death toll may have been much higher, if subsequent reports of diggers dying in the bush or being hunted down by vengeful troopers are to be believed. Around 20 more were wounded and 114 taken prisoner. Father Smythe read the last rites over smouldering corpses while Doctor Carr did his best for the wounded, before being arrested as a rebel sympathiser. Inevitably, in such a confused and bitter engagement, there were conflicting reports, particularly over the performance of both sides and the behaviour of the police units. One correspondent to the *Argus*, who described himself as a 'military man', wrote:

The Camp Officer says the police were first to enter the Stockade. He is wrong. There was not a single policeman killed or wounded during the whole affair. When Captain Wise fell the men cleared, and were over in the Stockade in a second, and then bayonet and pike went to work. The diggers fought well and fierce, not a word spoken on either side until all was over. The blacksmith who made the pikes was killed by Lieutenant Richards of the 40th. Honour to his name: he fought well and died gloriously.

It was rumoured that the police were cruel to the wounded and prisoners. No such thing. The police did nothing but their duty, and they did it well for men that were not accustomed to scenes of blood or violence. To my knowledge there was only one wounded man despatched, and he kept swinging his pike around his head as he sat on the ground. He was shot in the legs and had a ball in his breast. He could not live and it was best to despatch him. His name was O'Neill, a native of Kilkenny, Ireland. I heard this statement from a sergeant of police and I know it was correct.

Another correspondent recorded the aftermath:

The dead was buried the same day in the cemetery. The bodies of the insurgents, placed in rough coffins made hurriedly, were laid in a separate grave, the burial service being performed by the clergyman to whose congregation they belonged. At night we were again under arms, as constant rumours of an intended attack kept us on the alert. This is exhausting work, and a severe trial, especially for the military, as the men have had no real rest for several nights. Indeed, no-one within the lines has undressed for the last four nights at the very least.

Government men buried that first day were Privates Michael Roney and Joseph Wall of the 40th. The wounded wagons took away thirteen men, including Privates William Webb, Felix Boyle and John Hall, all of the 12th, who would subsequently die of their injuries. Captain Wise joked with his men that his dancing days were over. Gangrene infected his legs, and the *Argus* reported: 'Amputation is considered necessary. This is but the beginning of the end.' He died four days before Christmas. The governor praised the 'gallant and valuable officer'.

Around the wreckage of the Eureka stockade the dust settled to the cries of newly made widows and orphans, but the business of the day soon reasserted itself. The great chronicler Manning Clark wrote:

The shopkeepers were wondering when buying and selling would start again; the tipplers were wondering how long they must wait before they could get a drink. No-one on the field or in the camp detected any majesty in the moment or prophesied that the diggers would one day be heroes of the people and hailed as the founders of democracy in Australia. Law and order had been restored. The shutters of the shops could now be removed and the flaps on the sly-grog tent tied back.

★   ★   ★

Peter Lalor, buried under a pile of wood, slipped in and out of consciousness. He was found by Father Smythe and a manservant who took him to a trusted digger and his wife near Mount Warrenhelp. More dead than alive, he was treated by a Kilkenny man, Doctor Timothy Doyle, who decided that his arm was beyond repair – shattered fragments of bone protruded from the flesh. The following day the arm was amputated.

The digger prisoners were meanwhile squashed into the government camp lock-up alongside more common criminals, riddled with lice and fleas. Carboni wrote: 'This vermin, and the heat of the season, and the stench of the place, and the horror of my situation, had rendered life intolerable to me.' The authorities, fearful that some rebels would die before they could stand trial, eventually moved the Eureka men to the better-ventilated camp storeroom.

Major-General Sir Robert Nickle finally arrived at the Ballarat diggings with his field guns and howitzers. But instead of menacing the truculent diggers he visited their encampments, unescorted, and found 'not the slightest expression of feeling' against the Crown. Embarrassed by his report, Governor Hotham lifted Martial Law three days later.

Hotham, as ever egged on by Rede, was still convinced that the goldfields were about to explode in revolutionary fury. Posters were tacked up offering a £500 reward for Friedrich Vern, still supposed to be the ringleader – due to his own boasting, and £200 apiece for Lalor and George Black. He thanked the queen's faithful subjects for ending the anarchy created by 'strangers in their midst'. And he ordered that every one of the 114 prisoners should be charged with insurrection, a capital offence. Henry Seekamp, the editor of the *Ballarat Times*, responded with an editorial calling for vengeance for the 'foul massacre' inflicted on the Eureka diggers. Hotham had him thrown into a gaol on charges of sedition. The governor's tough reaction split the population. In Melbourne, which had been thrown into panic by the first reports of insurrection, people were divided into those who demanded the restoration of law and order, and those who condemned the government as a 'set of wholesale butchers'.

Gradually tempers cooled on both sides. On 6 December 6,000 people gathered next to the city's St Paul's Church and vowed that in future reform must be sought by peaceful, constitutional and moral force alone. It soon became clear, also, that Govenor Hotham had over-reacted. It was simply not feasible to feed and house over 100 prisoners and mount a full and fair trial of them all. The numbers had already been whittled down by pragmatic officers and by the intervention of Doctor Kenworthy, who negotiated the release of all captured Americans in order to avoid a diplomatic row with his country. The only exception was John Josephs, the blacksmith's assistant who had helped to make rebel pikes. He was black, and therefore his execution was hardly likely to provoke a storm at home.

On 8 December just thirteen of the Eureka prisoners were committed for trial at the Supreme Court in Melbourne on the charge of high treason. They appeared to

The thirteen indicted Eureka men. Left to right: Timothy Hayes, James MacFie Campbell, Rafaello Carboni, Jacob Sorenson, John Manning, John Phelan, Thomas Dignam, John Josephs, James Beattie, William Molloy, Jan Vennik, Michael Tuehey and Henry Reid. (*Melbourne Age*, 1885)

have been chosen more or less at random. Carboni, who protested that he had never fired a shot or raised a pike, was shackled to Josephs. Timothy Hayes, Michael Tuehey and John Manning were designated as ringleaders. The remainder appear to have played only small roles in the Eureka drama. The following Tuesday they were chained into three carts which set off for Melbourne under the command of Captain Thomas. He told them that if they so much as turned their heads they would be shot. They were guarded by over thirty troopers until they were safely locked up in the city gaol.

A campaign immediately began to win them amnesty. John Basson Humffray, who had taken no part in the fighting, presented a petition signed by 4,500 Ballarat miners. The document claimed that the Eureka men 'did not take up arms, properly speaking, against the government, but to defend themselves against the bayonets, bullets and swords of the insolent officials in their unconstitutional attack . . .'. The delegation argued that clemency would prevent further dissent from turning into a movement for separation from the Mother Country. Hotham remained, however, a stiff-backed Royal Navy officer, and to his mind there was to be no shirking the due process of law. That process, from his point of view, quickly became a shambles.

The state trials of the Eureka men began on 22 February. The first to stand trial for their lives were John Josephs and John Manning. After an impassioned speech by Butler Cole Aspinall, a brilliant young lawyer from Liverpool, the jury found them not guilty. They were carried out shoulder-high by a cheering crowd. Hotham and his Attorney-General, William Foster Stawell, delayed the subsequent trials in the hope that the public mood would swing against the diggers. The next were held on 19 March before Justice Redmond Barry, a graduate of King's College, Dublin. Timothy Hayes spoke in his own defence, saying: 'I did everything in my power to bring about a peaceful resolution of our grievances. But that final licence-hunt was the last straw and, from then on, we were overtaken by events beyond the control of mere mortals.' He walked from the dock a free man. So too, a little later, did Rafaello Carboni. Evidence from soldiers and policemen that he had picked up a pike in the stockade was contradictory, and the assertion that he was one of those who had burnt his digger's licence was refuted when the Italian flourished the intact, and correctly dated, document in the courtroom. Another bout of 'spirited, cutting and withering' defence from Aspinall ensured that the jury took only 20 minutes to clear him.

The governor and his law officers were lampooned in the Press and *The Age* reviewed the proceedings as it would 'an exceedingly successful farce'. A Dutchman, Jan Vennik, was cleared next, and then James Beattie, Michael Tuehey and Thomas Dignam from Sydney. On 27 March the remaining accused – Henry Reid, James MacFie Campbell, William Molloy, Jacob Sorenson and John Phelan – also walked free. The *Argus* reported that the men were 'escorted from the Court by a large company who frequently raised loud plaudits on their way down Stephen Street'.

This legal fiasco was a bitter blow to Hotham's pride and authority. It was followed, on the same day, by the report of the Gold Fields Commission which Hotham himself had set up as a delaying tactic, and which he was committed to

Crowds celebrate the acquittal of the Eureka insurgents.

implement. With one stroke the Ballarat Reform League won virtually all the reforms they had demanded before the bloodshed. The hated licence tax was abolished in favour of a Miner's Right, costing just £1 a year, which would act as the title deed to his claim and thereby give him the right to vote. Diggers were to be elected to local courts and the power of the 'gold lace' was over. The diggers, as part of a burgeoning democracy, would have the right to manage their own affairs. The loss of revenue to the government was to be made up from an export duty on gold bullion.

Further humiliated, Sir Charles Hotham continued to do what he regarded as his duty and thus became ever more unpopular. After a clash with the Legislative Council in 1855, he offered to resign, but before it took effect, he went to open the new Melbourne gasworks in December. Sadly for him, he caught a chill and died on New Year's Eve. The wily Commissioner Robert Rede fared better. He married the daughter of a renowned explorer, became Sheriff of Melbourne in 1877 and lived in the city until his death from pneumonia in 1904.

The collapse of the Eureka prosecutions and the commission's report allowed the fugitive rebels to come out of hiding. George Black and Thomas Kennedy had fled to Geelong, changing their clothes and cutting their hair as a disguise. Frederick Vern, who sent boastful letters to the Press claiming he had escaped tyranny by boat, had in fact tramped to his hiding-place in Melbourne dressed as a woman.

Peter Lalor, recovered from his amputation, emerged as a hero. He married his fiancée Alicia and bought a farm with a cheque for £1,000 from a fund raised by grateful diggers. He was the first digger to be elected to the Legislative Council in 1855. He was later appointed Postmaster-General and Commissioner for Trade and Customs. In 1880 he became Speaker of the House of Assembly. He died in Melbourne in February 1889.

Rafaello Carboni published a popular account of the events at the Eureka stockade from the diggers' point of view a year after the tragedy. He served on the new Local Court at Ballarat but left Australia for further adventures early in 1856. He travelled to India, China and the Middle East, promoting the cause of Italian freedom. He became an unsuccessful dramatist in Naples and died in Rome during the 1870s.

The two men whose villainy led directly to the tragedy of Eureka did not enjoy the peace. The crooked magistrate John D'Ewes emigrated to British Columbia, where he was arrested for embezzlement. He later committed suicide in Paris. James Bentley, his drinking companion on that fateful night in the Eureka Hotel, served only part of his sentence for the killing of James Scobie. After his release in 1856 he turned to the brandy bottle and the medicine cabinet. In April 1873 he deliberately took a huge overdose of laudanum at his house in Ballarat Street, Melbourne. He left a wife and five children.

A monument in the Old Cemetery, Ballarat, carries the inscription: 'Sacred to the memory of those who fell on the memorable 3rd December, 1854 in resisting the Unconstitutional Proceedings of the Victorian Government.' And schoolchildren are still taught the stirring words of Peter Lalor, the reluctant leader of the Eureka uprising, who wrote:

> I looked around me; I saw brave and honest men who had come thousands of miles to labour for independence. The grievances under which we had long suffered, and the brutal attack of that day, flashed across my mind; and with the burning feelings of the injured man, I mounted the stump and proclaimed Liberty.

However, Governor Hotham was right in one sense at least. After the shock of Eureka, moderates took over on both sides. The only call to revolution ever made on Australian soil was quickly snuffed out and the diggers became good, true capitalists. Their earnings increased and they spent their wealth freely, creating a new market for goods and a boom time for the young colony. It was a new colonial phenomenon and it was exploited to the hilt. Thus the real victors of Eureka Stockade were bankers, merchants and gold-buyers. In London Karl Marx mourned another lost opportunity.

CHAPTER SEVEN

The Defence of Kars, Turkey, 1855

'Firm as a rock on duty . . .'

A correspondent for the *Illustrated London News* reported:

> In a few minutes the whole force of the Russians charged up the hill with loud cries; they were received with a terrible fire of grape and musketry which mowed them down whole ranks at every volley. The position was attacked by eight battalions of the enemy; they advanced very gallantly to within five paces of the work, when so heavy a fire was opened at the head of the column that the whole corps wavered, halted, then turned and fled in the greatest confusion . . .

This account, though written in 1855, did not describe an action at Balaclava or any of the other well-remembered battles of the Crimean War. Instead, it concerned a generally forgotten sideshow to the main event, peopled by a handful of remarkable British adventurers and one of the most unjustly neglected generals of the Victorian era.

★　　★　　★

In 1854 a 21-year-old artillery lieutenant, Christopher Charles Teesdale, met up with a handful of British officers in the wilds of eastern Turkey. With the Crimean War raging on the other side of the Black Sea, it was a strange appointment for ambitious young soldiers eager for battle and advancement. Teesdale, the son of General Henry Teesdale of South Bersted in Sussex, had entered the Royal Military Academy at Woolwich at the age of fourteen and received a commission at eighteen. A conventional Victorian army career seemed inevitable. His first posting was to Corfu, but he then embarked on an unconventional adventure which was to win him glory and a favoured position by Queen Victoria's side . . .

Teesdale was appointed *aide-de-camp* to Colonel William Fenwick Williams, a 53-year-old fellow misfit with fourteen years' service in Turkey, who had just been appointed British commissioner to the Turkish army in Anatolia. It was not reckoned to be a very difficult task, hence the appointment of such junior staff. In fact, Williams and Teesdale were to play leading roles in one of the epic sieges of the nineteenth century.

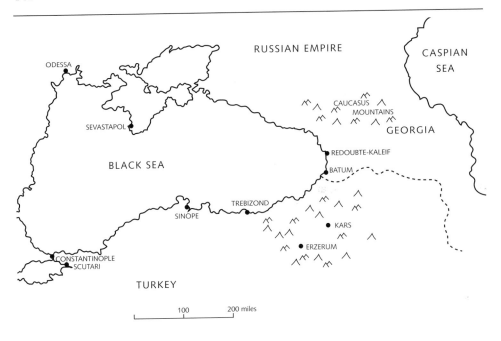

The Eastern Theatre, 1855.

Their role in what in London was called the 'War in the East' was the result of the complex power struggles between an ever-expanding imperial Russia and its neighbouring empires. The Ottoman Empire had been in decline for 200 years and Russia had been the main beneficiary. The early Russo-Turkish wars – and there were ten after 1676 – were generally sparked by Russia's attempts to secure a warm-water port on the Black Sea, then an Ottoman lake. In the war of 1768–74 the Russians captured the Crimea, Azov and Bessarabia and defeated several Turkish armies. The treaty which concluded that war gave Russia the right to maintain a fleet on the Black Sea, advanced her territory in the south and gave her vague rights of protection over the Ottoman Sultan's Christian citizens. Further wars saw Russia take control of much of the Balkans and the Ukrainian Black Sea coast, and her victory in the 1828–9 conflict threatened Turkish sovereignty over the straits which flowed into the Mediterranean. Britain and France viewed the Russian expansion as a threat to their own interests in the Middle East. The Treaty of Edirne gave Russia most of the eastern shore of the Black Sea, and Turkey recognised Russia's claim over Georgia and parts of present-day Armenia. Russian influence was creeping ever closer towards India.

The Crimean War was detonated by a row between Russian Orthodox monks and French Catholics over who had precedence at the holy shrines of Jerusalem and Nazareth. After some bloodshed, Tsar Nicholas I demanded the right to protect all the Holy Land's Christian shrines. To back up his demands he moved troops into the Ottoman provinces of Wallachia and Moldavia. His fleet sank a Turkish flotilla off Sinope in the Black Sea and again threatened the straits of Constantinople. British newspapers carried reports that the Russians had slaughtered Turkish wounded in the water. Propaganda or not, it prepared the populace for a 'just' war. Britain, deeply suspicious of Russian intentions in Central Asia, sided with the Turks. The French Emperor Louis Napoleon III, anxious to recreate the military glory of his illustrious uncle, in turn allied France to Britain. Both countries dispatched expeditionary forces to the region, which arrived in March 1854. Britain's military commander was Lord Raglan, who had last seen action at Waterloo. The French commander, General St Arnaud, fell victim to cholera and was replaced by the veteran General Canrobert. The allied forces swiftly drove the Russians out of the Balkans, and the war could have been over by the summer if the Allies had not believed that the great Russian naval base at Sevastapol posed a direct threat to the future security of the region. In September they landed on the Crimean peninsula.

The catalogue of disasters which followed does not need to be repeated here. Apart from their victory at Alma, the bloodbath of Inkerman and the heroic absurdities of Balaclava, the allies became bogged down in the long siege of Sevastapol. The Russian winter, cholera and other diseases, infected and rotten supplies, appalling generalship and even greater incompetence among the quartermasters, starvation and exhaustion, all killed more than enemy cannon and musketball. Only the work of Florence Nightingale and other nurses in the British hospital at Scutari offered any relief from the dismal saga of negligence and stupidity. The war became one of attrition, spadework and artillery.

But there was another war being fought beyond the eastern shores of the Black Sea, between another Turkish army and the Russian divisions under General Mouravieff. It was well away from the main theatre of action, but a Turkish collapse there would have had a devastating impact on the wider conflict. Early in 1854 the Turks were badly beaten at Kuruk-deri and their demoralized eastern army was fast turning into a rabble. British observers blamed the 'corruption, ignorance, prejudice, want of public spirity' of the Pashas or officers and chiefs. The troops were badly treated and died in droves from disease and starvation. The names of many of the dead remained on the muster rolls to allow the senior officers to collect their salaries and allowances. The Turks were fighting a better-trained but numerically inferior Russian army. Moreover they were fighting in their own mountainous homelands and could invoke Islam to obtain help from the fierce but devout hill tribes of the region. The Russians should have been beaten back but Kuruk-deri showed that training and discipline could far outweigh numbers and local knowledge. *The Times* correspondent wrote:

With a vivid impression of the whole engagement, from the first cannon shot to the last straggling discharge of musketry, I can use no language too strong to express my mis-approbation of nearly four-fifths of the Turkish officers present. In accounting for the defeat of an army numbering nearly 40,000 men of all arms by a hostile force of less than one half of that number, it is not sufficient to say that the management of the whole battle on the side of the

Turks was a series of blunders from the first to last; strategical errors might have protracted the engagement, and added to the cost of a victory, but downright cowardice alone – which no generalship could have reduced – gave the day to the Russians.

The conduct of the Turks on the Crimean peninsula itself gave the British and French good cause to have mixed feelings about their compatriots. Around 3,000 Turkish troops fought at Balaclava, and 500 of them put up a stout resistance on the Fedioukine Heights against 10,000 Russians, despite being subjected to bombardment from thirty guns. Their stand cost them 170 dead and gave the Allies an extra hour to rally their forces. But later in the battle other Turkish troops took fright under bombardment and fled from a rise near Kadikoi, leaving Campbell's Highlanders exposed. The British judged them fine enough fighters, but badly led by decadent officers.

Mouravieff was busy collecting a large and well-equipped army at Gumri and was advancing towards the key towns of Kars and Erzerum; his long-term aim was the capture of the port of Trebizond, through which the Turks were supplied. Kars was the gateway to Trebizond. At the end of July Colonel Williams was sent to represent British interests with the Turkish army in Anatolia, under the orders of Lord Raglan. He was to aid, inform and cooperate, but few initially saw him assuming effective command.

Major-General Sir William Fenwick Williams, the commander of Kars, from a photograph by John Watkins. (*Illustrated London News*)

Williams was well qualified for his new role. Born in Nova Scotia late in 1800, the son of the barrack-master at Halifax, he entered the Woolwich Royal Military Academy. His early career was held up by the reduction of the army following Waterloo and he did not receive his commission as a second lieutenant in the Royal Artillery until 1825. His advancement through the officer ranks was also slow, due to the lack of action and the few opportunities available in postings to Gibraltar, Ceylon and home stations. His big break came in 1841 when, already middle-aged, he was sent to Turkey to work in the arsenal at Constantinople. As a British commissioner he was involved in the conferences which preceded various treaties, both to end conflicts with Russia and to settle border disputes with Persia. By 1852 he was highly regarded as a peacetime soldier, diplomat and expert on Turkish affairs and, made up to brevet-colonel, was the natural choice for the task.

In discussions with Lord Raglan it was agreed that the Turkish army needed both practical support and advice. Neither Raglan nor Williams then fully realised the poor state of their ally's forces facing the Russian forces in the east. In September Williams, with Teesdale, arrived at Erzerum, where they discovered to their dismay that the Turkish troops in that strategically important city could not muster 1,000 men. Those who were standing to arms were nursing a grievance: none had received any pay for at least 15 months. It was a taste of things to come.

Williams then moved on to Kars where the Turkish army numbered 28,000 men, many of whom were 22 months in arrears of pay; Williams wrote: 'Their patience under so glaring an injustice was truly praiseworthy.' The defences at Kars were in a poor state and the troops, who had suffered famine the previous winter, wore tattered uniforms and disintegrating boots. The four regiments of cavalry were in a 'wretched plight' and the horses were 'small and in a bad condition'. Only the artillery passed muster, with 162 guns all in working order. Another witness wrote that the condition of the garrison was so wretched 'as to fill us with forebodings for the ensuing campaign'.

There is evidence that such sentiments were shared by senior figures in the Turkish government. Rizza Pasha, the minister for war, quietly recommended to the new army commander that 'the frontier fortresses should be abandoned, if he thought they could not be held'.

Williams also quickly realised that the Kars garrison would be no match for the Russians who were already beginning to move towards this pivotal town. Leaving Teesdale behind to winter with the Turkish army and establish what discipline he could, Williams returned to Erzerum. He could see a disaster in the making and was determined to prevent it. He got precious little help.

Williams petitioned the British Embassy at Constantinople and the Foreign Office to send the Turkish forces the supplies, clothing, ammunition and money they so desperately needed if the Russians were to be halted as they swept around the eastern shores of the Black Sea. His most urgent demand was for 20,000 pairs of boots and 10,000 shirts and drawers. He was blocked at every turn by the ambassador to the Turkish capital, Lord Stratford de Redcliffe. Unsurprisingly, His Lordship's main preoccupation was the provisioning of the British forces outside Sevastapol, themselves facing a harsh winter. His incompetence, however, was

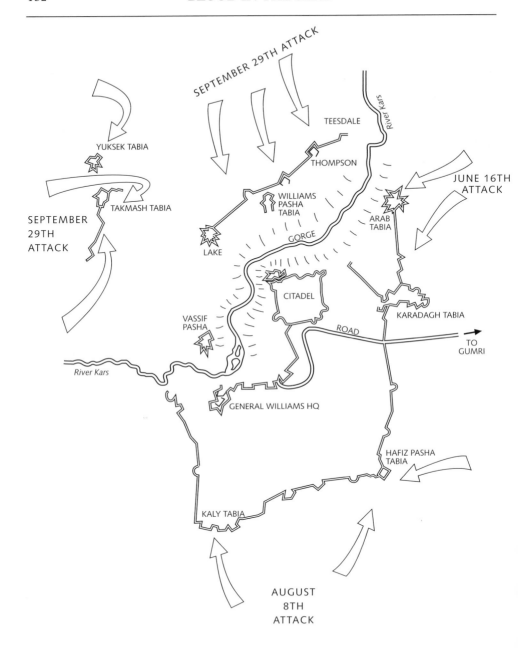

The defences at Kars and the Russian attacks.

The town of Kars, showing the river and the citadel. (*Illustrated London News*)

demonstrated by his stewardship, as senior British official, of the appalling conditions at Scutari, which Florence Nightingale first encountered. A long and bitter correspondence began, with Williams complaining angrily to Lord Clarendon, the Foreign Secretary, about Stratford's neglect and delay in providing material. Stratford in turn blamed the corruption of the Turkish Pashas and officials.

Williams's first full report on conditions at Kars caused consternation in the British Embassy at Therapia. His language was so blunt that the report could not be passed on to the Turkish authorities without risking a severe breach in the alliance. Williams demanded the sacking of several Pashas and other commanders for cowardice, theft and incompetence. He claimed that the wounded had been forced to become beggars while 'drunkenness prevails to a great degree among those of higher rank'. Kars could not accommodate more than 10,000 soldiers within its walls, he wrote, because of the risk from disease. Europeans should be employed to oversee the drills and sanitation. The Turkish NCOs did not bother with rifle and musket practice. 'Men much neglected as to their comforts. The great copper cauldrons dangerous from want of tinning. Butter rancid and musty – as bad as possible – though used for pilaff.' On and on went his catalogue of complaints.

Eventually even Stratford was forced to take notice. He lodged an official complaint with the Turkish government, couched in rather more diplomatic terms than Williams would have wanted, saying that Britain would not tolerate inaction or cowardice by the Pashas. The Grand Vizier, Reshid Pasha, promised to investigate, although little was actually done. But later, bombarded with further evidence of their own failings, the Turkish government agreed that Williams should have overall command of Kars, with the Pashas being subordinate to his orders.

During this frustrating period Williams also busied himself building up Erzerum's defences and fortifying the surrounding heights. His efforts so impressed the

Turkish commanders that he was made a *ferik*, or lieutenant-general, in their army. He was aided by another remarkable man, a 32-year-old army physician called Humphrey Sandwith. The son of a leading Hull doctor and surgeon, he at first followed his father and was appointed house surgeon at Hull Infirmary. Ill-health forced him to resign and he decided to seek adventure in the Near East. He made diplomatic friends in Constantinople, and spent nearly two years with archaeologists in Mesopotamia before he was incapacitated by a bout of fever. He was briefly a correspondent for *The Times* but its then editor Delane judged him too pro-Turkish. On the outbreak of the Crimean War he was engaged as staff surgeon to a British-officered corps of Bashi-Bazouks on the Danube. The corps saw no action but was devastated by sickness. Sandwith eked out his meagre medical supplies by gathering herbs in the meadows and leeches in the marshes. Joining Williams at Erzerum, he took charge of sanitation and the military hospital. He found the dispensary contained few drugs but was packed with cosmetics and scents.

Meanwhile Teesdale was doing what he could to improve the defences at Kars. A contemporary account illustrated some of the difficulties:

Kars is situated under a precipitous range of rocky hills which run east and west, and are divided by a deep gorge, through which flows the river Karachai. The western extremity of the range is called Takmash, and the eastern, Karadagh; the former is about two miles distant from the town, and the latter about a mile. To the south of Kars a wide level plain extends for several miles, until it meets the slopes of a line of low hills. The fortifications of the place consisted of a number of *tabias*, or redoubts placed in the most commanding positions.

On all four sides the outer defences were strengthened with small forts, breastworks and redoubts. The Turkish artillery commander, Tahir Pasha, was given clear fields of fire for his gunners. Some queried whether such preparations were justified to defend such an insignificant Asian town. Dr Sandwith himself had not been impressed on first sight. He wrote:

The streets are narrow and dirty, the people sordid in appearance, and the chief employment of the women appears to be the fabrication of *tezek*, or dried cow-dung for fuel, cakes of which are plastered over the walls of every home.

In fact Kars, sitting on a plateau 5,740 feet above sea level and dominated by an ancient citadel that overhung the river, had a bloody history which bore testimony to its strategic importance. The seat of an independent Armenian principality during the ninth and tenth centuries, it was captured by the Seljuqs in the eleventh, by the Mongols in the thirteenth and by Tamerlane in 1387. It was incorporated into the Ottoman Empire in 1514.

Throughout the winter Teesdale, aided by his interpreter Mr Zohrab, worked incessantly to improve moral, discipline and order among the Turkish troops. Dr Sandwith, in his memoirs, wrote that Teesdale 'exhibited such a rare

General Mouravieff, the Russian commander at Kars, from a photograph by Weingartner of Moscow. (*Illustrated London News*)

combination of firmness and conciliatory tact that he won all hearts'. The grey-bearded General Kherim Pasha 'never ventured on any act of importance without first consulting this young subaltern of infantry'. The Foreign Office later lauded Teesdale's efforts in 'averting from the garrison at Kars the horrors that they suffered from famine the previous winter'. The Turkish army at Kars, under the nominal command of the Mushir, Vassif Pasha, consisted of 13,900 infantry, 1,500 cavalry, 1,500 artillerymen and 42 field guns.

The Russian army gathering for the attack consisted of 28,000 infantry, 7,500 cavalry and 64 pieces of artillery. The commander, General Mouravieff, had been a young officer at an earlier siege of Kars in 1828 and knew the lay-out of the town. Mouravieff was the son of an ancient Russian family, distinguished in literature as well as arms. Even the London Press regarded him as a hero of the old school. Fighting with Paskiewitsch in the earlier Turkish war he gained a reputation for bravery, while later campaigns confirmed his good generalship. The British knew him as a canny, courteous and utterly ruthless opponent.

Against such an adversary Vassif Pasha was grateful for all the help he could get from his British experts and advisers. In the early spring of 1855 Teesdale was joined by 26-year-old Henry Langhorne Thompson, an Old Etonian who had served with the British Army in Burma and now a volunteer major in the Turkish army, and Lieutenant-Colonel Sir Henry Atwell Lake, Williams's second-in-command. Lake had previously served with the Madras Engineers, engaged mainly in irrigation works in India. His engineering skills were to prove invaluable in strengthening the defences at Kars.

On 1 June Williams, now promoted by Britain to major-general, heard that the Russian army was advancing on Kars. He rushed to the fortified town, arriving on the 7th when he reviewed the troops and inspected the defences. Despite the minor miracles worked by Teesdale, Lake and Thompson, vital supplies had still failed to materialise. There was food for three months but enough ammunition for only three days of serious fighting. More earthworks were constructed as agents reported the Russian advance. On the 16th, the beginning of the Turkish festival of Bairam, General Mouravieff's army finally arrived and launched their first attack.

Williams reported:

> Our advanced posts were driven in soon after daylight, and the Russian army appeared on the heights about half past 6 o'clock: its advance guard consisted of three regiments of regular Cossacks, supported by artillery and rockets. The main body of Infantry marched in three columns, flanked by three regiments of Dragoons and supported by six batteries of eight guns each. In the rear appeared a strong column of Reserve Infantry, then the wagons carrying, as I have since heard, three days' provisions. The whole force could not have been less than 25,000. Nothing could be more perfect than the handling of the enemy's army as it advanced upon the front of our entrenchments . . .

The first Russian attack on Kars. (*Illustrated London News*)

Mouravieff's cavalry crashed upon the Bashi-Bazouks posted on the plains to the south-east of the town, but the charge was checked and thrown into disorder by well-directed artillery fire from the Karadagh and Hafiz Pasha redoubts. The Turkish skirmishers halted a fierce Cossack attack on their camp. Teesdale, with Zohrab, was in the thick of the fighting and Williams recorded in dispatches that his 'labours were incessant'. The Russians brought up their artillery and blasted the redoubts without much effect for an hour. They then retired in good order. Williams reckoned their losses to be at least 100 men, compared to six Turkish defenders killed and eight wounded.

Williams wrote:

> The spirit of the Turkish troops was excellent, evincing, as they did, as much readiness to the defence as they had shown in the construction of their epaulements. If the enemy had attempted to carry his original intention into execution he would, I confidently believe, have met with equal disaster.

But Mouravieff's plan from the start was to invest the fortress and cut all supply lines. An isolated garrison, he calculated, would be taken with only light losses. He ordered his troops to move to the west and north, encircling the defences, while his Cossacks patrolled the surrounding countryside. By the middle of July Kars was completely blockaded and it was 'almost impossible for a single horseman to pass without capture'.

Williams managed to smuggle out some messages to his superiors. One said:

> The rain has been so heavy and incessant as to prevent the enemy from any attempt to attack our lines, but he has pushed forward large bodies of Cavalry, supported by guns, burnt the surrounding villages and destroyed one of our small depots of grain at Chiplaklee, eight hours on the Erzeroom road, and probably thinking that our entrenchments are too formidable to take by *coup de main*, he has sent to Gumri for eight heavy guns belonging to that fortress, which are now on their way to his camp.
>
> The duties of our garrison have been most trying, in consequence of the torrents of rain, but the spirit of the troops is good.

The epic siege of Kars had begun in earnest. The rain continued to pour down, hampering the enemy but also washing away earthworks and flooding trenches in the defences. Teesdale shared a dug-out in the Takhsap redoubt with the renowned Hungarian soldier of fortune General Kmety, to whom he acted as chief of staff. Kmety, also known as Ismail Pasha, was the son of a Protestant clergyman, who had turned soldier when his hopes of an academic career turned sour. Now aged forty-four, Kmety and Teesdale were continually engaged in skirmishing and harassing the enemy with parties of riflemen.

The defenders constantly repaired and extended their entrenchments, while the Russians constantly probed and tested them. General Mouravieff kept a close watch for any perceived weaknesses. Williams, in a typical dispatch on 14 July, wrote:

Yesterday the whole Russian army marched towards [the southern heights above Kars], and the force left by the enemy on the heights in our front moved up close to Kanly Tabia to engage our attention; but we were nevertheless enabled by our central position so to reinforce the menaced heights, so that General Mouravieff, after some hours of close reconnaissance, retired to his camp. As this visit was made with his entire army, I assume he would have assailed us if he had found such a step desirable to his future operation. The enemy remains quiet today, but our new redoubts on those hills are pressed forward with vigour, and, indeed, enthusiasm by the troops.

After a third such demonstration by the Russian commander-in-chief, Williams wrote a week later:

His powerful cavalry has not been inactive, having blocked up the roads. Fortunately we have in store nearly three months' supplies of biscuits, flour and wheat; we therefore may hope to be relieved before this amount of food is consumed. Any reinforcements sent by the Turks, from whatever quarter they may be, must come with convoys of provisions; otherwise such accessories of force would amount to positive loss to the chances we now feel of holding out until the allied Governments, by wise combinations and sufficient forces, can oblige the Russian army to retire into Georgia.

There were indeed plans to relieve Kars and its beleaguered garrison, but the Allied generals could not agree on the most feasible scheme while the Turkish sultan and his ministers could not agree on anything at all. Eventually it was decided that the Turkish general Omar Pasha could take up to 42,000 Turkish troops from the Crimean front to Redonte-Kaleh, a port on the south-east Black Sea. But, much to Omar's disgust, the Allied generals again prevaricated, not wishing to release Turkish troops from the Crimean front until Sevastapol had fallen. The French in particular regarded as sheer folly any plan that diverted troops from the main theatre of war. The emperor also suspected that Britain wished to gain postwar economic and strategic interests in Asia Minor and was prepared to risk allied lives outside Sevastapol to achieve them. Napoleon said:

We have 60,000 men at the siege, the English have 12,000. The Turks for whom we are fighting are never in the trenches . . . All this should be considered carefully. If now they still want to weaken the siege army by withdrawing Turkish troops, they will create a justified alienation in the French army. Furthermore, the great objective now is Sevastapol and not at Kars.

The wrangling continued as Omar Pasha fumed.

Lord Clarendon vehemently disagreed with the French. Early in August he wrote:

Her Majesty's Government consider the relief of the Turkish troops in Asia of such vital importance . . . It is plain that without assistance the whole Turkish force in Asia must be destroyed or captured. The force at Kars is surrounded, and even if able to defend its position against assault, which may be doubted, it must surrender when its provisions are exhausted, and that will happen in a few weeks. The immediate result would be that 13,000 Turkish troops would become prisoners of war, and a strong position be occupied by the Russians.

But, moreover, Kars taken, Erzeroom must share the like fate, and the whole of the neighbouring country would be in the hands of the Russians, while the season would be too far advanced for military operations to drive them out of it.

Clarendon recognised also that if the Allies failed to take Sevastapol before the winter, the Russians would, by occupying Asia Minor, be free to deliver a hammer blow to the heart of the Turkish Empire.

In Kars the defenders were again hard-pressed. The Russian troops destroyed vast areas of farmland. General Mouravieff continued to probe, moving 15 battalions and 40 guns to a new camp at Komansoor. Williams reported:

If we are to credit the reports brought in by our spies, General Mouravieff meditates an advance upon Erzeroom, but I believe his object to be the devastation of the country, and more especially the destruction of the growing crops, in which barbarous measures the army now in our front is daily occupied.

We steadily add to the strength of our field-works, and yesterday we seized the cattle of the surrounding villages, to prevent their falling into the hands of the enemy, and to add to the chance of our holding out till relieved by the allies.

Mouravieff led a portion of his army towards Erzerum and, during his absence on 8 August, his subordinates ordered another attack on Kars. The Official Report states that 'the enemy, losing sight of his usual precautions, advanced with large masses of Infantry, Cavalry and Artillery to within gun-shot of the Kanly Tabia, on the south-east angle of our entrenched camp, where a well-directed fire from the guns of that redoubt obliged him to retire with the loss of several officers and many men'.

General Mouravieff soon returned with Russian reinforcements, bringing his total strength up to around 50,000 men. He proclaimed his intentions to reduce Kars by starvation and take the city without another shot being fired. Mouravieff's reputation as a tough-minded veteran soldier was well known to the British officers. Lake considered him 'an officer of talent and energy who, during a long period of arduous service, had won for himself a name of which any soldier might be proud'.

Within the beleaguered garrison General Williams, given free rein by the Turkish commanders, imposed his iron will. They described him as a martinet 'with kind eyes'. But that resolve, normal and well respected at the time, meant that men died in front of firing parties or dangling from the hangman's rope. In an army of 20,000, facing such a powerful enemy, it was inevitable that some would desert – especially as they had not been paid for the best part of two years. Williams also understood that in a town located on the crossroads of Asia it was inevitable that some men would have split loyalties. His somewhat cynical response, understandable with hindsight, was to brand them criminals, cowards or spies. All who opposed him were condemned, and in that he had the enthusiastic support of the Pashas. Early in September he reported:

> The execution of two spies has, in great measure, broken up the party within our camp which gave the enemy information. A dangerous amount of desertions took place on the nights of the 4th and 5th instant, but having shot an Infantry and an artillery deserter, the mischief was arrested. The town and army now know that no spy or deserter shall escape his doom if taken.

A few days later, exasperated by further desertions, he told Yassif Pasha that all the culprits came from the regiment of Redif. The regiment was duly disbanded with great shame, the officers put on half-pay, and the men distributed among the companies of other corps. Williams said: 'The sentence was executed this morning, to the astonishment of the officers and soldiers of this unworthy regiment, and I trust we have now struck at the root of the evil, for the general disposition of the garrison is admirable.'

The lesson, however, was not learnt quickly enough for the general's taste. In his next dispatch to Lord Clarendon, dated 14 September, he wrote:

> In spite of the example exhibited to the troops in the disbanding of the regiment of Redif we had no less than six desertions yesterday; fortunately we recaptured two of them; they proved to be men of the corps in question. They were tried by a Council of War, and instantly shot. On their trial they denounced the parties [inhabitants of Kars] who had instigated them to this act of treason, and furnished them with peasants' clothes to enable them to effect their purpose. Three of these men were seized in a house where the musket of one of the prisoners who suffered yesterday was found, together with the clothes and appointments of seven more deserters. There can be little doubt that these wretches are in communication with the enemy, as proclamations were found on the last-captured spy, offering any deserters free passage through the Russian posts to their homes.
>
> A council of war has tried and condemned these men who will be hanged today in the market place; and the appointments of the seven deserters who have escaped by their agency will be exhibited on the gallows, as a further proof of their guilt.

The weather grew suddenly colder and snow fell. Every supply route to Kars was now cut off. The defenders' provisions began to run out and desertions became more frequent. An outbreak of cholera increased the misery and Dr Sandwith's resources were stretched thin. The horses began to starve to death and it quickly became evident that the cavalry – which Williams in any case regarded as next to useless – under the command of the Austrian Baron de Schwartzenberg could no longer exist as a fighting force. Williams decided to give the remnants at least a chance of survival. Around a thousand horsemen were assembled with the intention of cutting their way through the Russian lines. Under cover of darkness they trotted from the town by way of a defile pointing towards Oltee. When they reached the first Russian outpost the alarm was raised. Volleys of enemy muskets poured fire into them, and there were many casualties, but most got through.

Williams sent a cryptic dispatch regarding his decision, for reasons which soon became obvious:

> The enemy's Cavalry has received a reinforcement of 2,000 men, and presses, if possible, still more closely on our picquets and advanced posts, where a daily struggle takes place for forage, which has, for several days, failed to supply our wants; a large portion, therefore, of our Cavalry horses has been sent from the camp in order to seek subsistence beyond the mountains and out of reach of the enemy Cavalry, which cannot be estimated at less than 10,000. It is with the utmost difficulty that either horse or foot messengers escape the vigilance of the enemy, and I abstain from entertaining into details which might fall into their hands. The garrison preserves its health, notwithstanding the great difference of temperature between day and night; its spirit, I am happy to add, is excellent.

As September progressed General Mouravieff appeared to be pulling back, giving every impression that he intended to abandon the siege and retire to Georgia. That impression was given greater credence on the 24th when the Kars garrison received reports that Sevastapol had been taken and the Russian fleet was destroyed. Two royal salutes were fired from the cannon – the Russian commanders answered with a sham cannonade to disguise its import from their own men – and the details of what seemed to be the final act of the war were read to all troops.

Even though the reports were later confirmed, General Williams believed that Mouravieff's tactics were no more than a ruse, intended to put the Turkish garrison off its guard. At dawn on 29 September 1855 his suspicions were proved correct.

★　　★　　★

At 4 a.m. the Russians advanced in three columns, supported by 24 guns, each targeted on a different part of the defences. They hoped to surprise the garrison as they marched through the mist in faint light. But the defenders heard their advance and quietly prepared to meet it, charging their guns with grapeshot. The Russian left flank was met with a crushing fire of artillery from all points. They answered with 'loud hurrahs' and rushed up the hill against the redoubts and breastworks, to be savaged by destructive musketry fire. They faced a battalion of 450 Chasseurs armed with Minie rifles. These muzzle-loaders could be fired twice a minute – no faster, in fact, than the muskets of the Napoleonic wars, but much more accurate and with a far greater effective range. After a desperate struggle the Russian flank broke and fled in disorder back down the hill, leaving around 850 dead on the field.

The central column stormed the Takmash and Yukseh redoubts. Teesdale, returning from his early morning rounds, rushed to the most exposed battery of the Yukseh, the key to the whole position. There, too, the Russians battered hopelessly against a firestorm of musket balls, grapeshot and shell. The *Illustrated London News* reported:

> Takmash Tabia bore the brunt of the battle; about sixteen battalions, with many guns, were brought up against it, but the garrison was undaunted, and for a long time the Russians could not even get possession of the breastwork forming the left wing of the battery; but, at length, an overwhelming force obliged the Turks to retire within the redoubt. A scene of carnage now ensued perfectly terrible to behold. As the Russians came over the brow of the hill within the breastwork, to take the battery in the rear, Tchim and Tek Tabias and Fort Lake opened on them with 24-pound shot, which tore through their ranks, but they did not seem to heed this. They charged Takmash Tabia, which was one sheet of fire, over and over again, and so resolute were their assaults that many of the Russian officers were killed in the battery, but they could not succeed in carrying it.

Teesdale, General Kmety and the Turkish general Hussein Pasha won praise in dispatches for their courage in rallying their troops. Hussein Pasha was wounded in the shoulder and had two horses killed under him. For a while the fighting seemed to reach a bloody stalemate. But the Russian column, after heroic efforts and more desperate fighting, finally managed to turn the left flank of the Turkish defences at Takmash, and penetrated to the rear of the Turkish positions.

Teesdale turned some of his guns about and 'worked them vigorously'. The redoubts were enclosed so the Russians who had reached the rear had no way out and were subjected to close-range cannon fire which wreaked havoc. Nevertheless the Russians fought on ferociously, some climbing up the slippery breastworks to the gun positions. Williams reported that three were killed 'on the platform of a gun which was at that moment being worked by Teesdale, who then sprang out and led two charges with the bayonet, the Turks fighting like heroes'.

At the same time the Takmash defenders launched a sortie under Colonel Lake and attacked the wavering Russian column. An official account said that the reinforcements 'being hidden from the enemy by the rocky nature of the ground, confronted him at a most opportune moment. They deployed, and opened their fire, which stopped and soon drove back the enemy's reserves, which were then vigorously charged with the bayonet.' The two-pronged assault by Lake and Teesdale proved to be the turning point. Lake later wrote:

> This horrid carnage continued until the Russians, stopped by a mound of dead bodies and dislocated by the repeated discharges of grape, were brought to a standstill. The Turks there leaping over the breastwork and led on by the gallant Kmety, finished with bayonet the utter rout of their assailants.

The Russians fled down the hill, being chopped down as they ran through relentless cannon fire. Their central column, however, overwhelmed a portion of the defences while enemy cannon fire drove many of the Turkish artillerymen from their guns.

The battle of Kars. (*Illustrated London News*)

Teesdale rallied their gunners and by his own example induced them to return to their posts. Then, although hit by a piece of spent shell and suffering severe contusions, he led another bayonet charge. Williams wrote in dispatches: 'My aide-de-camp, Teesdale, had charge of the central redoubt and fought like a lion.' The young British officer was also later praised by the enemy commander, General Mouravieff, for saving 'at great personal risk' many of the Russian wounded lying outside the works from the fury of the Turks.

General Kmety, having joined up with Teesdale, saw that a battalion of Russian chasseurs were forming up behind the abandoned works of Yarem Ai and led his men in a wild charge which again sent the enemy tumbling down the hill. For that action alone, only one of many, Kmety was dubbed the 'hero of the day' by some London publications.

While the main battle was raging a Russian column of eight infantry battalions, three regiments of cavalry and 16 guns advanced from the valley of Tchakmak and assaulted the small redoubts commanding the eastern portion of the defences. The Turkish troops there were joined by townsmen and mountaineers from Lazistan who planted their clan flags on the ramparts before them. But this part of the battle

General Kmety, also known as Ismail Pasha, from a photograph by Fenton. (*Illustrated London News*)

was won by Turkish infantry under Captain Thompson, whose men poured down from the heights of Karadagh and Arab Tabia. Williams recorded:

> This reinforcement descended the deep gully through which flows the Kars river, passed a bridge recently thrown across it, and ascended the opposite precipitous banks by a zigzag path which led into the line of works . . . These battalions, joined to those directed by Colonel Lake, gallantly attacked and drove the Russians out of the redoubts at the point of the bayonet.

A heavy cannon, moved to a key point by Thompson, was then turned on the fleeing Russians.

After the Russian infantry had been thrown back from the eastern redoubts the entire attack collapsed. They retreated along the whole line and suffered more severe losses from round-shot bearing from every battery, each of which kept up an incessant fire on the crowded columns.

General Williams, in his dispatch to Lord Clarendon, said:

> During this combat, which lasted nearly seven hours, the Turkish infantry, as well as artillery, fought with the most determined courage; and when it is

recollected that they had worked on their entrenchments, and guarded them by night, throughout a period extending to nearly four months, I think your Lordship will admit that they have proved themselves worthy of the admiration of Europe, and established an undoubted claim to be placed amongst the most distinguished of its troops.

With regard to the enemy, as long as there was a chance of success he persevered with undaunted courage, and the Russian officers displayed the greatest gallantry. Their loss was immense; they left on the field more than 5,000 dead, which it took the Turkish infantry four days to bury. Their wounded and prisoners in our possession amount to 160, whilst those who were carried off are said to be upwards of 7,000.

As the garrison was afflicted with cholera, and I was apprehensive of a great increase of the malady should this melancholy duty of the burial of the dead be not pushed forward with every possible vigour by our fatigued and jaded soldiers, I daily visited the scene of strife to encourage them in their almost endless task; and I can assure your Lordship that the whole battlefield presented a scene which is more easy to conceive than to describe, being literally covered with the enemy's dead and dying. The Turkish dead and wounded were removed on the night of the battle. The dead numbered 362, the wounded 631. The towns-people, who also fought with spirit, lost 101 men.

His Excellency the Mushir has reported to his government those officers who particularly distinguished themselves – a difficult task in an army which has shown such a desperate valour throughout the unusual period of seven hours of uninterrupted combat.

$$\star \quad \star \quad \star$$

As General Williams reported, it took the Turks four days to bury the dead piled up around the town's ramparts. Each day the defenders heard distant volleys as the Russians buried, with military honours, those of their comrades killed by long-range artillery fire and those who had succumbed their wounds. Williams's original estimate of the Russian dead was later upgraded to almost 7,000 and even that may have been too modest a count as more wounded died. Mouravieff's report to the Tsar cited the loss of 6,517 men. But although the Russians had lost a costly battle, General Mouravieff had no intention of retiring. He reverted to his plan to invest Kars with 'pertinacious obstinacy', determined to starve the garrison into capitulation.

The defenders, once the heady brew of victory wore off, now faced cold, famine and disease. The heaviest burden fell on Humphrey Sandwith as Inspector General of the Kars hospitals. He had under him fifty surgeons, physicians and apothecaries, 'ignorant practitioners, surgeons, ignorant barbers, preferring to bleed, draw teeth and dress wounds'. Dr Sandwith first had to tend the large number of wounded, both Turk and Russian, in his overcrowded and poorly stocked wards. He relied mainly on horseflesh broth to bring his patients round, and he succeeded in keeping his charges free of hospital gangrene and epidemic typhus. There was, though, no defence against the cholera which swept through the lines and the town, and hit all ranks. There were 2,000 cases during the siege, and by the end of October the men were dying at the rate of 100 a day. But the biggest concern was starvation. Sandwith's diary paints a vivid picture of the sufferings endured:

> October 17th – Our troops suffered fearfully from their diet of bread and water. They are no longer the stout and hardy men who fought for seven hours against overwhelming odds, and drove back a magnificent Russian army. A visible emaciation is observed throughout the ranks, and the newly-opened hospitals are filling daily with men whose only disease is exhaustion from want of nutriment. The high price of bread, too, in the town induces many poor fellows to sell half their rations; and those who yield to this temptation inevitably sink at their posts and die.
>
> October 21st – Swarms of vultures hover round our lines, preying on the corpses that the hungry dogs, which have forsaken the city, have scratched out of their graves. These dogs gorge themselves with their foul banquet, while within the city every man, woman and child is searching for food. The grass is torn up in all the open spaces, and the roots eaten by the soldiers and the people. Crowds of women besiege the public offices for bread, which is dealt out to them with a very sparing hand.
>
> October 28th – The wretched remains of our cavalry are inspected; and as the horses can scarcely stand, much less support the weight of their riders, their throats are cut.
>
> November 16th – A small quantity of snow falls; the rapid mountain stream which runs through the town, the Karsachai, is already almost entirely frozen over. Old women are moaning and crying out that they are dying of starvation; the children have a gaunt and famished look . . .

In his memoirs Sandwith sometimes could not disguise a forensic fascination with the symptoms he saw all around him:

> The emaciation is wonderful, yet in most no diarrhoea or other symptoms of disease is observable. Their veins are excessively feeble – a clammy cold pervades the surface of the body, and they die without a struggle. Surgeons are posted in every part of the camp with the broth of horse-flesh in the form, and under the name, of medicine. I have again and again seen men watching the batteries at midnight, some standing and leaning on their arms, but most coiled up under the breastwork during cold as intense as an Arctic winter, scarce able to respond to or challenge the visiting officer, and, in answer to a word of encouragement or consolation, the loyal words were ever on their lips, *Padishah sagh ossoum*. Long live the Sultan! It would seem that the extremity of human suffering called forth latent sparks of a loyalty and devotion not observed in seasons of prosperity.

The dispatches of General Williams over roughly the same period were more laconic, as was the Victorian soldier's way, but carried hints of the same despair:

October 12th – Notwithstanding the severe defeat experienced by the enemy, he still blockades us closely, and the erection of huts in his camp this morning shows that he intends to continue this course. He knows that all our Cavalry horses are dead of starvation, and that we cannot take the field; he is also aware that cholera inflicts severe losses on us, which are aggravated by the difficulty we have of burying the horses.

October 19th – I regret to say that desertion has again commenced, and, with it, military executions, for I am determined that no deserter who again falls into our hands shall escape the punishment due to his infamy.

October 23rd – All our horses are dead of starvation, and we have not carriage for a load of ammunition, if we are ultimately obliged to abandon Kars. The garrison has been without animal food for more than a fortnight.

November 19th – We divide our bread with the starving townspeople. No animal food for seven weeks. I kill horses in my stable secretly, and send the meat to the hospital, which is now very crowded. We can hold out . . .

Williams and the Turkish commanders were holding on in the hope of a relief. It never came. There was, indeed, a strong Turkish force in Erzerum, but the defence of that city was considered to be too important to risk. The Russians threw out bodies of troops into the neighbourhood and kept the garrison there in check. James Brant, the British Consul in Erzerum, blamed the Turkish commander Selim Pasha for not going to the aid of Kars. He wrote to Lord Clarendon: 'Selim Pasha now pretends that he fears danger to Erzeroom from the [Russian] Byazid division and talks of advancing to attack it, but this is a mere pretext to cover his cowardice. I fear there is nothing to be done to help this neglected army in Kars.' Vely Pasha made several bids to march upon Kars from Trebizond, but each time he was met by Russian detachments under General Sousloff and compelled to retire. The Turkish authorities in Constantinople and Ankara haggled about the cost of relief expeditions, quarrelled amongst themselves and prevaricated when urged into action by the British generals, although the latter could hardly boast of their own track records of indecision and incompetence. In another letter to the Foreign Secretary Brant said: 'Is the Kars army to be allowed to perish? Is nothing to be done to relieve it? I now fear it must surrender, and to confer honours on its gallant defenders, while they be left to perish is a cruel mockery, and an indelible disgrace to the Turkish Government, as well as to those of the allied Powers.'

Early in November Williams wrote: 'I have on my shoulders the management of the starving population, as well as that of the army. I take from the rich, and give to the poor, but am now obliged to issue corn from the public stores. I hope Omar Pasha is at least acting like a brave resolute man.'

Omar Pasha had landed his relief force at Redoubte-Kaleh and Chopi, and was busy creating depots to provision his men. Around 10,000 of his troops manned the depots while the main body of 20,000 pressed forward. But the expedition had been badly delayed by the indecision of the generals in Constantinople. *The Times*'s man on the spot wrote:

It is much to be regretted that this expedition was not undertaken earlier in the year. It will be impossible now before the winter to do more than advance upon Kutais. Under the most favourable circumstances the army cannot commence the march before the beginning of November; at that late season of the year the advance of a large army for more than 100 miles through a difficult and almost unknown country is, to say the least of it, a hazardous undertaking.

On 4 November the Turkish general sent several bodies of men to find passable fords across the river Ingour. One body under Major Simmonds advanced steadily under heavy fire through water up to their shoulders and took Russian entrenchments. Another body under Osman Pasha, lower down the river, marched against up to 12,000 Russian infantry who, happily for the Turks, had few cannon. A British account of the battle said:

> The Russians, who kept up a heavy fire of musketry while the troops were crossing the river, were charged at the point of a bayonet, and driven into the woods; so that soon after dark the Turkish army was in complete and undisturbed occupation of the whole of the left bank of the Ingour, so far as their line extended.

The British correspondent put the Turkish casualties at 68 dead and 242 wounded, while the Russians left over 400 dead on the field and 40 prisoners. A Russian account of the action said that their two battalion commanders, Colonels Josselian and Zvanboi, were killed in the first exchange of shots. It went on:

> Our reserve, on arriving on the ground, continued the combat for some time but, after an obstinate struggle of six hours' duration, in which the enemy had been four times driven back into the river, our troops were finally obliged to give way before the Turks, eight times their number, and, as some of the artillery horses had been killed, our detachment was under the necessity of sacrificing three guns. Accordingly, after three murderous rounds of grape fired into the dense columns of the enemy, our gunners dismounted the guns and, having rendered them unserviceable, abandoned them.

By 19 November the Russians had evacuated much of the area, burning bridges and culverts behind them. That rendered Omar Pasha's progress steady, but slow – too slow to save Kars.

The following day Consul Brant wrote: 'I am apprehensive Omar Pasha will not advance rapidly enough, and General Mouravieff seems determined to hold out as long as possible. The season favours him signally. I am in a great state of anxiety, for bravery and skill will soon be unavailing, and they cannot stand out against famine.'

At Kars the garrison's hope of relief was fading fast. Sandwith reported how on 16 November the men heard some distant firing and 'a thrill of joy and excitement runs through the population at the idea of the near approach of a succouring army; but their hopes are doomed to disappointment'. Coded dispatches rolled up in quills were carried out each night by disguised couriers, urging the relief force to make speed 'as we cannot hold out much longer'. It was another five days before the defenders realised that the earlier reports of imminent rescue were false. Selim Pasha sent a chilling message: 'I fear you have no hope but in yourselves; you can depend on no help in this quarter.'

General Williams, in his last dispatch from Kars, wrote:

> We had suffered from cold, want of sufficient clothing, and starvation, without a murmur escaping from the troops. They fell dead at their posts, in their tents and throughout the camp, as brave men should who cling to their duty through the slightest glimmering of hope of saving a place entrusted to their custody.
>
> From the day of their glorious victory, on the 29th September, they had not tasted animal food, and their nourishment consisted of two-fifths of a ration of bread and the roots of grass, which they had scarcely strength to dig for; yet night and day they stood to their arms, their wasted frames showing the fearful effects of starvation, but their sparkling eyes telling me what they would do were the enemy again to attack them.

On 23 November Williams, ignorant of Omar Pasha's movements and hearing that Selim Pasha would not advance, called together the Turkish commanders. They told him that all hope had vanished. Soldiers were dying of famine at the rate of 100 a day. 'They were mere skeletons,' Consul James Brand reported, 'and were incapable of fighting or flying. The women brought their children to the General's house for food, and there they left them, and the city was strewed with dead and dying.' The besieging Russians were well provisioned and, with the onset of winter, were warmly housed in huts rather than tents and showed 'no inclination to retire'. Williams asked the Pashas whether they could resist longer or retreat, and they all replied that both were impossible.

The following lunchtime Williams sent Teesdale to General Mouravieff's camp to arrange an appointment to discuss terms of surrender. He also sent the gallant General Kmety to sneak through the Russian lines to report to his superiors the intended capitulation. Mouravieff immediately agreed to see Williams the following morning, the 25th. Williams was acting as Plenipotentiary with the authority to negotiate on behalf of Vassif Pasha, the nominal commander of the Kars defences and the actual commander-in-chief of the Turkish forces in Anatolia.

The meeting between the opposing generals duly took place. Mouravieff told Williams: 'You have made yourself a name in history, and posterity will stand amazed at the endurance, the courage and the discipline which the siege has called forth in the remains of an army. Let us arrange a capitulation that will satisfy the demands of war without outraging humanity.' The *Annual Register* recorded:

> The conditions agreed to were highly honourable to both parties, and the conduct of General Mouravieff was marked by chivalrous courtesy towards his brave but unfortunate foes. The terms included: the surrender of the fortifications with the remaining stores, arsenals and guns intact; all the

surrendering prisoners of war to be treated in accordance to the rules of civilised warfare; non-combatants and militia should be allowed to return to their homes provided they swear on oath not to take up arms against the Tsar; the occupying forces would not loot, plunder or damage the town's mosques or other public buildings.

The document further pledged: 'It being the principle of the Russian Government to respect the customs and traditions of the people subject to its Government, and especially the buildings devoted to worship, it will not allow any damage to be done to the religious monuments or historical souveniers of Kars.'

On the 28th, Williams, Vassif Pasha and the garrison discharged their muskets and marched out of Kars in full uniform, with drums beating and colours flying. Of the 20,000 men, including civilians, still drawing their meagre rations, only around half were fit to fight. The officers were allowed to keep their swords as a mark of respect. They assembled near the ruins of the nearby village of Gumbel where they were fed by the Russians. General Mouravieff wrote in his official report how he received Vassif Pasha, General Williams and the other English officers when they presented themselves to him at 2 p.m.: 'Our troops were drawn up in line of battle on both banks of Karschai. The colours of the Turkish regiments were then brought to the front of our lines by a detachment of Toula Chasseurs, and received with the bands playing and repeated cheers from our troops.'

The town was occupied that afternoon and 130 cannon, unspiked under the terms of the surrender, were taken, along with a 'great stock of arms'. Those arms included 2,000 good Minie rifles, several thousand muskets, 340,000 rounds of ball cartridge and 500 rounds for each cannon and field gun. The final victory, won by attrition and dogged determination, cancelled the shame of the earlier Russian defeat on 28 September.

In his report to the Tsar Mouravieff took full credit but also, in his chivalrous manner, shielded the reputation of his opponent. He complimented the garrison on its long defence, adding:

The besieged founded their hopes on the arrival of aid from Erzeroum. In fact Vely Pacha [sic], coming from Trezibond, had attempted to advance on Kars, but at each attempt he was met by General Souslott's detachment, which threatened his rear. Our patrols skirmished with these troops, keeping them in a state of alarm as far as the vicinity of Erzeroum. Meantime the provisions at Kars were diminishing; the cold weather was coming on; snow had fallen; cases of death, of weakness from want of nourishment occurred in the garrison; desertion increased, and despondency became general. All these circumstances decided General Williams, who directed the defence of Kars, to surrender the fortress.

The bitterness of the defeated was not aimed at their military vanquishers. Dr Sandwith wrote: 'We lay down our arms to our conquered enemy, starved by the dishonest jobbery of rascally factions, and the bribed apathy and unworthy intrigues of modern Byzantine officials.' Mouravieff issued an Order of the Day to be read to all troops:

Companions in arms, I congratulate you! As Lieutenant of our Sovereign, I thank you. At the price of your blood and your labour, the bulwark of Asia Minor has been placed at the feet of His Majesty the Emperor. The Russian standard floats on the walls of Kars. It proclaims the victory of the Cross of the Saviour. The whole of the [Turkish] army of Anatolia, 30,000 strong, has vanished like a shadow. Its Commander-in-Chief, with all his Pashas and officers, and the English General who directed the defences, with his staff, are our prisoners. Thousands of Turkish prisoners who return to their homes will proclaim your deeds of arms . . .

Despite his triumphant tone, Mouravieff was a generous victor. Around 6,000 Turkish soldiers and militiamen, including the oldest, those most weakened by starvation and those on unlimited leave, were paroled and allowed to go home. The sick and wounded were well tended. The remainder, between 7,000 and 8,000, were fed and, where necessary, clothed and shod before being marched to prisoner-of-war camps.

But it was the British officers who were shown the most respect. Dr Sandwith was set free in recognition of his humane treatment of wounded and sick Russian prisoners during the siege. Teesdale was personally thanked by Mouravieff for saving the Russian wounded from butchery below the redoubts on 28 September. Thompson was saluted for his bravery on that same day, and General Williams was wined and dined by his admiring captor. Two days later, Williams and the other English officers were sent under guard to Tiflis, where they were to sit out the remainder of the war as prisoners and honoured guests.

★　★　★

The Russian victory at Kars came too late to affect the course of the wider Crimean War. The harsh winter set in and Mouravieff had to wait until spring to strike deeper into Asia Minor. By then events had overtaken him.

Sevastapol had fallen on 6 September 1855, but it was only after Austria threatened to join the Allies that the Tsar agreed to negotiate peace terms. Lord Palmerston, fearful that Kars might become a negotiating counter over the winter, proposed sending a Turko–Egyptian force from Eupatoria to Trebizond. But he would not consider sending British troops and nothing happened. The Asia theatre of war was not reopened. The Treaty of Paris, signed on 30 March 1856, saw Russia forced to return southern Bessarabia and the mouth of the Danube to Turkey. Moldavia, Walachia and Serbia were placed under an international, rather than Russian, guarantee. The Russians were forbidden to maintain a navy on the Black Sea. The Treaty's third and fourth articles testified to the importance of Kars: the town was restored to Turkey, while Russia in exchange received back Sevastapol, Balaclava, Kamiesch, Eupatoria, Kertch, Tenikale and Kinburn.

The war marked the collapse of the arrangement under which the victors over Napoleon – Britain, Russia, Austria and Prussia – had cooperated to maintain peace in Europe for four decades. The break-up of that coalition allowed Germany and Italy to break free from Austrian dominance and to emerge as independent nations.

For the Russians, the shock of defeat was a catalyst for the internal reforms introduced by Tsar Nicholas's successor, Alexander II.

In military terms the myth of Russian might and invincibility was brought crashing down, not least by the gallant defence of Kars. Few British commanders emerged from the blundering, hugely wasteful war with their reputations enhanced or even intact. The exceptions included the Britons at Kars. There was an inevitable post-mortem on the failure to relieve Kars. The *Illustrated London News* described it as

> a dismal blotch on the fair fame of a war whose results have generally been so glorious . . . Enough is known of the heroic endurance of the little garrison, during a long and dreary blockade – the culpable neglect of which rests with those who were responsible for their succour and relief – to excite at once the enthusiasm and the indignant reproaches of the world.

Lord Stratford blamed the Turkish court and Pashas for his own tardiness. The Turks blamed the British and French. The Allied commanders blamed one another. A more level-headed assessment was made the following year by Brigadier-General W.R. Mansfield, in a memorandum to the Foreign Office:

> If I may be allowed to offer an opinion on the real cause of the disastrous issue of the Turco-Asiatic campaigns, I should say that it must be found in the nature of the alliance, which absorbed all the really available means of action, whether French, British or Turkish, in the invasion of the Russian soil, to the exclusion of attention to the hostile operation on Turkish territory. The contest pursued in the former required every practicable means to ensure success, perhaps even military safety.
>
> The garrison of Kars performed a great duty in arresting the march of the Russian columns till the resources of the allies could be turned to Asia . . .
>
> Some months since I ventured to predict, in private conversation, that we should have to be satisfied with such an issue; and that, assuming the allies to be prepared to take advantage of what has been thus achieved by the devoted garrison, we should have no reason to be disappointed when viewing the two theatres of war as one comprehensive whole. I have no reason to depart from the opinion then expressed.

In other words, the real victory at Kars was in tying up an efficient and extremely dangerous Russian army for so long.

There was an unsuccessful attempt to prosecute Selim Pasha for failing to relieve Kars. Two other Pashas were held to account for not properly provisioning the garrison. They escaped blame because they were noblemen. Instead, the blame was put on the shoulders of a former Commissary, now dead. His son was thrown into prison as an accomplice.

The Sultan sent his effusive thanks to the townspeople of Kars who had shared with the troops the hardships and dangers of the siege. They were more grateful for his more practical reward – three years' exemption from taxes.

Williams and his staff were well treated during their captivity, first at Riazan and later at Tiflis in Russia. He wrote:

> We were conveyed in carriages furnished by the Russian Government, and under the charge of Captain Baschmakoff, of the Imperial Guard, whose kind and friendly care of us demands our best thanks; indeed, nothing can exceed the warm and flattering reception which we have received from the authorities, military and civil.

Williams was presented to the Tsar even before the peace was signed and by the end of March he and his officers were on their way back to England.

One of their comrades was already there. Dr Sandwith, on being released by Mouravieff, had travelled, mainly on foot, to Constantinople and crossed the Armenia mountains, undergoing great hardships and dangers on his way. He arrived in London on 9 January 1856 and became 'the lion of the season'. He related the story of the siege to Queen Victoria and her ministers, and his narrative, rushed out by the end of the month, became a bestseller. He was made a CB and Oxford gave him an honorary degree. In August that year he went with Lord Granville to Moscow for the coronation of the new Tsar, where he was presented with the Russian order of St Stanislaus for humanitarian service. The French also answered him the Legion of Honour.

Sandwith had no wish to practise medicine comfortably in England and early in 1857 he became the colonial secretary in Mauritius. The climate there did not suit him and he returned less than two years later. He became active in politics as an ardent reformer and tried, unsuccessfully, to become MP for Marylebone. A visit to Serbia and Bulgaria reversed his previously pro-Turkish sympathies. He wrote about Turkish misrule and the threat of a massacre hanging over the region's Christians. When Serbia declared war on Turkey in 1876 he went to Belgrade and devoted himself to the relief of the wounded and the refugees. On a return visit to England he raised £7,000 for refugee relief and campaigned to prevent Britain again taking sides on behalf of Turkey and against Russia.

During his later years he agitated for improved water supplies for Londoners. His health and that of his wife Lucy deteriorated and in 1860 they were advised to winter in Davros. It was disastrous for both of them. Sandwith died in Paris the next May, aged fifty-eight. His wife and one of his five children followed him to the grave the following year. Tributes flooded in. Professor Max Muller wrote: 'I never heard him make a concession. Straight as an arrow he flew through life, a devoted lover of truth, a despiser of all quibbles.' An eminent churchman said that no other Englishman had done more to help the Christian population of European Turkey. An obituary said he had 'the one-sidedness of a strong partisan'.

Henry Thompson was honoured by the Turks and by Britain. He had no time to enjoy the accolades. He died, aged just twenty-six and unmarried, in London on 13 June 1856, just days after he returned from his captivity. He was buried in Brompton cemetery and a memorial tablet was erected to his memory in St Paul's Cathedral by public subscription.

Colonel Lake received the thanks of Parliament, the Legion of Honour from the French and a sword and silver salver from the people of Ramsgate, where his mother lived. He was made a major-general in the Turkish army. A year after his return he retired from the British army to take up his appointment as chief commissioner of police in Dublin. He retired twelve years later and died in Brighton, aged seventy-three, in 1881. He had outlived two wives. Of his five sons, one became an admiral and three were officers in either the Artillery or the Engineers.

Teesdale, although still a mere artillery lieutenant, was made a CB on his return. The queen later presented him with the Victoria Cross for his courage during the battle of Kars. For three years he continued as *aide-de-camp* to General Williams until he was promoted first to captain then to brevet major for distinguished service in the field. Further promotions steadily followed, and by 1887 he was a major-general. Always a royal favourite, he had by then also served ten years as *aide-de-camp* to the ageing queen and for longer as equerry to the Prince of Wales. He died in 1893 from a paralytic stroke, aged sixty, at his bachelor's home in Sussex after returning from a trip to Germany. He is buried in South Bersted churchyard.

General Williams deservedly returned a hero. His marathon defence, despite its ultimate failure, showed that not all senior British officers in the recent war had been nincompoops. He was created Baronet of Kars with a pension of £1,000 a year for life, was made a Knight Commander of the Order of the Bath, and received the freedom of the City of London with a sword of honour. The French gave him the Grand Cross of the Legion of Honour and the Turkish sultan followed suit with the first class of the Order of the Medjidie.

He was general-commandant of Woolwich garrison from 1856 to 1859, during which time he was also MP for Calne. In 1859 he went to Canada, where he served for six years as commander of forces, becoming governor of Nova Scotia. From 1871 to 1876 he was governor of Gibraltar and in 1881 he was appointed constable of the Tower of London. He died at eighty-two, unmarried, in Garland's Hotel, Pall Mall, on 23 July 1883. He was buried at Brompton cemetery.

His Kars comrade and devoted friend Sir Christopher Teesdale said:

He had marvellous self-reliance and perfect fearlessness of responsibility. He trusted his subordinates, but only consulted with them on points of detail. He would walk for hours alone at Kars, working out plans and ideas in his mind, and, once settled, they were never departed from. Every one knew that an order once given had to be obeyed without comment. Firm as a rock on duty, he had the kindliest gentlest heart that ever beat.

But perhaps the most fitting tribute to Williams was spoken to Dr Sandwith by an unnamed Turkish soldier and survivor of Kars: '*Veeliams Pasha chock adam dur,*' he said. Williams Pasha is no end of a man.

CHAPTER EIGHT

The Fenian Invasion of Canada, 1866

'And we'll go and capture Canada, for we've nothing else to do.'

On 13 December 1862 the Irish Brigade swarmed up Marye's Heights above Fredericksburg. They had already witnessed from afar other regiments of the Union Army being slashed to ribbons by the Confederate Virginian Division firing musket balls, canister and grapeshot from behind a stone wall on the summit. Their fate was to be no different. The Irishmen got further than any others had done on the corpse-strewn hillside but they were still 50 yards short of that terrible wall.

Thomas Galway, a young officer in another company, embracing the ground under the lethal hailstorm, wrote:

> Every man has a sprig of green in his cap, and a half-laughing, half-murderous look in his eyes. Poor fellows, poor, glorious fellows, shaking goodbye to us with their hats. They reach a point within a stone's throw of the stone wall. No farther. They try to go beyond, but are slaughtered.

The correspondent for the London *Times*, not noted for many Irish sympathies, wrote: 'Never at Fontenoy, Albuera or at Waterloo was more undaunted courage displayed by the sons of Erin than during those six frantic dashes which they directed against the almost impregnable position of their foe.'

An Irish officer serving on the Confederate side at Fredericksburg, one of the most savage battles of America's Civil War, wrote to his wife: 'My darling, we forgot they were fighting us, and cheer after cheer at their fearlessness went up all along our lines.' General Robert E. Lee himself, watching from above, famously remarked: 'It is well that war is so frightful. Otherwise we should become too fond of it.' An officer of the Irish Brigade saw no glory, only the bodies of his men. 'It was not a battle,' he wrote, 'it was the wholesale slaughter of human beings – sacrificed to the blind ambition and incapacity of some parties.'

That night the brigade's commander, General Thomas Francis Meagher, went ahead with a previously planned banquet in Fredericksburg town. American staff officers, unused to the Irish custom of a wake, were horrified to witness the general and others quaffing the regimental cocktail of whiskey and champagne around a cannon ball on a silver salver.

The following morning there was a roll call. Meagher wrote: 'Of the 2,200 men I led into action . . . 218 now appeared on that ground.' Three Irishmen standing alone were ordered to join their company. They replied: 'General, we are our company.'

In the minds of Meagher and many other survivors of that dreadful day a significant change of attitude towards America began to develop. Most of them were first-generation migrants who had left Ireland to escape the potato famine, with its dreadful poverty of the body and spirit. Some, including Meagher, had been the victims of political oppression and had escaped from penal colonies in Australia with the help of their American friends. All shared a great feeling of gratitude to the United States, which was one reason why they fought so heroically and enthusiastically for the Union. After Fredericksburg, they felt that they had repaid their debt in full, with interest. Some felt that America owed them help in a new enterprise which could serve all their interests and would strike at the heart of the swelling British Empire – which they had good reason to detest. That adventure was to be nothing less than the invasion of British Canada.

$$\star \quad \star \quad \star$$

By the time the opening shots of the American Civil War were fired in the spring of 1861 the population of Ireland had fallen by two million. Half of those had died in the Great Famine, the result of potato blight, failed crops, absentee landlords, the ignorance of the people and the callous greed of the English and Anglo-Irish gentry. Most of the rest had emigrated, preferring the uncertainty of death-trap steamers and strange lands to the certainty of on-going squalor and religious persecution.

The majority crossed the Atlantic, taking advantage of the 'passenger trade' in which empty cargo vessels filled their holds with emigrants on the outward journey, before returning to Britain laden with more precious cargo, such as timber. Most landed in Quebec and New Brunswick, north of the Canadian border, but few of them wanted to settle on British sovereign territory. They had had enough of that back home. Such sentiments were not shared simply by ragged, embittered refugees. Lord Durham, High Commissioner and Governor-General of Canada, understood the attractions of the new nation being forged south of the border. In his 1839 report he said:

> On the American side all is bustle and activity . . . on the British side of the line, with the exception of a few favoured spots where some approach to American prosperity is apparent, all seems waste and desolation. The ancient city of Montreal which is naturally the commercial capital of Canada, will not bear the least comparison in any respect with Buffalo, which is the creation of yesterday.

Thousands more were transported to the penal colonies of Australia, charged by an over-zealous and often panicky British administration with sedition, riotous assembly and affray. These were the men who formed the Fenian Brotherhood, committed to freeing Ireland from British rule. One of these was Thomas Francis

General Thomas Francis Meagher at the battle of Fair Oaks. (New York Public Library)

Meagher, born in 1823, the son of a prosperous Waterford merchant. As a law student in Dublin he became a radical, an anti-slavery campaigner and a Republican. His views were formed by the memories, still fresh among his elders, of the Irish rebellions of 1798 and 1803, put down with great harshness, and shaped by the zeal for civil and religious rights that he witnessed in the revolutionary wars of America and France. As a 'stripling' he took on the great Daniel O'Connell in debate, famously advocating Irish independence by violent rather than political means. One particularly robust speech in 1846 earned him the popular title 'Meagher of the Sword'. He said:

> I look upon the sword as a sacred weapon. And if . . . it has sometimes reddened the shroud of the oppressor, like the anointed rod of the high priest, it has, at other times, blossomed into flowers to deck the freeman's brow . . .

After the 1848 Young Ireland Uprising, fuelled by famine but woefully misjudged, Meagher was sentenced to death. This was later commuted to transportation for life to the prison colony on Van Dieman's Land, later renamed Tasmania. In 1852 he escaped, controversially breaking his parole, and took a ship to New York. There he was welcomed as a hero, and lectured to crowds grown starry-eyed about the Old Country and the boundless freedom and opportunities of the New.

After the bombardment of Fort Sumter sparked the war between the States, Meagher was fired with the idea of forming an Irish Brigade to pursue the Union cause and their own. For 150 years after the Battle of the Boyne there had been a fine tradition of Irish exiles fighting the British in the armies of France and Spain. Now it was time to fight for the 'land of freedom'. Moreover Britain seemed to be siding with the Confederacy, with its strong ties of cotton to English milltowns, and there seemed every chance that Britain would go the whole hog and send military aid to the South. Meagher argued for a fighting force to be recruited from the Irish communities growing rapidly in New York, Philadelphia and Boston. He was joined, at first reluctantly, by General James Shields, an Irishman who had commanded a brigade in the US Army in the Mexican war. Shields had the ear of the president. He once challenged Abraham Lincoln, long before he entered the White House, to a duel over an alleged libel. When asked to choose weapons, Lincoln opted for 'broadswords at seven feet'. The two men broke down in laughter and became firm friends. That friendship helped to win over Washington sceptics who did not hold the Irish in high regard, and permission was granted. Meagher was given the colonelcy of the 69th New York State Volunteers, which became the nucleus of the Irish Brigade.

Recruiting started in earnest at the end of August in a New York pleasure-ground known as Jones's Wood, at what was ostensibly a picnic held to raise money for the widows and children of those killed at Bull Run. Meagher told the crowd to put aside the petty party divisions to which they were prone and unite in a great cause. The defeat of the Union, he said, would encourage European royalty and the enemies of democracy. Victory would be another blow struck for the cause of a free, independent Ireland. In 1861 the Irish made up 87 per cent of all foreign-born New Yorkers and there was no shortage of volunteers. They were labourers, navvies, railway workers, streetcar drivers, clerks, waiters, doctors, priests, schoolteachers and academics. Many were active Fenians and, like the young Meagher, had histories of violence and sedition.

By Christmas Eve 1861 the brigade, swelled by volunteers from neighbouring states, was complete, with full complements of infantry, artillery and cavalry. They camped in a downpour in North Virginia, part of the Army of the Potomac, poised to take part in General George McClellan's advance on Richmond. This huge military operation began in unassailable optimism – and ended in disaster.

At Fair Oaks, 4 miles from the Confederate capital, Meagher's Brigade broke a rebel assault designed to split the Union lines. The Irishmen charged through woods and swamp, yelling in their native tongue. Their first fatality was Private Michael Herbert, a devout Catholic and nationalist. Herbert had served in the British Army suppressing the Indian Mutiny before joining the Papal Brigade in Italy (where he served alongside Meagher's brother). He enlisted in the Irish Brigade shortly after arriving in New York.

McClellan's blundering and over-cautious approach turned the campaign in favour of the Confederates and the Irish Brigade was caught up in the battle of White Oak Swamp, as 'Stonewall' Jackson and General Robert E. Lee tried to destroy the Army of the Potomac. After seven days of intense marching and fighting Lee's hopes were shattered by heavy losses at Malvern Hill. Meagher led his men in shirtsleeves, suffering a graze from a musket ball. He reported proudly: 'Coming into contact with the enemy, the Sixty-Ninth poured in an oblique fire upon them with a rapid precision and an incessant vigour.' Afterwards he showed a fellow general the regiment's bullet-ridden colours, saying: 'That is a *holy* flag.'

Such victories boosted the reputation of the Irish Brigade in the eyes of officers who had previously considered them little more than a rabble, whose fighting prowess was confined to bar-room brawling. Meagher was a heavy drinker and often laid himself open to reports of drunkenness while campaigning, if not during actual battles, but many of his men were paid-up members of the Temperance League. In many other ways too they did not fit the stereotype forged by those hostile to their cause. One cavalry officer said: 'I preferred the Irish; they were more intelligent and resourceful as a rule.'

In September 1862 the brigade marched 50 miles to take part in the bloodiest battle to date on American soil. At Antietam Creek near Sharpsburg the brigade's three New York regiments and the 29th Massachusetts were ordered to attack. Five times they charged the strong rebel position along the infamous Sunken Road. Those who reached the lane found themselves in a brutal mêlée in which the clubbed musket was the chief weapon of necessity. Two of the New York regiments lost 60 per cent dead and wounded. Meagher's horse was shot from under him and he suffered serious concussion in the fall – although some American officers later wrongly attributed his confusion to drunkenness. The 69th alone left bodies on the field. In all, the brigade's casualties were 540 men, including 75 new recruits who had begged to be let off provost duty so they could take part in the fighting. Meagher wrote to his wife Libby:

It was an awful battle. Fancy a deafening storm of artillery and musketry ranging along a line of over two miles in length, and when at last it subsided, the glorious Stars and Stripes flying triumphantly three miles beyond where the Rebel colours had been planted in defence. The poor little Brigade was woefully cut up – I have not more than 750 in camp today – the best of my officers too, killed.

General McClellan wrote in his report:

The Irish Brigade sustained its well-earned reputation. After suffering terribly in officers and men, and strewing the ground with their enemies as they drove them back, their ammunition nearly expended, and their commander disabled by a fall from his horse, this Brigade was ordered to give place to General Caldwell's brigade . . . The lines were passed by the Irish Brigade breaking by company to the rear as steady as on drill.

The depleted brigade was reinforced by the 116th Pennsylvanians and was back up to strength in time to meet its greatest challenge – and heaviest losses – at Fredericksburg. The night after that battle, while Meagher was knocking back his lethal cocktails, a Cork-born Union captain, Dennis Downing, began singing the Fenian marching song 'Ireland Boys Hurrah.' The chorus spread from his campfire, voice to voice, 6 miles down the river. Irishmen in the Confederate Army on the far bank joined in.

The return of the less seriously wounded helped to rebuild the Irish Brigade but it was still a sadly reduced force which faced a further test at Chancellorsville in May. The Confederates pounded the Irish with cannon. Meagher, recovering from a leg ulcer, stayed with his men under fire. One shell burst on the spot he had vacated moments earlier, killing four men. The rest of the Union Army had been ordered to retreat northwards and the brigade's 88th regiment was the last to leave. Meagher, dispirited by the seemingly endless carnage tendered his resignation. He wrote that the Irish Brigade

> no longer exists. The assault on the enemy's works on December 13th last reduced it to something less than a minimum regiment of infantry. For several weeks it remained in this exhausted condition. Brave fellows from the convalescent camp and from sick beds at home gradually reinforced this handful of devoted men.

Such weariness grew widespread among those Irishmen mourning friends, brothers, fathers and sons. Battle-scarred veterans grew sick of fighting a war to benefit the Federal States, and recruitment dropped. The thoughts of many turned towards fighting their own, unfinished, war.

Such sentiments were exacerbated by the Federal government's reluctance to recognise the heroic sacrifice of its Irish recruits. Meagher's resignation letter was cancelled after some prevarication but no new command was offered. General Winfield Scott Hancock, who would have been happy to serve alongside him, said: 'The War Department seems to regard the Irish general as a communicable disease.' Late in 1863 Meagher, now a reluctant agitator, joined the Fenian Brotherhood. He solemnly pledged 'my sacred word of honour as a truthful and honest man that I will labor [sic] with earnest zeal for the establishment of a free and independent government on Irish soil'. As the Civil War reached its final conclusion, with the crushing of the South, Meagher used his political friends and outstanding reputation to become acting governor of Montana, a state conveniently bordering Canada.

Those left in the brigade fought on, and encountered some of the fiercest fighting below Little Round Top during the war's pivotal battle at Gettysburg. Facing an enemy line barely 15 yards away they drove the Confederates from the summit, only to be surrounded. They retreated through a cornfield, loading and firing as they ran. Given their hopeless situation, the brigade suffered no dishonour.

The end of the Civil War in 1865 saw the disillusioned survivors of the Irish Brigade and their families thirsting for their own cause. The courage of the brigade in battle inspired men who shared the same blood but who had never themselves seen action to become increasingly bellicose. Many of the veterans who inspired them, however, had seen enough action to last their lifetimes. The Fenian Brotherhood was by now hopelessly split. That division, ironically, propelled thousands into backing an equally hopeless adventure.

James Stephens, who fled to France after the Young Ireland rebellion, had in 1858 formed the Irish Revolutionary Brotherhood which aimed at nothing less than the complete overthrow of British rule in Ireland. Later that year he visited America to raise funds, and left behind the nucleus of the Fenian Brotherhood under his lieutenant, John O'Mahony. A Kilkenny man, born in 1825, Stephens was a former engineer on the Limerick and Waterford railway. O'Mahony was born, in 1816, into a strongly nationalist family and both his father and uncle had fought in the 1798 Irish rebellion. As the American conflict closed, the British rulers in Ireland cracked down hard on the movement. Their numerous spies told them, correctly, that Stephens was plotting armed insurrection. In the meantime a leadership battle erupted among their American supporters. O'Mahony, Stephens' choice, wanted to continue putting all their efforts into backing, with cash, arms and men, the planned revolt on Irish soil. When the Irish revolt was postponed, O'Mahony and Stephens were prepared to wait but others, strengthened by the intake of many Irish Brigade veterans, were not. The rival faction was led by the Irish-born Colonel William Randolph Roberts, a dry goods merchant in Manhattan, backed by General Thomas W. Sweeny, who had lost an arm while serving in the US Army during the Mexican War, and who had also commanded a Union division in Sherman's campaign against Atlanta. They wanted an attack on Canada, which was closer and a poorly defended flank of the British. Such an invasion, even if the territories won could not be held, would complement any Irish uprising and see the British fighting on two fronts. Roberts and his followers argued that an Anglo-American war was imminent because of naval disputes, British support for the Confederacy and the revolutionary fund-raising activities of Americans. Whether he truly believed this himself is debatable, but the often-repeated claim helped to stiffen the sinews of his men and boosted his bid for control of the Brotherhood.

O'Mahony grew concerned at the number of brigade veterans deserting him and conceived a scheme to win them back. His aim was to restore credibility by seizing Campobello Island, which was claimed by both Britain and America. Close to the coastline of Maine and New Brunswick, this island could be used as a base for Fenian troops on their way to Ireland, and as the port of privateers who would prey on British shipping. Brigade veterans began to congregate on the north shore of Maine. Their transport was to be the small ship *Ocean Spray*, bought from the Confederates by O'Mahony's treasurer, Doran Killian.

The vessel, manned by naval veterans, was in place by April 1866. Spotting a British man-of-war on patrol, *Ocean Spray* ran for cover and some of the crew captured a British flag on nearby Indian Island. At Calais, Maine, there was an exchange of fire across the bridge which joined the two nations. Britain complained bitterly about the incidents and the American government, which had been busily rebuilding relations with London, reacted to prevent an international crisis. Three warships were sent to the scene while Federal troops under General Meade disarmed about 200 Fenians. The disappointed Irishmen were sent away from the planned invasion point on board the steamer *New Brunswick*. The 'Border Scare' ended ingloriously. The *Tribune* newspaper reported: 'Hundreds of fine young men left their homes, threw up their situations, gave up everything to join, heart and soul, in this movement, and it was a truly melancholy sight to see them leave by the boat.'

O'Mahony was discredited and the débâcle resulted in the Fenians being held up to ridicule in the Press. It also strengthened the support for Roberts and Sweeny among members who wanted to wipe the smiles from their tormentors' faces. Ominous events began to alert the American authorities, and the British across the border, that something rather more serious was in the wind. Rumours circulated that 100,000 Union and Confederate veterans were willing to fight for Ireland's freedom. A thousand Irishmen heading for California made a detour and assembled in Buffalo. Another 500 left Boston for the same destination. And Federal marshals in St Albans, Vermont, seized a 1,000-strong stand of Fenian arms. An invasion anthem was composed:

> We are the Fenian Brotherhood, skilled in the arts of war,
> And we're going to fight for Ireland, the land that we adore,
> Many battles we have won, along with the boys in blue,
> And we'll go and capture Canada, for we've nothing else to do.

★   ★   ★

General Sweeny's plan of campaign was to drive four separate forces across the Canadian border early in June 1866. To the west, a small Fenian army would set off from Chicago, cross Lake Huron and draw off thousands of British regulars and Canadian militia from the main targets on the Niagara and Vermont borders. Some 5,000 more men would embark on a similar feint across Lake Erie to threaten towns on the Toronto road. The main attacks were to be from Buffalo, where Fenians were to be towed across the Niagara River to take the Niagara Peninsula and the Welland Canal, while the right wing would move through Vermont to seize Montreal and Quebec. Swift success would, Sweeny reckoned, result in the collapse of British defences and the US government's recognition of a new Fenian administration followed, possibly, by the long hoped-for Anglo-American War. He also believed that his armies would be welcomed by Catholic and French-Canadians. In an address aimed at them he said: 'We come among you as foes of British rule in Ireland. We have no issue with the people of these provinces. Our weapons are for the oppressors of Ireland, our bows shall be directed only against the power of England; her privileges alone shall we invade, not yours.' Sweeny was, however, relying on the element of surprise, and the time for that had long since passed. Only one of his four planned thrusts became reality.

This was the Buffalo assault, led by the 32-year-old, red-haired Colonel John O'Neill from Drumgallon, who had emigrated to America when he was just fourteen. Well regarded for his bravery and good humour, O'Neill had become an officer in the Federal Army after an unsuccessful career in publishing and selling books, and had campaigned with the 13th US Coloured Infantry and the 7th Michigan Cavalry. He had resigned his commission after being passed over for promotion, due, he believed, to anti-Irish bigotry. Unlike many others involved in this enterprise, he was a capable tactician and led his men with confidence.

Around 3,000 Fenians were gathered in Buffalo under his command. To confuse the American authorities and British spies, they marched up and down apparently at random. One night, however, 1,200 of them slipped away from the town and congregated on the banks of the Niagara river close to its source on Lake Erie, expecting the balance of their force to join them after daybreak on 1 June. From Black Rock they boarded canal barges and were towed across the river to land at the wharves in front of Fort Erie, an old stockade garrisoned by a handful of soldiers. When they landed the Irish sent up a wild yell and unfurled a green flag. The British were swiftly over-run in the darkness and taken prisoner. The small village nearby was also captured without casualties. Canadian propaganda and some history books depict the Fenians embarking at this point on a drunken rampage of looting. In fact, they simply employed the tactics learnt while on campaign during the Civil War – cutting telegraph lines, foraging and confiscating horses. In compensation householders were offered Irish Republic bonds printed by Roberts. There must have been some infractions, however, as O'Neill threatened to bayonet a soldier who stole a girl's shawl from an inn. The British Press reported that two houses were burnt and 60 dollars was stolen from a Customs officer. O'Neill then occupied the fort and waited for the rest of his men to catch up. They did not come.

The anti-Fenian mayor of Buffalo had ordered that the Niagara river ferry should stay on the Canadian side overnight to deny the Irish the chance to board it. Moreover, the armed steamboat USS *Michigan* had been ordered out on patrol to prevent any crossing by small vessels. It ran between Black Rock and Tonawanda, where the beginnings of the rapids above Niagara Falls make the river uncrossable. The steamer cut off all communications and O'Neill's men roared their anger as it passed back and forth in front of their own positions. O'Neill decided to march downriver, closer to the Falls, hoping that his reinforcements might somehow be able to cross over beyond *Michigan*'s reach. On the way he captured the small village of Waterloo. The steamer kept pace with him, and although crowds of Fenians and curious onlookers also marched along the opposite shore, none dared attempt the crossing. O'Neill stopped at Frenchman's Creek, where he ordered the building of a breastwork of fence rails. From behind those defences he proclaimed himself the 'Commander-in-Chief of the Army of the Irish Republic in Canada'. That night the American authorities across the river received firm orders from Washington that no Fenians should be allowed to join the invasion force. Two armed tugs were sent to reinforce *Michigan*.

In the meantime the Canadian authorities had not been idle. Canada's populace was outraged by the invasion, and Irish-Canadians had little or no sympathy for the interlopers. The statesman Thomas D'Arcy McGee, who, like Meagher, was a veteran of the Young Ireland uprising, warned that Fenianism was not welcome in Montreal. He declared: 'This filibustering is murder, not war.' The alarm was sounded in Toronto and across the province. Thousands of militiamen were called out. The Queen's Own Rifles paraded 450 men who boarded the ferry *City of Toronto* and sailed for Port Dalhousie. From there they travelled by train to Port Culborne.

Some 25 miles to the north of the Fenian invasion force Lieutenant-Colonel George Peacocke of the 16th Foot, the British commander on the Niagara front,

The reception of the Canadian Volunteers at Montreal. (*Illustrated London News*)

disembarked from a train with men of the Royal Artillery and two infantry regiments. His plan was to move south-west across the peninsula to meet up with the Canadian militia regiments and the Queen's Own from Fort Colborne, drive the invaders back to Fort Erie and wipe them out. However, the militia commander, the Canadian surveyor Colonel John Dennis, left his men before dawn that day to travel in an armed tug to Fort Erie. Alfred Booker, an English merchant, was left in charge of 600 Volunteers. Booker, the recently appointed commander of the 13th Volunteer Battalion, was a military incompetent. On receiving a telegram from Peacocke directing him to move his force to meet the regular soldiers, Booker decided to take 480 men by train 10 miles east to the village of Ridgeway, set in gently rolling farmland. His force was a mixture of militia, the Queen's Own Rifles, a battalion of the Royal Hamilton Light Infantry and the York and Caledonia Rifle companies. It was later claimed that by the time they left the train his men were 'well-liquored'. Local farmers warned Booker that the Fenians were nearby but he dismissed their reports because his own spies told him that the enemy had been camped at Black Creek the night before. That was true, but O'Neill had decided to move up to meet Booker's weaker column before it could join with Peacocke's stronger force.

O'Neill's scouts certainly heard Booker's Volunteers laughing, shouting and blowing bugles as they formed up. The Canadians marched along a road running parallel to a long, limestone ridge about 8 miles west of Fort Erie. It was a fine, hot morning and the road was flanked by fields of tall new corn. No. 5 Company of the Queen's Own was first to come under fire and the troops returned fire with their Spencer repeating rifles. Fenian skirmishers ran down the slopes and reached a crossroads ahead of Booker's column. The Canadians did precisely as O'Neill expected and enthusiastically rushed the small band of Irishmen. The Fenians pulled back, tempting the Canadians to follow them to the next crossroads. Here the main Fenian forces were waiting in the cover of the ridge and woods. As Booker deployed the men of the Queen's Own Battalion they were suddenly met by a scattering fire from O'Neill's skirmishers concealed in a clump of low bushes. A Canadian ensign was the first fatality. He was hit in the stomach and died after 20 minutes of agony.

Both sides opened an intense fire but the Canadians soon ran short of ammunition because Booker had neglected to unload most of the munitions from their train. A *Times* correspondent wrote grudgingly: 'It appears that the Fenians fought with great desperation, taking off their coats, vests and even their shirts, and fighting half-naked with great ardour.' Booker's men also fought bravely, however, and began to put pressure on the Fenians around the intersection. The Volunteers charged three times but were repulsed each time by the Irish, who launched a counter-attack. Booker then saw some horsemen – probably either onlookers or Fenian scouts – and panicked. He formed his men into a traditional British infantry square. Canadians pressing the Fenians with some success were dragged back into the stationary, purely defensive position. When Booker realised that there were no massed ranks of Fenian horsemen threatening him, his buglers ordered the men back into a fighting line. As they attempted to do so they were blasted at close range and, in confusion, began to retreat. Booker had little option other than to order a general withdrawal but that order was delivered late to the Highland Company and the University Rifles on the far right. The Rifles were forced to retire across the Fenian front and suffered heavy casualties.

The adjutant of the Queen's Own, Captain William Otter, wrote in his official account:

> The fire of the now pursuing Fenians became hotter than ever, and the Volunteers being crowded up in a narrow road, presented a fine market to their rifles, causing our poor fellows to fall on all sides. It was in vain the officers endeavoured to rally the men . . . several times as quads, and even a company, were collected, but never in sufficient force to check the pursuit, though a constant fire was kept up until the Fenians ceased following. For the first two or three hundred yards it was a regular panic, but after that the men fell into a walk, retiring in a very orderly manner, but completely crestfallen.

The Fenians chased the Canadian rearguard for a quarter of a mile beyond Ridgeway. The whole action had taken 20 minutes. The Canadians lost 23 men, and around 30 wounded, of whom at least two died a week later: Sergeant Hugh Matheson, shot in the thigh, and Corporal William Lakey, who took a bullet in the mouth. Private Charles Lugsdin was hit in the arm, chest and lung but miraculously survived. The Fenians lost 6 dead and 15 wounded. The Irish dead included at least one Irish Brigade veteran, James Geraghty. According to Otter, General O'Neill praised the performance of the Queen's Own, saying that 'we behaved splendidly and were mistaken by them for regulars, owing to our steadiness'.

By now it was about 9 a.m. and O'Neill heard reports that Peacocke's main body of Regulars was behind him, and approaching fast. He called off the pursuit of Booker's men and ordered that the wounded from both sides be quartered with local farmers and with two doctors to tend them. This was efficiently and humanely done within an hour. But reports of Peacocke's speedy advance were false; he let his men rest in a field north of Stevensville, rather than rush to the aid of the militia.

Another militia column from Suspension Bridge captured the abandoned Fenian camp at Frenchman's Creek and advanced on the Irish rear at the hamlet of Waterloo. In a skirmish in which about a hundred men fought on either side and which was later dignified by the name 'Battle of Waterloo', the Canadian Volunteers broke against the Irish muskets. But O'Neill's men gained little advantage and the main Fenian body retreated back towards Fort Erie. With a shortage of men and the whole countryside against them, it was a tactical withdrawal, not a rout, and was conducted in good military order as befitted the veterans of the brigade. Most were in exuberant mood, heartened by the victory at Ridgeway. The tracks of the Grant Truck Railway were pulled up behind them.

Meanwhile the Canadians suffered another setback. Colonel Dennis, with 70 artillerymen and sailors, landed at Fort Erie to pick up Fenian stragglers captured by local farmers. Instead of marshalling his forces, swelled by militia men after their run from Ridgeway, he left his command and travelled by road back to Fort Colborne. Dennis was later tried for cowardice but acquitted. O'Neill and his little army now marched on the Fort Erie and took it. The Canadian defenders blasted away from the cover of firewood stacks and from the house of the local postmaster. A Fenian was bayoneted to death as he tried to kick in the door of the postmaster's home. Another, Colonel O'Bailey, was shot, non-fatally, in the chest as he led his men in a mounted charge against a tug in the river shallows. Outside the fort O'Neill's force, whittled down to 800 by casualties, capture and desertion, camped rough and again waited for reinforcements.

Again, they were disappointed. When 700 Fenians tried to cross from Buffalo in a skow they were arrested by the USS *Michigan*. O'Neill sent a message across the river by a small boat, urging that the main Fenian army should join him as speedily as possible. He was told that because of the transport difficulties only one more regiment could be sent. O'Neill refused that as inadequate but said that he was prepared to sacrifice himself and his command to tie down substantial British forces on the peninsula to aid the rest of the invasion across the Canadian border. He was unaware that those forces to the west and in Vermont had not yet moved. The other invasion forces did nothing, confused by conflicting orders and dissuaded by the presence of the US generals Grant in Buffalo and Meade in Eastport. Grant issued orders to prevent anyone, Irish or American, aiding the Fenians. President Johnson issued a proclamation declaring 'the Fenian expedition an enterprise unlawful. All good citizens are warned against aiding or abetting it. The civil and military authorities are ordered to prevent, defeat and arrest all persons engaged in violating the neutrality laws.' The Fenians who had flocked to Buffalo as news of the attack spread were eager to join O'Neill but were stuck in open scows on the shore of Lake Erie, waiting for tugs that never came. General Tevis, who was supposed to be in charge of transportation, was later found guilty of cowardice by a Fenian court-martial.

All the time Colonel Peacocke's Regulars and the Canadian militia were gathering strength and moving closer to O'Neill's encampment, until they completely trapped the Irish in the toe of the peninsula. Their line extended from the bank of Lake Erie on the west to the shore of the Niagara river on the east. As well as Peacocke's men and the Volunteers, the Canadian government was mobilising the 16th and 45th Regiments and two batteries of Royal Artillery. They were descending on the Irish by road, rail and canal boat.

In a sideshow to the main action, 90 artillerymen under Captain Richard King and Captain L.M. Cullum were armed with swords, bayonets and muskets and attacked a band of Fenian stragglers. After a 'spirited action' 66 of the invaders were captured. Another group of Fenians tried to rescue their comrades and were repulsed. But in the confusion 20 Canadians became detached from their comrades and were in turn captured by the Fenians. Captain King was severely wounded and abandoned on the field; he survived but one foot had to be amputated.

O'Neill knew that as long as he was denied the promised reinforcements, his position was hopeless. One correspondent wrote: 'The Fenians had no idea of being caught this way, and imprisoned in Canadian dungeons, or hanged perhaps on Canadian gallows.' In the early hours of 3 June O'Neill ordered the destruction of their ammunition dumps. He and his men clambered into a flotilla of small tugs and canal barges and tried to escape to the American shore. In their haste they left behind 32 men on picket duty, all of whom were captured by the Canadians. Almost all the escapees were halted in mid-river by the USS *Michigan* with two armed tugs and several other smaller armed vessels. Shots were exchanged and at least five Fenians were killed. Around 700 were arrested. The remainder either drowned or escaped in the confusion. O'Neill and his staff were held aboard *Michigan*, while the men were confined in flat boats. *Michigan*'s commander telegraphed Washington to ask what he should do with the prisoners. The *New York Times* man wrote: 'From a cursory examination of these prisoners I judge them a wretched-looking lot, totally deficient in uniform, and composed of the roughest-looking specimens of humanity.' Another correspondent wrote:

They are a woe-begone set of fellows, and they tell most mournful tales of their experience as invaders. They say that having no artillery, and finding that the Canadians had Armstrong guns and were closing around them, with no prospect of reinforcements and no supplies, they concluded not to be 'gobbled up' and perhaps hanged, as they say all those captured in Canada will be, and so they 'skeddaddled' as best they could. They were completely worn out, had been constantly on the march since they crossed over to Fort Erie, had no camp equipage or shelter, very little to eat except what they captured in Canada, and no sleep.

Other accounts, however, suggest that the captured men were still in high spirits and regarded their arrest by their former compatriots in arms as merely a temporary setback. They only grew despondent when informed that the main Fenian army, under General Spears, was not marching on Toronto. They were also shocked to discover that Roberts, the architect of the invasion, had never even left New York, while General Sweeny, the military commander, had got no nearer to the Canadian border than Albany. O'Neill said simply: 'Our people are glad they didn't fall into the hands of the Canadians.'

Across the border about 80 captured Fenians were sent to Toronto and Hamilton. Highly exaggerated reports sparked a more widespread scare, while other correspondents far from the scene painted lurid pictures of drunken Irishmen going on a spree of murder, rape and looting. Still others reported that the invaders had been massacred in their hundreds. Britain sent grateful messages to the American government which had stifled the invasion before it could be properly born. *The Times* man reported:

> The invasion was sprung upon us, but as soon as anything could be done the most vigorous measures were taken to prevent aid of any kind being sent across the Niagara River. And thus ended the great 'Fenian War' which lasted just 48 hours from midnight on 31 May to midnight of 2 June; which resulted in the killing, wounding and drowning of about 100 persons, the capture of 800 more, and the plain development of the fact that the Fenians are utterly unable to carry on an offensive campaign. Their 'army' never got more than eight miles from Fort Erie. It is confidently believed that nine-tenths of the Irish in America denounced this invasion as a foolhardy enterprise, of no advantage whatever. Its sudden collapse, were it not for the bloodshed, would certainly provoke a smile.

The *New York World* on 4 June neatly summed up the affair:

> The Fenian invasion of Canada has come to a speedy and inglorious end. After a spirited and gallant fight on Saturday, in which the Fenians did no discredit to the Irish reputation for uncalculating courage, they retreated to the Niagara River by nightfall; made themselves drunk by liquor taken on empty stomachs in the early part of the night; lost their resolution before morning; attempted to recross to the American side; and were captured in the attempt by the United States' authorities, in whose custody they remain. The first act of this drama – conceived in folly, displaying gallantry in its progress – ends in a finale, to be followed probably by a tragedy.

★   ★   ★

Despite the shambles, or perhaps because of it, Fenians continued to muster at Buffalo and other points close to the border. On 6/7 June General Spear's Fenian force finally crossed into Canada from Vermont. It was a brief incursion. They

The funeral of Canadian Volunteers killed in a skirmish with the Fenians and buried in Toronto. (*Illustrated London News*)

planted the green flag at Pigeon Hill and some of the Irishmen, unpaid and hungry, looted some farms. By the 8th the advance of a strong British and militia force had driven them back across the border. President Johnson deployed Federal troops to close it behind them, ending any hopes of another such adventure.

O'Neill and his captured men remained under American arrest for only a brief period. Roberts and Sweeny were also arrested and then released. Those in Canadian hands, perhaps 80 men in total, faced a much more uncertain fate. The Irish invaders were portrayed as murderers, incendiaries and drunken brigands. There was a widespread public call for their mass execution. The Canadian authorities, however, rightly feared that the creation of martyrs would only boost Fenian support in America. The *Rochester Union* commented: 'The execution of the first man now under arrest in Canada for Fenianism will be the signal for a movement here that will wrest Canada from the men who now control it, and make it part of the American Union.' That was not a universal view in the American Press, however. The *New York Times* described the attempted invasion as 'a mere conspiracy of lawless ruffians to create international disturbance and secure plunder, under the guise and pretence of a patriotic uprising'. It concluded:

The news of this untoward event will cause disappointment among us here. If there was one thing that we Americans have prayed earnestly for since these bandit gangs were first formed, it was that every ruffian that crossed the frontier might be straightaway caught and hung. The prospect of this was a sort of compensation for the intolerable nuisance of being obliged to listen to their blather day after day.

In October those Fenians held in Toronto and Sweetsburg were put on trial. An Indiana priest, John McMahon, claimed that he had been travelling to Montreal to collect a legacy from his brother when he was captured by the Fenians and press-ganged into being their chaplain. Few believed him. He and six others were sentenced to hang on 13 December. A further 26 were acquitted, given five dollars going-home money and booted across the Suspension Bridge back onto American soil. The remainder who could prove American citizenship were quietly released before the trials. There were also reports, disputed then and now, that five Fenians were shot after summary drum-head trials on the night of 2 June.

Despite the attitude of the *New York Times*, the death sentences sparked outrage in the US, especially as one of the condemned men was a priest whose only proven action was to administer the last rites to the dead on both sides. The Canadian government commuted the sentences to twenty years' hard labour, although in the event most were released after six years. Thirty more captives, including the hapless Fort Erie pickets and others taken on the Vermont border, were tried later. They were all found guilty and imprisoned. In 1872 they were pardoned and sent home, save for 23-year-old Thomas Maxwell who had died in custody on Christmas Eve, 1869.

The Canadian expedition held the Fenians up to contempt and ridicule, and destroyed the Robert–Sweeny power bid. Much was made of their decision to stay well away from danger, confining their own activities to issuing pompous and vainglorious calls to arms. At the Philadelphia conference of the Fenian Brotherhood Stephens, the Republican hero who had arrived in America too late to stop the raid, condemned such foolish actions and 'any breach of the Neutrality Laws by which this country might be compromised, and the cause of Ireland ruined beyond redemption'.

Stephens did not stop advocating an imminent rising in Ireland itself. The Canadian episode was, he believed, a damaging distraction. He realised, however, that the proposed revolt would have to be delayed yet again because of a shortage of arms and ammunition in Fenian arsenals across the Atlantic. His caution did not go down well with American Fenians eager to halt the contemptuous laughter heard after the Canadian fiasco. They deposed him as Leader of the Brotherhood and replaced him with another Civil War veteran, Colonel Thomas J. Kelly.

Kelly and his lieutenants, all experienced soldiers, decided to go to Ireland to help lead the revolt. They headed first to London, where they began preparations for an Irish rising the following February. They hatched an audacious plot to seize arms and ammunition from the English army garrison at Chester Castle, forcibly take over all the trains in the garrison town and rush the arms by rail to the Holyhead mailboat for Ireland. Unfortunately for the Fenians, there was at least one informer in their midst.

At dawn on 11 February 1867, 1,000 Fenians began to arrive in small parties at Chester. Before any action could be taken the leaders learnt that the British authorities knew of the raid. It was immediately halted, but it was too late to stop hundreds of Irishmen being arrested in a joint police and army swoop. The chief informer was John Corydon, but there may have been others.

The disaster left 14,000 Fenians in Dublin and 20,000 in Cork desperately short of weapons. The revolt was delayed until 5 March but again they were betrayed by Corydon, who had not yet been unmasked. Several leaders were arrested but the news did not travel fast enough and there were small uprisings in Dublin, Cork, Tipperary, Drogheda, Clare and Limerick. These were easily suppressed by the Irish police force, whose diligence was rewarded by the addition of the word 'Royal' to their title. The revolt, which was meant to instigate guerrilla warfare all over Ireland, simply disintegrated. In April, far too late, the ship *Erin's Hope* left New York with Fenian officers, rifles, cannon and ammunition. Twenty-eight officers were landed at Waterford – and all were arrested almost at once.

The main participants in the disastrous Canadian invasion enjoyed different fortunes. Colonel Booker, who refused to accept blame for the Ridgeway fiasco, retired from the Volunteers in 1867 and reopened his shop in Montreal. He died four years later, aged forty-seven. John Dennis, who had abandoned his command before hearing a shot fired, faced a court-martial. The court heard evidence that he had disguised himself as a labourer, but found him not guilty. He returned to his surveying career.

In 1870 John O'Neill attempted a raid on Eccles Hill, on the border of Vermont and Quebec, with over 350 men. Forewarned, the Canadian militia force attacked them before all the Fenians were across the border. The main Fenian body returned fire from the American side. But as more Canadian reinforcements arrived, the Fenians turned and fled. The Canadian commander, Lieutenant-Colonel Osborne Smith, had to restrain his men from pursuing them on to American soil. The Canadians suffered no casualties, the Fenians mainly wounded pride. Another minor incursion was repelled two days later near Huntingdon by a combined Canadian–British force, again with no casualties. O'Neill was arrested by a US marshal, but again he was released. However, his fighting days were over and he died eight years later.

General Thomas Meagher continued as governor of Montana and tried, unsuccessfully, to become a senator. He coninued to court controversy and remained a Fenian to the end. His Irish Brigade was long held as a glorious example of what the Irish could do in arms, untarnished by the Canadian débâcle. After watching from a distance the failure of the Irish uprising, Meagher, in June 1867, set out on a gruelling 200-mile journey to Fort Benton to collect Federal muskets. He arrived on 1 July and told friends he feared assassination. His enemies later put it about that he then went on a drunken spree, a version of events still widely accepted, but he was sober enough to compose clear-headed letters to colleagues. He took a state-room on the moored steamer *G.A. Thompson*. That night several people heard a cry and a splash. A watchman said he saw a man leaning over a rail vomiting, before he fell into the water and his body sank under the keel of another boat. The body was never found. Meagher died ingloriously, though whether it was through drink, simple accident or murder remains unclear to this day.

Apart from a minor foray into Manitoba, which had no support, the Fenians' Canadian incursions were over. The Brotherhood set aside its cross-border ambitions and concentrated on rhetoric, political pressure and fund-raising. It is a process which has continued, behind different front organisations, to the present day.

A proper uprising in Ireland, followed by civil war and partial independence, would have to wait until the twentieth century.

CHAPTER NINE

The Battle of Orange Walk, Belize, 1872

'Our Queen has much reason to be annoyed.'

It was like a scene from a John Ford western movie. So-called 'Indians' surrounded a log cabin in the wilderness, attacked its occupants and tried to burn them out before being driven off with heavy losses. But this was neither the Wild West of America nor an invention of Hollywood. The venue was the Central American frontier of Belize. And the heroism involved cannot disguise the tragic nature of the events of which this siege was a bloody chapter.

★　★　★

Up to two million natives once lived within the borders of what is now Belize. The Maya built massive stone cities, including Caracol, Xunantunich and Lamanai, and farmed the lush but hostile land in between. The collapse of their great civilisation from the ninth and fifteenth centuries saw them retreat from the region to neighbouring Yucatan. When Hernan Cortes conquered Mexico in 1520 his lieutenants moved south and east, driving the Maya before them. The conquistadors had less success with Mayan settlements which had returned to the thick jungles and treacherous swamps of Belize. The Mayan chief of Chetumal, close to present-day Corozal Town, told the Spanish that their only tribute would be 'turkeys in the shape of spears and corn in the shape of arrows'. The Maya fought back throughout the next hundred years, retreating into the forest and tributaries when outgunned, then returning to burn the Spanish settlements and dismantle their Mission churches.

Daumier described the 'Indians' with admiration: 'They are tall, well-made, raw-boned, lusty, strong, and nimble of foot, long-visaged with lank black hair, look stern, hard-favoured and of a dark, coffee-coloured complexion.' Supposedly civilised soldiers had the advantage in weaponry, but the Maya knew how to hide and strike from the countless rivers, streams and alligator-infested lagoons. The Spanish never conquered Belize with arms, but the diseases they unwittingly carried with them had a much more devastating effect. Of a population of around 400,000 when the Spanish came, only an estimated two-fifths survived.

The survivors withdrew inland and the British saw few of them when they arrived around 1638. They assumed that the disease-ridden shore was largely uninhabited. Most of the early settlers were pirates and buccaneers, who raided Spanish galleons

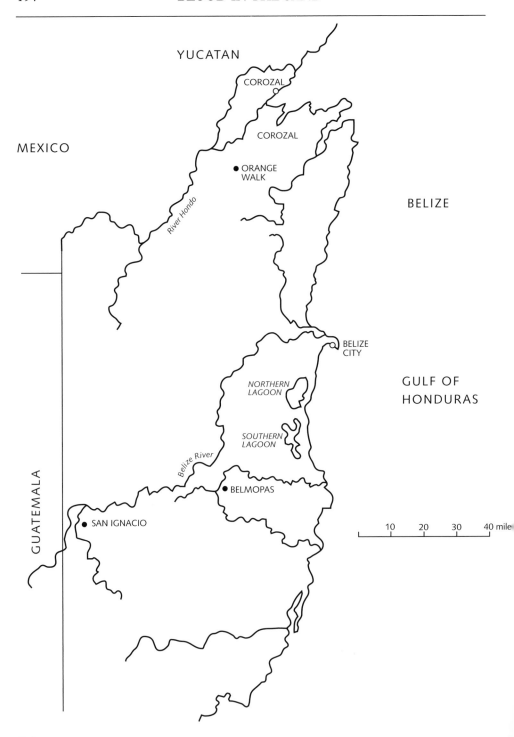

Belize.

carrying gold, silver, hardwoods and other loot from their Central American conquests. The British Settlement in the Bay of Honduras was their base and the coastal coral reefs and sandbars were their hunting-grounds, offering both cover for surprise attacks and an escape route from pursuing warships and deep-hulled vessels. Sometimes they were joined by individual native warriors. Daumier wrote:

> They are esteemed and coveted by all privateers, for one or two of them on a ship will maintain 100 men . . . They do not love the French, and the Spaniards they hate mortally. When they come among privateers they get the use of guns, and prove very good marksmen. They behave themselves very boldly in fight, and never seem to flinch or hang back. They will never yield nor give back while any of their party stand.

But the 1670 Treaty of Madrid made piracy and privateering against the Spanish much more difficult. The white settlers were encouraged to cut logwood, from which was extracted a valuable dye used to colour woollen cloth for the growing domestic market. The land was treacherous for Europeans and natives alike, but rich in resources. Swamps gave way to jungle and, finally, to mountains up to 3,675 feet high. All were crisscrossed by innumerable water-courses which provided the main transport routes. A British official reported: 'It is easy to count the rivers which throw themselves into the sea, but if a line were to be drawn parallel to the coast at a distance inland of 25 miles it would cross an infinite number of Creeks or rivulets navigable for wood and boats which, after intersecting the country, lose themselves in lakes or larger rivers.'

Britain and Spain clashed repeatedly during the eighteenth century over the rights of the British to settle in Belize. The first attack, in 1717, saw Spanish soldiers marching from what is now Guatamala. Several times the British were forced to leave after strong attacks, but each time they returned. The profits from logwood, supplemented by some piracy, were too good to abandon. British warships were repeatedly sent to protect the small communities. The settlers themselves formed irregular militias, strengthened by hired Indian warriors and African slaves from Jamaica. Gradually the British trade expanded and their settlements grew more prosperous, especially around St George's Caye. When the value of logwood began to decline, they developed a new trade in mahogany. Finally, in 1763, the Treaty of Paris gave the British the right to cut the export wood, but Spain still claimed sovereignty. In 1779 the Spanish captured St George's Caye, seizing 140 prisoners with their wives and children, and 250 slaves, all of whom were shipped to the dungeons of Havana. Most died there. The settlement remained deserted for four yeras until new treaties were signed. The loggers, or Baymen, were given the right to cut logwood only between the Hondo and Belize rivers. The settlers petitioned the British government and a new agreement was reached which allowed them to cut both logwood and mahogany as far as the Sibun river. The Spanish refused to allow them to build forts, or to do any work other than woodcutting. In 1786 the Governor of Jamaica appointed Colonel Marcus Despard as superintendant of the settlement and commander-in-chief of its defence forces. Belize had begun its long journey towards self-government.

An uneasy peace held until 1798 when the Spanish again attacked the Belize
settlements in force. The onslaught was fierce, with 32 vessels, 500 seamen and
2,000 troops, but the Baymen were better able to navigate the narrow channels and
inlets of the coast. Helped by their African slaves, the armed sloop *Merlin* and three
companies from the West India Regiment, they defeated the Spanish in the Battle of
St George's Caye. The Negro slaves, most armed only with palm spears, fought
bravely for their British masters from a flotilla of small craft. Many had been
promised their freedom if they fought well. An English correspondent wrote:

> You will be astonished to hear that our Negromen who manned the fleets gave a
> hearty cheer on coming into action, and in the midst of firing of grape kept
> upon them by the Spanish vessels, these Negroes in an undaunted manner
> rowed their boats and made every exertion to board the enemy.

The Spanish retreated after two hours of hard fighting and lost all claim to Belize.
The Maya watched the clash of the Europeans from afar, shunning the sounds of
muskets and cannon. But they did not retreat when woodcutters' camps began to
appear deep inside their inland territory. Repeated Maya attacks against the
encampments were reported and in 1802 a contingent of troops was ordered upriver
'to punish the Indians who are committing depredations upon the mahogany works'.
European arms, technology and numbers had pushed the Maya back into the forests
around San Ignacio by 1839, but their attacks continued. Some were lethal, others
not. A typical dispatch in the colony's archives, dated 17 March 1848, concerns a
raid on the mahogany works in New River Lagoon and Irish Creek, a settlement of
around 100 men and their families:

> The Indians crossed from Rio Hondo, armed with bows and arrows; several
> arrows were fired at the people at Hill Bank who were in charge of the
> provisions. The Indians were kept off by fire-arms in possession of the men
> there. No bloodshed had so far occurred, the objects of the Indians being
> confined to plunder.

Meanwhile Belize was transformed into the dominion of British Honduras. The
slaves were freed, new laws were introduced; Belize City was founded as
the administrative capital, while more towns were built with protective forts, and the
whole region flourished. Spanish power in neighbouring regions waned, however,
and Central America was thrown into a series of bloody revolts. In 1847 the Mayan
descendants in southern Yucatan rose against their Mexican rulers and Spanish
overlords in what became known as the Caste War. With bows and arrows they
defeated the local garrisons, stormed Bacalar and burnt it to the ground. A small
British naval force intervened and brokered a truce, which was promptly broken by
Spanish soldiers. The war lasted, on and off, for twenty years.

The town of Corozal was founded just inside British territory by survivors of the
Bacalar massacre, who introduced the sugar industry. The Maya in the region were
barred from owning their land, being allowed only to rent property or to live on

reservations. Most were small farmers, however, and they too prospered for a while, growing rice, corn and vegetables in North Belize. The borders of Belize and neighbouring Mexico and Guatamala were still either ill-defined or hotly contested. The refugees caused further strain between the British and the Mexican administration. Mexican officials complained that some of Corozal's inhabitants returned across the border to attack their former masters. The Commandant of Bacalar wrote to the British Superintendant:

> An attack was made on the 22nd instant at Juan Luis, Cayo Obispo [sic] and other places. Robberies were committed, murders committed and many other atrocities perpetrated. On the 24th instant Chac was surrounded and a poor man burnt alive. Troops sent succeeded in driving them out. Many fled back to British Territory.

He asked the Superintendant to 'endeavour to prevent a recurrence, as it might be found necessary on a future occasion to pursue them into British Territory which would affect the friendliness hitherto existing between the two Governments'. He was told in reply that the British would do their utmost to 'restrain Spanish and English alike' from crossing the Rio Hondo to join what was effectively civil war in Yucatan. But the Mexicans were warned that any cross-border incursions by Mexican forces, or by any others, would be met with 'the promptest and most decided steps to punish the offending parties'.

Back across the border Indian outrage at the harsh tactics employed by Mexican soldiers erupted again in what became known as the Yucatan Indian Mutiny in 1857. A force of Chinchenha Indians slaughtered 1,800 Spaniards at Tekax. Bacalar was again seized and its streets became a morgue. The Yucatan rebels established their own fledgling republic and the frontier was in flames as the Mexican government savagely suppressed it. An Indian raiding party killed 16 Britons south of the Rio Hondo. More raiders followed them across the border, menacing Corozal and the British settlements of Orange Walk, New River and Spanish Creek. Envoys sent to deal with them were abused at the Temple of the Speaking Cross. Parties of braves several hundred strong attacked isolated communities and melted back into the forest when confronted with troops or organised woodcutters. The sporadic fighting dragged on without conclusion, crisscrossing the deep and sluggish Rio Hondo.

The Belize administration's Blue Book for 1856 noted:

> The Hondo is interesting as being the boundary between this territory and Mexico; or more correctly – between us and the revived Maya republic which is now supreme in Southern Yucatan. The one side presents a scene of total ruin and devastation. Not a house standing, not a Spaniard left alive. The other is still happily enlivened by the industry of the English woodcutters.

In 1864 Corozal, by now a town of over 4,500 citizens, was again raided by Icaiche Indians, with three Britons murdered and 24 kidnapped. They and other European captives were ransomed. The leader of the raiders was Marcos Canul, a chief who rapidly acquired legendary status. He styled himself 'General' and claimed he had the authority of the Mexican government, which still laid claim to the frontier region of British Honduras. He demanded rent from the woodcutters, who regarded his demands as blackmail. Many, however, paid his 'protection money'. The colony's new governor, John Austin, insisted that Mexico relinquish all claims to any part of British Honduras and annul any commission, if any existed, held by Canul. Campbell Scarlett, the British Minister in Mexico City, was given such assurances – but they were then withdrawn. Months of feverish diplomatic activity followed and Scarlett came close to winning Mexico's recognition of the Rio Hondo boundary between British Honduras and Yucatan. The negotiations collapsed when the execution of the Emperor Maximillian severed diplomatic relations between Britain and Mexico.

Canul was spurred to greater activity by the wrangle over Mexico's claim to 'British' soil. He believed the land belonged to his people, although he found it convenient to wave the Mexican flag. In May 1866 he attacked the mahogany camp at Qualm Hill on the Rio Bravo with 125 of his followers. Two men were killed and 79 prisoners taken, including a number of women and children. Canul demanded 12,000 dollars ransom. The British Honduras Company demanded military protection. Governor Austin believed that the woodcutters were themselves to blame for straying outside their boundaries and failing to pay the tribes rent, which had previously been agreed. He asked a leading citizen, Mr Von Ohlafen, to act as intermediary. This former Prussian officer managed to beat down Canul's ransom to 2,000 dollars, a sum which was raised by public subscription. The prisoners were released after a month's captivity.

Later that year there was an even more serious incident. In the western part of the colony around 1,000 Indians, also refugees from Yucatan who had little wish to become British subjects, established several small towns, of which San Pedro was the largest. Its mayor, Ascension Ek, was supplied with arms by the British as defence against attacks. But a British reconnaissance patrol discovered that Ek was acting in collusion with Canul, and that the guns supplied were to be turned on the colony's forces. At the end of December an expedition under Major MacKay was sent to drive Canul and his new allies from San Pedro. The column walked straight into an ambush. The *Official Report* said:

> On approaching San Pedro after 14 hours march by truck passes rendered almost impassable by heavy and continuous rain, the column, which appears to have been in no sort of fighting formation, and was marching without advance or flank guards, was suddenly and heavily attacked from the bush by Indians estimated at between 300 and 400 strong, from all sides, Major MacKay, it appears, attempted to lead his men into the bush in a counter-attack, but failed to make way. After an action lasting half an hour, having lost five men killed and sixteen wounded, Major MacKay gave the order to retire.

MacKay later claimed that his men were exhausted by the long march and that the dense bush hid the enemy. The column was forced to flee, leaving behind all their baggage. The Civil Commissioner, Mr Rhys, was also abandoned to his fate in the confusion. Governor Austin bitterly accused MacKay of cowardice, particularly for leaving Rhys behind. A court of inquiry held later in Jamaica found that MacKay, far from being a coward, had 'shewed no lack of presence of mind or courage'. But he was to blame for not providing an advance guard and displayed 'lamentable lack of firmness and judgement in sounding the retreat'. The court found that his men had 'behaved throughout in a most creditable manner'.

The defeat of a British force caused shame and panic in the colony and an armed steamer was sent to patrol the Rio Hondo, although only after much haggling over who was to pay for it. Late in January the Governor of Jamaica and overall commander of the region, Sir John Grant, arrived to assess the situation, bringing with him reinforcements from the West India Regiment, 13 white officers and 300 disciplined black men in red uniforms under the command of Lieutenant-Colonel Harley. Canul's forces seized the villages of Indian Church and Mount Hope. On 9 February Harley hit back with an all-out attack on San Pedro. His column marched for four days over swollen rivers and hard roads in continuous rain before they reached the small town. A rocket tube firing six-pound incendiary missiles was used for the first time. Canul's men, seeing the terrible effect, fled into the forest. So too did Ek, who left letters laying claim to rent for the disputed border areas. Harley left a letter condemning the murder of Mr Rhys. The column moved on, marching 32 miles in 11 hours. San Jose was taken and burnt, with three casualties. The troops found some of Rhys's personal equipment and loot from Indian Church. Mayan villages, provision stores and granaries were burnt in a bid to starve the natives into either flight or submission. Martial law was declared in the region but lifted in April when it seemed that peace was resumed.

Across the border Canul recovered from the shock of defeat and rebuilt his forces. He again launched repeated attacks on Corozal, which the British refused to garrison fully despite its increasing importance as a trade centre. In 1870 the town was captured by Canul without bloodshed, its white Yucatan and Indian inhabitants being disinclined to fight. Canul marched into the town with 116 men, shouting 'Mexico forever'. Finally a strong detachment of troops, supported by the warship *Lapwing*, was dispatched and the Indians melted back across the border. Canul still would not give in, and by 1872 the area north of the colony was a virtual no-go area, with trade at a standstill and settlements on perpetual armed stand-by. Canul then decided on one last push to drive out the white men. His target was Orange Walk, the largest settlement in the north, a logging centre 66 miles from Belize City.

*   *   *

Canul was a charismatic leader, a natural guerrilla fighter who knew the country and the value of swift, surprise strikes. On 31 August 1872 he led around 150 warriors across the Rio Hondo near Corosalito. His targets were the settlements at Orange Walk, August Pine Ridge and Water Bank. At the latter place they sought out and killed a Spanish woodcutter called Gonzalez before camping for the night.

At 8 a.m. the next day they advanced on Orange Walk, which contained a garrison of 38 soldiers of the 1st West India Regiment under Lieutenant Smith. As the Indians approached the outlying buildings the alarm was raised; seeing that they were heavily outnumbered, the garrison barricaded themselves within their one-roomed barracks, constructed from stout logs. The military report to the governor said:

> The Indians opened a heavy fire from the buildings around and occupied piles of logwood, dumped ready for embarkation, which lay by the riverside about 75 yards from the barracks. The troops replied, using at first the 20 rounds which had fortunately been issued to every man, and later ammunition from the portable magazine which Lieutenant Smith and Sergeant Belazario very gallantly succeeded in bringing into the room.

Smith was shot and wounded after 10 minutes of the firefight but remained at his post for two hours until weakness forced him to relinquish active command to Belazario and the detachment's surgeon, Doctor Edge. The attackers crawled to within 25 yards of the barracks and kept up their heavy fire for six hours. The defenders picked off their enemies one by one. Canul, seeing that his men could not dislodge the soldiers, then tried to burn them out. The kitchen, standing just 5 yards from the barracks building, was successfully fired and burnt to ashes. The military report continued:

> At about 2.30 p.m. the fire of the troops began to tell and a party of Indians commenced to retire. Sergeant Belazario led six men round to the other side and drove the Indians out of their positions [in the logwood pile], killing three and wounding many more. A general retirement of the Indians commenced and the troops followed them up as far as the outskirts of the town; they were then recalled and commenced to prepare a stockade in anticipation of a renewed attack.

Inside the garrison almost half the men had been hit: 2 soldiers died and 14 other men, apart from Smith, were wounded. Most accounts agree that the Indians lost 15 dead and many more wounded. Canul himself was seriously hurt, and lived just long enough to be dragged back across the Hondo. The so-called 'War of the Colours' was over.

Canul's place was taken by Rafael Chan, who wrote to the Lieutenant-Governor, William Wellington Cairns, asking for peace. He urged that the faults committed by his predecessor Canul be forgiven. Chan protested that he had always advocated peace with the British but had to obey his chief while he was the latter's second-in-command. He craved the pardon of 'our Queen who has much reason to be annoyed'. Cairns agreed, but there was little need. The Indians had disappeared and were no longer a threat. Cairns told his Legislative Council that 'the lesson lately taught at Orange Walk by both Civil and Military defenders of that post [were] not likely to be lost upon them.'

Just in case, however, he strengthened the garrisons in the North, improved their defences and ordered a road built from Corozal to Orange Walk to render the route fit for the quick transport of troops, light guns and stores. Corozal became the colony's main military headquarters, in place of Belize City; Orange Walk became its second garrison, with a minimum of 3 officers and 50 men housed in new barracks behind new earthworks. Fort Cairns was erected a few years later. The members of the Legislative Council, safe in their houses in Belize City, were unwilling to levy extra taxes for the provision of a permanent frontier force, but the British government insisted they should finance their own defence. Diplomatic pressure was put on Mexico to 'restore order' on their side of the Hondo. The last major Indian incursion was in 1874; this time they were unarmed, starving and begging for food.

★　　★　　★

There were a few small border raids after the Battle of Orange Walk, but these were regarded as simple banditry. A group of Icaiche Indians kidnapped several civilians but their chief, Santiago Pech, was seized and held as a hostage for their safe return. In August 1879 the governor told his council that 'the Colony has been almost free from anxiety in regard to Indian raids; no bar exists to trade and barter with the various Tribes by which we are surrounded'.

The territory, which had been subordinated to Jamaica since 1862, became a separate colony in 1884. In the preceding years its population was swelled by Chinese labourers, sepoys from India and former Confederates who arrived after the American Civil War. A proclamation declared: 'No Indians will be at liberty to reside upon or occupy or cultivate any land without previous payment or engagement to pay rent whether to the Crown or the owner of the land.'

The Indians who returned to Belize were the poor and dispossessed, and most became Catholic. Their customs intermingled with other cultures as they inter-married and became subsumed into the general Creole population, which remains the majority of Belize's people. The colony suffered civil strife rather than military attack. In 1894 mahogany workers rioted when their wages were cut as a result of currency devaluation. They were easily subdued by visiting British soldiers. In 1919 demobilised Creole soldiers, returning from service in the First World War with the British West India Regiment, rioted in protest against high prices and the lack of both jobs and homes. They proved harder to subdue and order was only achieved by the imposition of martial law.

During the 1950s Belize, like much of the remaining British Empire, saw the growth of an independence movement. Britain granted the colony internal self-government in 1964 but kept control of its defence because of Guatamala's continuing claims on its territory. Several times Guatamala threatened invasion – and was only kept at bay by the presence of 8,000 British servicemen and RAF fighters. Full independence was finally achieved on 21 September 1981, with Britain continuing to provide defence guarantees. The descendants of the proud Maya, having lost their land and their freedom, now enjoy some control over their destinies once again.

CHAPTER TEN

The Hut Tax War, Sierra Leone, 1898

'Here the Englishman must give the black man the lead.'

The poll-tax riots and non-payment campaigns across Britain in 1989 led, indirectly, to the downfall of premier Margaret Thatcher. As she left Downing Street, sobbing, she may have reflected that there were many precedents – not least the civil disobedience that followed the imposition of a similar tax in a British colony a little more than 90 years previously. In Sierra Leone, however, the outcome was a lot more lethal.

★   ★   ★

Portuguese seamen named the rocky peninsula at the mouth of West Africa's Rokel River the Serra Lyoa, or Lion Mountain, because of its resemblance to the beast. This name was gradually corrupted to Sierra Leone, covering the hinterland of dense forest and grassy plain. From the later fifteenth century European vessels traded manufactured goods for slaves and ivory from local chieftains. The two largest tribes in the following centuries were the Mendi, who gradually inhabited central and southern Sierra Leone, and the longer-established Temni who occupied the north. The Temni were subdivided into over 40 chiefdoms, each ruled by a chief and his council. They were farmers and fishermen, fighters and slavers. Both men and women belonged to secret societies which helped to maintain law and order, and settled disputes. A later British visitor claimed:

> The greater part of the natives lived in stockaded towns guarded by armed men night and day; each chief was in mutual dread of his neighbour, and intestinal broils and organized raids for the purpose of obtaining slaves and plunder were common. Human sacrifices and cannibalism were practised, together with all the barbarous customs of the savage.

Although English trading posts were established on Bunce and York islands during the seventeenth century, the newcomers came under the protection of friendly chiefs and trading partners. Much of the country was deemed uninhabitable by white men, while the coast was the haunt of pirates and slave dealers, until it was cleared by the British Navy. Both Britons and Temni were content to trade, but otherwise left each other alone.

That began to change in 1787 when the English abolitionist Granville Sharp embarked on a scheme to found a colony for freed slaves, which he called 'The Province of Freedom'. The first group arrived that year, and the following spring a Royal Navy captain, John Taylor, bought some land from a Temni subchief called King Tom. His successor, King Jimmy, drove the former slaves away in 1789. The survivors, sponsored by William Wilberforce and the other benefactors of the Sierra Leone Company, created a new settlement at what later became Freetown in 1791. The company brought freed slaves, English-speaking and mainly literate Christians, from Nova Scotia and later from Jamaica.

At the beginning of 1808, following the British abolition of the slave trade, London took control of Freetown for use as a naval base against slavers and as a haven for slaves freed from vessels captured in mid-Atlantic. In less than sixty years the Royal Navy brought in over 50,000 such 'recaptives'. More came from all over Africa. The British government, unwilling to expand its colonial interests in West Africa, encouraged them to create a self-governing, Christian community. Schools for boys and girls were established, while the freed slaves and their children set up their own trading stores, bartering European goods for palm products from the neighbouring tribes. Treaties of friendship were exchanged with the tribes. Gradually, however, the British extended their authority along the coast, fearful that the area would be snatched by the French, who laid claim to northern Sierra Leone from across the Guinea border. Frontiers were agreed but the ever-present French threat led, in 1896, to the proclamation of a British Protectorate.

The Temni chiefs were not alarmed. They had slowly relinquished their rights to make war, take slaves and sign foreign treaties, but in their own lands they still retained absolute power. The loss of some authority was more than balanced by the boost in trade which followed the building of roads throughout the interior. They were also fearful of falling into the hands of the French, having seen what that nation was capable of elsewhere. They only became seriously concerned when the British established travelling commissioners and the Frontier Police Force, both designed to keep the peace in disputed areas. They took over from the chiefs responsibility for free passage and trade along the roads. The rights of chiefs to freely enter Freetown were also curtailed, robbing them of direct access to the governor, Sir Frederick Cardew, to voice any grievances. Such grievances were exacerbated by the arrogant behaviour of the Frontier Police, some of whom were escaped Temni slaves who used their new powers to flog, plunder and wrongly imprison their old masters. New regulations only increased the bitterness. A new court system was set up which the chiefs had earlier agreed to, only belatedly realising that it robbed them of the right to try their own domestic cases, including those concerning land titles, witchcraft, slave dealing, raiding, murder and rape. It was the beginning of the end of the chieftains' political power, and they knew it. One of them, Pa Suba, complained: 'The king of a country however small, if he cannot settle small matters, is no longer king.' The regulations also gave the government rights over mineral exploitation and what it termed 'waste lands'. The

Sketches by Lieutenant H.E. Green depicting the rising in Sierra Leone. Clockwise from top left: women waving off a patrol; Bai Bureh; a patrol returning with prisoners; dancers rejoicing over the capture of a rebel chief, Hey Nani, a minor insurgent leader. (*Illustrated London News*)

Temni chiefs, employing English lawyers, interpreted the regulations to mean the 'total dispossession of their country'.

Such objections paled into insignificance compared with the next phase of Cardew's programme. London made no financial contribution to the running of the Protectorate, and Cardew needed to raise money. His solution was a tax on all houses, from the smallest huts of the poor to the more extensive structures of the chiefs. The tax was initially fixed at 5 shillings a year for two-roomed huts and 10 shillings for larger properties, later reduced to a flat 5 shillings for all houses of two rooms or more. Cardew's ignorance of the tribes under his 'protection' could not have been better demonstrated. Having lost much of their tribal powers, the chiefs saw the tax as a means of depriving them of authority over their own homes. To them it meant having to pay the government for a place to sleep; it meant no longer owning their own property. The proposed seizure of 'waste land' also included sacred grounds and tribal meeting-places, all of which the chiefs regarded, if not as their own, then as communal property.

The chiefs initially opposed the tax through a series of legal petitions. They professed their loyalty to the queen and said they understood the expense the government had undergone to keep the country prosperous and at peace. But they complained that the tax was an unacceptable infringement of ancient rights, reducing a tribal chief and his council to the rank of peasants who could, under the new arrangement, face imprisonment or flogging for non-payment. Most blamed Cardew directly. They claimed that his administration was 'so unlike the spirit of the English people, with whom they have had to deal now over one hundred and ten years'. One later reported: 'There is a difference between the white people who come now and those before; those that come now do not respect the Chiefs.'

Cardew would not listen. He refused to believe that a land rich in rubber and gum, and with good transport to the trading centres, was too poor to sustain his tax. He was also contemptuous of the chiefs and barely bothered to hide that contempt. He believed that any isolated resistance could quickly be suppressed by the Frontier Police, which had recently been strengthened to 10 officers, 40 NCOs and 550 privates armed with Martini-Enfield rifles. He wrote to the Secretary of State: 'I do not apprehend that the chiefs will combine to forcibly resist the collection of the tax, for they lack cohesion and powers of organisation, and there are too many jealousies between them for concerted action. . . .' His district commissioners were also dismissive. One wrote:

> Great discontent has existed amongst the chiefs since the abolition of slavery. Nearly all their wealth formerly consisted of their slaves, and the chiefs derived a large income from the sale of their surplus stock. . . . The tax is not peculiarly obnoxious or opposed to the habits and customs of the people, inasmuch as their own chiefs levy similar contributions on their subjects when they wish to raise money for any big event such as the coronation of a paramount chief, or when they consider that there is too much money amongst their people.

Such reports from Temni country convinced Cardew that there would, at most, be surly but passive resistance, which could quickly be dealt with by rounding up and jailing a few ringleaders. He was quickly proved wrong. Cardew was fifty-eight and a product of Sandhurst and the Bengal Army, where he reached the rank of colonel. No one doubted his courage: as a young officer he was mentioned in dispatches during fighting on the North West Frontier and during the Zulu War. He had served also in South Africa, China, the Transvaal and Natal. He had been Governor and Commander-in-Chief of Sierra Leone since 1894. He was a keen tactician with a good reputation for logistics and for putting first the welfare of those under his command. But he was also a classic late Victorian, ready to trample over any native sensibilities in the name of progress.

Nor was he able to grasp the objections of the Sierra Leone traders and the Freetown Press, all of whom added their voices to the clamour of discontent from the bush. Cardew – and, to be fair, most of his advisers – regarded the traders as unscrupulous crooks who exploited the natives by keeping them in ignorance of the value of the coin of the realm. One district commissioner reported that the general view was that the Hut Tax would 'ruin the traders as the natives would no longer deal to such an extent in goods when they found that they would have to pay a certain amount of coin annually to the Government, and that when the natives learned the value of coin they would send to Freetown and purchase goods for themselves'. The Press were regarded simply as trouble-makers who exaggerated the degree of opposition to the tax.

Conflict was now inevitable, partly due to the emergence of one of West Africa's most renowned warriors.

★   ★   ★

Kebalai, a veteran warrior with some Temni blood in his veins, took the title by which history knows him, Bai Bureh, meaning 'a man of importance'. He was the leader of a loose alliance of Temni chiefdoms in the northern region around the Great Scarcies River. His first battle honours were gained in 1865 when he helped to lead a holy war called by the Islamic leader Bokhari. He was prominent in intermittent tribal and religious conflicts over the next twenty years. In 1886 he became chief of Kasseh, a small chiefdom 25 miles from Port Lokko. His influence spread, leading to several diplomatic clashes with the British, who on at least two occasions tried to arrest him. In 1892 the British reluctantly recruited Bai Bureh and his warriors to take part in an expedition against the Susu leader Karimu, whom the French were encouraging to revolt to strengthen their claims to northern Sierra Leone, on the grounds that the British had lost control. Bai Bureh and his men greatly impressed British officers with their discipline and enthusiasm. Bai Bureh, for his part, closely watched the tactics of the Frontier Police and the recently deployed West India Regiment. His observations were of great value in the conflict to come.

The Times later reported that Bai Bureh was not like the other chiefs who negotiated happily with British officials, giving up some authority in return for roads, better trade and other advantages of civilisation: 'With men of the Bai Bureh type, who are constantly starting up and, by the aid of either religious fanaticism or of a warlike personality, contrive to acquire a large following, it is practically impossible to deal satisfactorily.' But the newspaper conceded: 'He is a clever and experienced fighting man, and reputed to be an adept in the native system of military organisation.'

Bureh was by then a famous war chief, while his men were experienced bush fighters. A Frontier Police officer, C. Braithwaite Wallis, wrote:

> If Bureh was an unusually smart man, so did the Timini [sic] prove to be. Savages they might be, but even in their way of fighting they betrayed such admirable qualities as are not always to be found in the troops of the civilised nations. They loved their chief, and remained loyal to him to the very last, while they understand bush fighting as well as you and I do our very alphabet.

Temni boys were trained for war, serving several grades of apprenticeship with proven warriors. Warriors were recruited for specific campaigns from among allied tribes and were rewarded with a share of the plunder and domestic slaves. A correspondent wrote:

> All along the West Coast the native tribes have a regular system of mobilization, and when it is completed 'war-paths' are cut through the bush and connected by communicating paths. When concentration is desired the war-drum is beaten and scattered parties of war-boys hurry by the war-paths to the rendezvous. Thousands can be collected in this manner in two or three hours.

The tribesmen were mostly armed with Birmingham trade guns, but some weapons of greater precision had been obtained. A year earlier the British had banned the importation of arms, but this royal proclamation was widely defied. It was a war-like society, held in check by the British until Bai Bureh was ready to challenge their authority.

Bai Bureh, now approaching old age, was insulted by the arrogance of the British. He saw the old order that rewarded fighting men being replaced by slavish allegiance to a foreign flag. Late in 1896 the British ordered him to the small garrison town of Karene to help build the barracks. He complied, ordering his men to complete the work, but he spent the next year coordinating resistance to the British and their hated hut tax. He sent his sub-chiefs through the chiefdoms of Sierra Leone, recruiting warriors. Other chiefs reached private agreements with him to block river traffic and barricade the roads. Spies were sent out to note the strength and numbers of British garrisons.

Meanwhile the British were already experiencing great difficulty in collecting the hut tax. Captain W.S. Sharpe, District Commissioner at Karene, even had trouble levying it from his own police contingent for their rented accommodation. Sharpe moved on to Port Lokko, the largest town in his district and the main trading depot on a tributary of the Rokell river. The local chiefs stalled and it soon became clear they had no intention of paying. Bai Bureh was nearby, ready to aid them against any British show of force. On 9 January 1898 Sharpe lost all patience. He summoned the chiefs to a meeting, watched by a thousand of their resentful followers. The main chief, Bokari Bamp, again refused to impose the tax on local traders who rented their homes from him. He and four sub-chiefs were arrested and convicted that same day of incitement of disobedience. They were sent as prisoners to Freetown and put to labour as felons in the town gaol. Their treatment roused bitter indignation. Bokari later eloquently expressed that bitterness:

> Since the time of our ancestors up to the present time there has never been such disgrace to one of our Chiefs as this prison dress which I wear. No Chief crowned by the Queen has been put into prison without disobeying the law, except this year. We have had to break stones. As I am telling you now, my heart is bleeding with tears. We have been brought to prison by the Hut Tax and our country is being destroyed.

A British puppet, Sorie Bunki, was installed as the new chief of a largely deserted town. The next night Bunki, clearly terrified, told Sharpe that Bai Bureh intended to attack the town and slay him as a usurper. Sharpe took the reports seriously. He wrote to Governor Cardew saying that he could not return to Karene until Port Lokko was secure. He next wrote to Bai Bureh, ordering him to levy the hut tax in Kasseh. When Bureh refused even to see the messenger, Sharpe prepared to arrest him. Sensibly, he first asked Freetown to send more police reinforcements. Both sides waited uneasily until the fresh contingent arrived in the town under the command of Major Tarbet. Sharpe now determined to carry out his threat. His police column set off on the march, accompanied every step of the way by the jeers of Temni warriors lining the route. Some warriors hurled stones from slingshots. One stone, thrown by a Temni called Thambaili, hit a British officer on the head – and this blow was later credited with starting the war. Tarbet ordered his rearguard to open fire. His advance guard, hearing the shots, rushed back to help, leaving their carriers unprotected. The Temni fell on them, killed some and carried off others to be sold as slaves in French territory in return for gunpowder.

The planned arrest of Bai Bureh was put on hold as the British and their policemen were harassed all the way to the village of Kagbantama, where they were met with another British party from Karene. The entire countryside around Port Lokko and Karene was now openly in support of Bai Bureh. Almost every village between the two towns was eerily deserted, and the road itself was only passable by large and well-armed parties. A small police garrison was left in Port Lokko. The policemen, poorly commanded by an inexperienced junior officer, panicked and killed an innocent citizen, the nephew of Bokari Bamp, who refused to hand over his sword. A subsequent inquiry found that he was 'practically murdered in cold blood' by a policeman who struck the lad on the back of the neck with the butt of his rifle. The unfortunate Bunki deserted and headed for Freetown. He was overtaken by townspeople who saw him as a traitor. His body was thrown into the Rokell river, weighed down with stones.

By 19 February Bureh's forces had completely cut the British lines of communication between Karene and Port Lokko, and even threatened the route to

The West India Regiment with a seven-pounder in action on the Meli river. (*Illustrated London News*)

Freetown. Three days later Tarbet led a 48-strong raiding party to burn Temni canoes at Bokupru as punishment for closing river traffic. His force was badly cut up by warriors who first retreated ahead of the British rifles, then silently circled around to hit the police as they attempted to re-cross the river. It was the first indication that the Temni were both well disciplined in guerrilla warfare and better armed than the British, with trade guns bought from the French. It was now clear that this was no simple policing action, but out-and-out warfare.

★   ★   ★

At Karene the garrison of Frontier Police was under siege, surrounded on all sides. Incorrect rumours reached Freetown that the town had been burnt. On 24 February Governor Cardew dispatched a company of regular soldiers under Major Norris with a seven-pounder, a Maxim machine-gun, camp equipment and 500 carriers. Even that number of porters was insufficient for the terrain and Norris was forced to leave some of the baggage at Robat. The column was unopposed on its four-day march to Karene, but was constantly trailed by warriors who stayed just out of range. Sharpe handed control of the Karene district to Norris, who promptly declared martial law.

After a few days Norris marched his force to Port Lokko in order to establish proper communications with Freetown. This time his column was constantly harassed, suffering 20 men wounded including 2 officers and 7 privates. The Temni

suffered severely, according to the official report, because of their foolhardly tactics
of rush attacks which exposed them to the rifle fire of the West Indian Regiment
soldiers. However, the warriors quickly learnt their lesson and did not repeat the
mistake. Once at Port Lokko Norris sent a carrier pigeon to Freetown requesting
two more companies. Early the following morning an attack on the town's *laager* was
repulsed by the Frontier Police with the loss of only one wounded carrier. Further
attacks were discouraged by shells from the gun-launch H.M.S. *Alecto*. Later that
day Major Stansfield with one company arrived on board the steamer *Countess of
Derby*. Norris again sent urgent messages demanding another company at least as
the entire district appeared to be in open revolt. His aim was to station one company
apiece in Karene and Port Lokko, with the third acting as a flying column to keep
open communications between the two. The third company, with 215 carriers and
another seven-pounder, arrived on 9 March.

After further unsuccessful attacks on the two towns, the Temni concentrated on
attacking the British columns employed in keeping open supply and
communications routes. They fired from ambush – seemingly with an inexhaustible
supply of ammunition – and rarely exposed themselves. They learnt to pick off the
white officers rather than the West Indian soldiers. Bai Bureh and his war-chiefs
developed bush-fighting into what would later be called guerrilla warfare. The
British front-line commanders had too few fighting men and too much baggage to
do anything but stay on the defensive. The only aggressive action during that March
had serious repercussions. A flying column under Major Burke was sent out from
Port Lokko to destroy every village along the road which showed any sign of
hostility to the British. There was no opposition on the first day, as Bai Bureh had
concentrated his forces from the village of Mahera onward. As the column
approached Mahera on the second day it met a ferocious fusilade from the trees.
After a full day's fighting, against warriors led personally by Bai Bureh, the column's
heavier firepower allowed Burke to take the village but his casualties were beginning
to mount. On the third day Bai Bureh held his men back until the column
approached Kagbantama. There the British found heavy stockades blocking the
approach roads, from which the Temni attacked in numbers. Burke was hard
pressed to resist. After several hours the Temni did retreat, but Burke's force was by
now too laden with wounded to give chase. When the warriors realised they were
not being followed they set fire to the grass on the windward side of the road,
hoping to engulf the British. Burke's men swiftly ignited the bush to the leeward side
of the path to create a firebreak. The countryside was soon swept by flames. The
column, choking and smoke-blinded, sat out the inferno through a lurid night. The
next day the column moved off again, meeting stiff resistance at the stockaded
towns of Romaron and Katenti. Burke's men were able to deploy their machine-gun
to good effect, and from then on the Temni confined their attacks to sniping.

When Cardew heard reports of the march he was alarmed, not by the risk of
massacre that his men had faced, but by the systematic burning of towns and
villages by the forces of the queen. He feared that such tactics would permanently
alienate the civilian population. He ordered Sharpe and Norris to confine such
scorched-earth methods to Bai Bureh's strongholds. The two officers closest to the

An officer and troops rushing a stockade. (*Illustrated London News*)

action, however, were reluctant to obey. They believed such tactics to be their only option, given their own small numbers and the fact that the whole countryside was up in arms against them. Cardew got his way only because Temni resistance was now so strong that the British were forced back on the defensive. Norris reported that it would be impossible to defeat Bai Bureh with just the Frontier Police and three companies of soldiers, of whose officers more than half had been killed, wounded or incapacitated by sickness. He asked for greater use of the heavily armed West Indian Regiment. Cardew again disagreed, arguing that the Regiment was better employed manning the garrisons while the more mobile Frontier Police could be deployed in the field. Officers seethed as Cardew constantly interfered for political rather than military reasons. Moreover, he repeatedly under-estimated the strength of Bai Bureh's well-armed forces and the difficulties of a terrain which was hostile in terms of both geography and population.

Such over-confidence was seen at first-hand by Major Stansfield when he led a column charged with ferrying large numbers of sick soldiers, police and carriers from Karena. He was forced back by the sheer weight of numbers opposing him, while his own soldiers were hampered by the need to safeguard their stretcher cases. Cardew could no longer ignore or under-rate the peril. Consequently he sent Colonel Bosworth, the commander of all British troops in West Africa, to take a fourth company to Karene and assume command of operations.

Bosworth, a cautious man, decided to wait at Port Lokko for reinforcements from Captain Carr Smith, but three days later word arrived that due to a strong attack at Matiti he had been forced to retreat. Bosworth decided to press on to relieve Karene. He suffered heavy resistance from the Temni warriors at Malal, Romeni and Kagbantama, and lost 35 men dead or wounded. The column, bloody, parched and exhausted, did not reach Karene until late that night. Bosworth stumbled into the beleaguered town's British headquarters, collapsed and died of 'heat apoplexy'.

His successor was a career soldier already en route to the war zone. Colonel John Willoughby Astell Marshall was a 44-year-old veteran of operations across West Africa, including the Gambia and the Ashanti wars, during which he had served with distinction and was mentioned in dispatches three times. His colonelcy was a field promotion. On 1 April he travelled on board *Alecto* to Port Lokko. In the river port, long deserted by the civilian population, he found the troops and Frontier Police demoralized, the hospital full of sick and wounded and the officers exhausted by constant fighting and sniping. In the previous two weeks eight officers had been either killed or seriously wounded. They told Marshall that as the rainy season had already begun it would be impossible to provision Karene and that the garrison there should be withdrawn. Major H.C. Bourke reported:

The men here at present cannot be used for anything except to garrison this place; they are nearly all suffering from fever and could not march or do any hard work; they are therefore not available for sending out as a flying column or any like duty. I am still more of the opinion from what I have learnt here that Karene should be evacuated and at as early a date as possible. The whole time of the expedition is spent in sending convoys of supplies up there, each time with the result that more and more men are killed and wounded; at present there are about 40 or 50 wounded there, which number will of course increase as long as we keep sending up supplies to that place. Out of the six companies in this district, not more than four are really available for duty, owing to the amount of casualties which have occurred in conveying supplies and communicating with Karene. Officers' and men's lives have been wasted in the most futile manner, in my opinion, in maintaining this station, with the result that the enemy appears to be more vigorous and in greater numbers than ever.

Marshall reported: 'It was evident that the course hitherto adopted, that of sending columns up from Port Lokko to Karene, could not be continued indefinitely without involving the sacrifice of the life of every officer in the battalion and those of a great number of NCOs and men.' Marshall would not, however, countenance a withdrawal from Karene which would have enhanced the power of the rebel chiefs, but he agreed that 'the delay caused in communicating between the posts gave the enemy ample time to complete new stockades, so that each force moving to the relief of Karene met with as much resistance as the force which had preceded it'. He decided to establish two intermediate posts between Port Lokko and Karene, reducing the length of marches and providing flying columns with several bases. This plan he put into effect immediately, establishing one post at Romani, 15 miles from Port Lokko, which swiftly took delivery of 18 days' supplies for 400 men and 'an equal number of carriers'. But the creation of another post at Kagbantama proved a tougher task.

On 7 April two companies of West Indian soldiers marched to Romani and camped for the night. The following morning the column split, taking two parallel paths to Kagbantama, followed three hours later by a protected convoy under Major Donovan. The column following the main road under Major Bourke, already the holder of a Distinguished Service Order, was forced to attack 12 strong stockades grouped in twos and threes on either side. In his graphic official report Marshall described the difficulties facing the British and their men throughout the war:

These stockades are composed of short logs ranging from 10 to 14 inches in diameter, or sometimes even more. The logs are imbedded in the ground to a depth of between two and three feet, leaving a length of six feet above ground, and are solidly bound together. In front of this large boulders of latterite stone are piled to a thickness of between three to four feet. Funnels made of pieces of bamboo are pushed through to form a row of loop-holes near the ground, and others are placed at different heights above them. Inside a trench of four feet is dug, which gives absolute protection to those firing below. These stockades are placed in dense bush at from 7 to 10 yards from the pathway. It is absolutely impossible for European eyes to discern them by an outward sign; occasionally an exceptionally quick-sighted native will discover the locality of a stockade by some indication, such as a dead twig or some drooping leaves overhead. The places mostly chosen are the crossing of fords and rivers, thick gullies, a sharp turn in the road, the top or bottom of a hill, so long as it commands the path, and the densest bush in the vicinity of their towns. They are often built in groups, giving mutual support. The shells of the seven-pounder break to pieces on coming in contact with these boulders, but the morale effect of the gun is good. A sheltered line of retreat down some small slope leading to a pathway cut in rear enables the defenders to retreat in comparative safety; owing to the density of the bush it is impossible to rush them as it would take 5 to 10 minutes to cut through the bush to the stockades, during which time the assailants would be under the direct fire of the enemy at very close range. Our only plan is to engage them in front while flanking parties cut their way into the bush. It was found necessary, whenever possible, to burn the woodwork, as otherwise the enemy came back, carried off the logs and rebuilt them in another spot.

An officer with Marshall's column also described the difficulties:

The attack must be made in single file, as these stockades are always built in the narrowest part of the path. Here the Englishman must give the black man the lead. This class of bush-fighting becomes wearisome to all concerned. Almost every hour a gun goes off at someone or other in the column – sometimes in front, then again in the middle of the column, or perhaps in rear, even at night the enemy creep up to the camp and fire their guns, which are usually loaded up to the muzzle with all sorts of bits of iron, or pot-legs as we call them.

As the main column approached Rotifunk the enemy opened fire from the bush and the troops replied with sectional fire which, together with several rounds from the seven-pounder, quickly scattered them. The column arrived at Kagbantama in the early afternoon and destroyed four more stockades there. A temporary *laager* was formed in the smoking ruins of the town. During this period the garrison at Karene was ignorant of the rescue operations. A column that had set off under Major Burke now joined up with Marshall's force, and Marshall followed Burke back to the town. There he set up a regular service of convoys, using the staging posts, to keep the entire line of communications open. He had close to 700 fighting men in the field.

Marshall now embarked on the scorched-earth campaign which Cardew had earlier tried to veto. Given the lack of fit officers, he took personal charge of a flying column which set out each day. At first he confined his operations to the villages close to Kagbantama and along paths running parallel with the main Karene road, but extended the range throughout much of April. As the neighbourhood was blackened by plumes of smoke and more and more villages were destroyed, the Temni resistance increased in determination and ferocity. Skirmishing turned into fast and furious fights in densely wooded ravines and tangled shrub which shredded uniforms and flesh alike. Major Donovan was mortally wounded trying to carry his hammock-boy, who had been shot down, out of the line of fire. Casualties piled up at Rogambia, Winti and other stockaded towns. Marshall described the period from 15 April as 'the most stubborn fighting that has been experienced in West Africa'. The fighting was continuous. Every village the column reached opposed them.

Scenes by Lieutenant Ramsay from a column marching towards Falaba. Clockwise from top left: troop carriers going upriver; a 'war-boy'; Port Lokko; a crew member; the barracks at Port Lokko; a prisoner. (*Illustrated London News*)

Up to 20 stockades were attacked and destroyed each day. As soon as they were levelled others sprang up in the rear, as if by magic. The flying column began its march at daybreak and rarely bivouacked before 5 p.m. The men were allowed 30 minutes for breakfast and a 90-minute halt was permitted during the noon-day heat. These were the only stops. 'The rest of the day was occupied in marching and fighting,' said one officer. 'It was no uncommon thing to have four or five stubborn fights during the day, while a day rarely passed without two or three.'

The surviving white officers of the West Indian Regiment began the campaign with little knowledge of the terrain or the enemy, having landed in West Africa only a few months before. A large number of their men were young, barely trained recruits. The battalion had recently given up many of their best NCOs and most experienced men to form the nucleus of another force heading for Lagos. At least some of those left were considered too raw or unfit for active service. But they learnt quickly, those that lasted long enough. Marshall later wrote:

> The behaviour of the troops throughout the operations was admirable. Before the commencement of the flying column the tornado season, which precedes the rains by about three weeks, was already well advanced. The men were constantly soaked to the skin on the marches, and as they had no change of clothes, were obliged to remain in their wet garments; nearly every night the bivouacs were deluged with rain; it was comparatively seldom that the troops were sufficiently fortunate to sleep in towns, for if the last town attacked during the day was not set on fire by the shellfire of the attacking party, it was frequently burnt by the enemy on being driven out, so as to leave no shelter for the troops. These discomforts were not only borne uncomplainingly by the men, but even cheerfully.

The precise thoughts of teenage lads from Jamaica and Trinidad, shivering in sodden camps, prone to sickness and at risk from sniper fire, is not recorded. Early on in the operation, only one blanket was carried for each man. Later, when the rains became even worse, a waterproof sheet was also carried by the porters. Marshall continued:

> The conduct of the troops under fire was excellent, although they knew the enemy was sheltered behind stockades which were proof against shellfire and very nearly so against rifle fire (for occasionally a bullet would find its way through the interstices or through the bamboo loopholes of the boulders), they nevertheless fiercely faced the enemy's fire, sectional volleys being delivered with a steadiness that would have been creditable on parade. . . . The small number of casualties when compared with the intensity of the enemy's fire is partly accounted for by the celerity with which the flying column came into action, and so disconcerted the pre-arranged plans of the enemy. The men of the column were sometimes changed, but the same officers remained, and as section after section came up, a word or two from an officer was sufficient to ensure the right impulse and direction being given to it.

During the course of the campaign the columns were divided into sections of 10, the highest number one officer could eventually keep under his command because of the density of the scrub and forest. A constant source of grief was the ignorance or, it was suspected, the treachery of some of the native guides. A report said:

> They were constantly leading the troops astray, and the maps supplied were too misleading to afford much assistance. The Police know the main roads, but are quite ignorant of the by-paths by which the enemy could be followed to his more remote retreats.

Another massive problem, as always in colonial wars when Europeans relied on natives to sustain them, was the casualty rate among the bearers. Their numbers were regarded as 'inadequate' from the start; even more so when over 100 were killed or wounded along the trails. This figure, though, was dwarfed by the enormous numbers who fell sick. Exasperated, Marshall blamed the lack of proper medical examinations when they were rushed to the front: 'Men with all kinds of complaints rendering them unfit for transport were enlisted.'

Smallpox broke out among the carriers, and there were daily desertions. Marshall made up the shortfall by ordering each carrier to carry two 30lb loads of biscuits, beef, ammunition and other supplies. Marshall's logic was impeccable: 'Light loads mean more carriers and more food to be carried for them.' He added: 'Everything depends on the compactness of the load – for instance the small bags of rice weighing 60lbs were eagerly sought after by the carriers, and boxes of S.G. ammunition weighing 80lbs were borne by one carrier throughout the expedition.'

The subsequent inquiry largely cleared the British forces of atrocities and there is little evidence of rape and plunder. But such a brutal form of warfare inevitably produced allegations of excess. Witnesses claimed that Captain Moore and a party of Frontier Police rampaged through several districts carrying 'fire and sword through the land, fusillading the inhabitants and burning their towns and villages'. Moore was accused of shooting one native in cold blood because he refused to drop a sword. A sick woman perished when her house in Mafouri was burnt around her. Cardew later dismissed such reports as fable or exaggeration. But Major Norris told Cardew that inhumane acts *were* committed, if not by those in uniform, then by discharged carriers who 'ravish women, steal the root crops and loot houses'.

The Temni fought with great valour and stubbornness – the hardest resistance was at the town of Mafouri on 25 April – but Marshall's tactics of attrition began to work. Most of the Kasseh district was subdued. Operations included the rescue of three white missionaries and nine black colleagues being held by one of Bai Bureh's allies at Rogberi. They were lucky; the local chief failed to carry out his threat to massacre them if the British column approached the undefended town. Bai Bureh and his men were pushed back from one stronghold to another until they became fugitives rather than an organised foe.

A vivid account of the fighting was given in dispatches by Captain E.D.H. Fairclough, who commanded a flying column sent deep into the Kwaia district:

Arriving close to the town of Mafuluma about two a.m. we found a big war-dance in progress. Whilst crossing the stream, which supplies the town with water, we were attacked but soon dispersed the rebels with a loss of six killed and several wounded. Reinforced by the natives of Maseracouli close by, the insurgents made a determined attempt to regain possession of the town about 3.30 a.m. but were driven off with the loss of seven killed. None of the Frontier Police were hurt but one of our friendlies was killed and one wounded.

After destroying Mafuluma and Maseracouli I moved towards Mayumera, meeting the war-boys gathered in force at Batipo, a village half-way. These were dispersed with a loss of several men, and we reached Maumera only to find it deserted. The insurgents having, however, collected again, attacked the town several times during the afternoon, and a night attack about nine p.m. was repulsed mainly through Fula Mansa's boys [Yonni native allies] who, walking around the bush, fell upon the rebels in the rear, killing their leader Pa Umri and several others. Hearing that the rebels had retired upon Fonde, I moved against this place on the 8th, meeting natives in ambush nearly all the way. At almost every town in the road groups of natives were posted, concealed in the bush, and fired upon us as we advanced, but as their feelings were naturally much upset by well-directed volleys from the Frontiers, their aim was very erratic, and none of our people were touched. We found the rebels collected in force at Fonde, but these were soon dispersed, the chief Pa Kuan and 14 followers being killed and several wounded. During the afternoon a village close by was destroyed and a large war-party dispersed, nine being killed, one friendly wounded. A night attack on Fonde was defeated with loss.

On the 9th I drove the rebels from Rofuta, close to Fonde, and destroyed the village but the friendlies, going too far into the bush in pursuit, lost two men killed. After destroying Fonde I proceeded to Forodugu, destroying a big gathering at Marifa en route. Here a strong mud fort and watch-tower had recently been constructed, but the fire from the loop-holes being silenced by volleys from our men, the rebels were quickly cleared out and scattered through the bush, pursued by the friendlies. Half-way to Forodugo I encountered and dispersed a large party in ambush close to Romabing which I destroyed. After driving the rebels from Rolia, and burning the town, I reached Forodugo, dispersing a war-party in this town with a loss of five killed and many more wounded.

The rebels under Suri Kamara attacked us in Forodugo during the afternoon but were repulsed and followed to Magbeni, lower down the river, Nyanba, a head warrior, and 25 men being killed. Suri Kamara and some 15 followers put off in a canoe for the Karena shore of the Rockelle [sic], but a volley from our men killing six of the crew, the canoe was upset and the Chief only escaped by swimming. . . .

And so it went on.

By the end of April Marshall decided to punish the chiefs of the neighbouring districts who had also rebelled. The territory of Alimany Amarah was the next to suffer punitive columns, burning villages at any sign of opposition. The road to Little Scarcies rivers, up to 150 yards wide and swollen by the heavy rains, were forded, the men struggling through water up to their chests under hot fire from stockades on the far banks.

The fighting in the territories beyond was often as rough as anything experienced so far. Ronula, the chief town of the renowned war-chief Alimany Lahai, proved a particularly hard nut to crack. Marshall wrote in dispatches:

> Here was a very fierce fight. Captain Harvey was dangerously wounded. It was found necessary to shell and fire the town in rear of the enemy's position, before the enemy could be driven out. A large number of rifles were used by the enemy, but the bullets whistled harmlessly overhead. A native can seldom use a rifle at short range, for he thinks the higher the sights are put up, the more powerfully does the rifle shoot. At last the enemy were driven from their stockades and from the town with considerable loss, and as the country on the far side of the town was comparatively open, were pursued with greater loss for some considerable distance. A large quantity of powder and slugs were taken, and also Alimani Lahai's drum, which was abandoned in the bush when the pursuit became hot.

At every village officers assembled, when they could, the local people. They gave graphic and lurid accounts of what their West Indians had done in the fire-blackened townships of Kasseh. They warned that further resistance would result in the same treatment. It was another early form of the 'hearts and minds' cajoling which was later deployed by western armies on other continents. Marshall's columns swept through Kambia and headed back towards Karene. On 13 May a young officer, Lieutenant Rickets, was shot dead. He was the last Briton slain among the convoys. Marshall now controlled the whole of the northern territories of the Temni. At Rokell Marshall, after three weeks of frustrating delays, negotiated the surrender of the Massimera chiefs. He wrote peevishly: 'Great difficulty was experienced and much time spent in the endeavour, owing to the timidity of the chiefs.'

But Bai Bureh himself remained at large, and other chiefs proved almost as troublesome. As the rainy season began to ease in September two companies of the newly formed West Africa Regiment were sent by rail into the hinterland. *The Times* reported:

> It has been decided to patrol thoroughly the Protectorate by bodies of troops, and clearly the chief offenders in the recent troubles, whereby so many lives were sacrificed, cannot be allowed to remain at large but must be brought to justice. The weakened authority of the Government must be re-established, and not till an object lesson has been given will the country be pacified.

Sporadic fighting continued for several months as the British crisscrossed the devastated countryside. Marshall knew that until Bai Bureh was safely in custody the war could not be conclusively won and his own reputation would be that of a town-burner rather than a victorious general. A reward of £100 was offered for Bai Bureh's capture. The Temni warrior reciprocated by offering £500 for Cardew's head. The governor was not amused. The heavy rains hampered pursuit and mopping-up operations. Muslim leaders in Freetown offered to mediate and passed on correspondence from Bai Bureh offering talks. Both his offers were rejected, with Cardew insisting on unconditional surrender.

Meanwhile Bai Bureh's defiance encouraged a sympathetic uprising by the Mendi people in the south. The Mendi, like the Temni, used secret society terror tactics, or *Poro*, with 'one word' oaths which meant that any of their people who did not join them would be killed. Creole traders were slain, and the body of a frontier officer buried at Bandasuma was dug up and burnt, to rid the earth of his evil influence. Christian missions were attacked and their occupants slaughtered. In Mofwe children attending the Methodist school were burnt alive when warriors set fire to an adjoining house where frontier policemen and some traders made a last stand. Two British columns were sent against Rotifunk and Bombi, where there was fierce resistance. Further operations included the relief of a besieged garrison at Panguma and a battle at Yomundu on 6 July.

The Mendi campaign, led by Lieutenant-Colonel George Cunningham, in many ways matched the expedition against the Temni. Cunningham, a decorated veteran of six campaigns, in which he suffered three wounds, wrote:

> The only means of advancing are along narrow roads bounded by thick bush. Occasionally the path widens a little and a clearing is reached in the centre of which stands a town. The Insurgents post their men armed with trade guns in a clump of thick bush by the side of the road, having cut narrow tracks behind them to retire by. As our column advanced, invariably the first notice of the enemy's presence was a discharge of guns at close quarters which almost invariably hit some of the leading rifles. It may be imagined under the circumstances how trying was the work of the advanced guard. Nevertheless the greatest keenness was always shown. . . .

After two months and the relief of Panguma, the enthusiasm of the Mendi chiefs began to flag as villages and towns went up in flames. But the British still feared further revolts as long as Bai Bureh remained at liberty.

Finally, the elusive Bai Bureh was betrayed by informers. After 23 weeks in the rain-soaked bush, he was tracked to swamplands on 11 November. A small party of the West African Regiment attacked the war chief's bodyguard. The warriors chose to fight rather than surrender but two men broke away. A local sergeant gave chase and overtook the slowest and oldest man. He was Bai Bureh. It was an anti-climatic end to a hard-fought war.

⋆   ⋆   ⋆

The British government was shocked by the outbreak of the war and by the cost in human terms. Long before Bai Bureh's capture, in July, Sir David Chalmers was charged with investigating the insurrection and its causes. A retired Scottish judge, he had served as a magistrate in the Gambia over thirty years before. He was the first Chief Justice of the Gold Coast in 1876 and later held the same post in British Guinea. Shortly before his return to Sierra Leone, where he had been a Queen's Advocate, Chalmers judged a fraud prosecution in Newfoundland. He was a roving legal eagle with a special knowledge of, and fondness for, the people of West Africa.

From the start Chalmers knew the practical difficulties he faced. He wrote:

> Travelling in the country was practically impossible, by reason of the rainy season which was then in full force. During this season (which continues to November) roads become water-courses, streams are swollen into torrents, drenching rains of a character not known in temperate regions are almost constant.

Added to those physical impediments was the impracticality of seeking evidence from natives in their own homes, 'nearly all of them being scattered and taking refuge in the bush or forests'. Nevertheless Chalmers was known to have a sympathetic ear and many chiefs trekked to Freetown to give him their account directly.

His conclusions were devastating for Cardew and his officials on the ground. Chalmers said bluntly that the Hut Tax and the brutal methods used to enforce it were the main cause of the insurrection. 'The tax was obnoxious to the customs and feelings of the people,' he said, 'There was a widespread belief that it was a means of taking away their rights in their country and in their property.' The tax was considered oppressive and unjust, and was higher than most of the people could afford. Hostility to the tax was aggravated by the actions of police, officials and, by implication, Cardew himself. 'The inherent repugnance to the Hut Tax would by itself most probably have led to passive resistance,' he continued. 'The sense of personal wrong and injustice from the illegal and degrading severities made use of in enforcing the Tax, coupled with the aversion to the Tax in itself, produced in the Timinis [sic] a resistance enforced by arms.' Cardew blundered by targeting Bai Bureh, a legitimate war chief with a large personal force, who subsequently became the focus for more widespread resistance. Chalmers wrote that it grieved him to point out so many 'grave errors' in his report. If he could have found that the insurrection was the result of an 'inevitable conflict between ancient barbarism and an advancing civilisation' he would have done so, but he could not.

He recommended that the Hut Tax, or any alternative, should be dropped as unworkable and the British administrators should concentrate on rebuilding both the shattered countryside and the confidence of the native people. 'Let the Colonial Officers realise that the subjects of a Protectorate *have rights* [his italics], and that it should be a work of forbearance and patience, rather than of overpowering force, to instruct them that they also have obligations and duties towards the protecting power.'

Chalmers died in August 1899, barely a month after he presented his damning report. He did not live to see the Colonial Office reject its main recommendations.

Officials and ministers accepted Cardew's assertion that the commissioner had over-stated the grievances of the natives. Furthermore, there was no more money forthcoming for the colony. The hated Hut Tax was reintroduced throughout Sierra Leone in 1900 at a minimum rate of 3 shillings a year. Much blood had been shed for the sake of a few shillings. Four more British columns marched through the back country in a show of force designed to cow the defeated natives. Paramount chiefs regarded as pro-British were appointed. And the Frontier Police were amalgamated into the West African Frontier Force, which was for military purposes only.

Cardew retired that year to his Tudor cottage in Oxfordshire. He enjoyed a long and peaceful retirement and he died in 1921. There is evidence that he was haunted by some degree of guilt. In his response to the Chalmers Report he wrote:

> I do not desire in any sense whatever to shift the burden of responsibility for all that has passed on any shoulders from my own, but at the same time I hope it will not be thought that I lightly or recklessly entered on the task before me . . . The thought of the many valuable lives which have been lost, of the gallant officers and men who have fallen, of the devoted missionaries who have been sacrificed, of the Sierra Leoneans who have been massacred, and of the many natives who have been killed, must ever remain to me a sad regret, the recollection of which can never pass away.

Given the small number of men involved, it was an expensive war. Casualties among the Karene expeditionary force totalled 277, including native carriers. Most were wounded and the fact that few died of their wounds is a tribute to the teams of medical officers and supplies of medicines given top priority by Marshall. The smaller force sent to suppress the Mendi uprising suffered 58 casualties, with 6 killed in action, 5 drowned crossing swollen rivers, and 2 more lost in the bush. The number of Temni and Mendi warriors and civilians who were killed or maimed is not recorded.

The war left a legacy of bitterness and racism which ignored Freetown's philanthropic birth. In April 1899 Freetown's mayor, Sir Samuel Lewis, a native African, boarded the first train on the newly completed Sierra Leone railway. Of the 600 people on board, 10 were white. Lewis, unaware of any restrictions, took a seat in the whites-only carriage – and he was forcibly ejected by a white NCO. The event caused much ill-feeling and the soldier was later fined 30 shillings for assault.

Marshall, who had deployed his flying columns and scorched-earth policies to a successful conclusion, was well rewarded for his ruthless drive. He was made a general and put in command of British troops in Jamaica. He retired to his home overlooking Hyde Park in 1911 and died ten years later.

After his capture Bai Bureh was first held at Karene but was later moved to Freetown gaol after a Temni soldier in the West African Regiment plotted his escape. He was later transferred to more comfortable confinement in a house on the outskirts of Freetown. Crowds gathered there to see the legendary warrior who had defied British military might for so long. Commissioner Sharpe wanted to try him on a charge of treason but he was overruled by the Colonial Office because there

Bai Bureh, shortly after his capture.

was some doubt whether Bai Bureh could be treated as a British subject. In captivity Bai Bureh, sick of war, said that he and his people wanted only to live in peace with their 'mother', the Queen of England. Proceedings dragged on until London decreed that he owed no allegiance to the queen and therefore his actions could not be deemed treasonous. He never faced a trial but was considered too dangerous to release. The British believed that to grant his request to be allowed to return to Karene district would be regarded as a sign of weakness. Sir Matthew Nathan, standing in for Cardew, then on leave, ordered his deportation to Gambia, along with two other chiefs. All other 'insurgents' were given a general amnesty.

Bai Bureh had proved that natives could organise effective resistance to colonial rule. His defiance proved that 'savage' people could demonstrate moral superiority when faced with unjust burdens. He showed that paternalistic rule could not stifle proud and independent peoples. Full independence, however, was not granted to Sierra Leone until 1960.

Bai Bureh's companions sickened and died in exile. The old war chief, frail and crippled by disease, twice petitioned, unsuccessfully, for his own release. Finally, in 1905, he was allowed to go home, provided he accepted severe constraints on his activities and movements. He died three years later, enjoying the respectful worship of his people.

Bibliography and Sources

General

Briggs, Asa, *The Age of Improvement 1783–1867* (Longman, London, 1959)

Callwell, Colonel C.E., *Small Wars* (London, 1906)

Chandler, David (general editor), *The Oxford History of the British Army* (Oxford University Press, 1996)

Dictionary of National Biography (Oxford University Press, 1921–2)

Farwell, Byron, *Queen Victoria's Little Wars* (Allen Lane, London, 1973)

Featherstone, D., *Colonial Small Wars 1837–1901* (Newton Abbot, 1973)

Haythornthwaite, Philip J., *The Colonial Wars Source Book* (Arms & Armour Press, London, 1995)

James, Lawrence, *The Savage Wars – British Campaigns in Africa, 1870–1920* (Robert Hale, London)

Morris, James, *The Pax Britannica Trilogy* (Faber & Faber, London, 1968)

Pakenham, Thomas, *The Scramble for Africa* (Weidenfeld & Nicolson, 1991)

Spiers, Edward M., *The Late Victorian Army* (Manchester University Press, 1992)

Strawson, John, *Beggars in Red – The British Army 1789–1889* (Hutchinson, London, 1991)

——, *Gentlemen in Khaki – The British Army 1890–1990* (Secker & Warburg, London, 1989)

The Gurkha War

Annual Registers, 1815–16

Bredin, A.E.C., *The Happy Warriors* (Blackmore Press, Dorset, 1961)

Chant, Christopher, *Gurkha – An Illustrated History of an Elite Fighting Force* (Blandford Press, Dorset, 1985)

Gould, Tony, *Imperial Warriors – Britain and the Gurkhas* (Granta Books, London, 1999)

Hastings, Lord, *Dispatches*

Moon, Sir Penderel, *The British Conquest and Dominion of India* (Duckworth, London, 1989)

Ochterlony, Sir David, *Dispatches*

Parker, John, *The Gurkhas* (Headline, London, 1999)

Brooke and the Borneo Pirates

Annual Registers, 1846, 1851

Brooke, Sir James, *Private Letters*, edited by John C. Templer (London, 1853)

Hann, Emily, *James Brooke of Sarawak* (Arthur Barker Ltd, London, 1953)

Jacobs, Gertrude L., *Raja of Sarawak* (London, 1876)

Keppel, Captain Henry, *The Expedition to Borneo of HMS Dido* (London, 1848)

Parliamentary Reports, 1844–51

Rutter, Owen, *Rajah Brooke and Baroness Burdett Coutts* (Hutchinson, London, 1935)

Saunders, Graham, *A History of Brunei* (Oxford University Press, 1994)

St John, Spenser, *Life of Sir James Brooke* (London and Edinburgh, 1870)

Tarling, Nicholas, *The Establishment of the Colonial Regimes*, part of the Cambridge History of south-east Asia, Volume 2 (University Press, 1992)

Madagascar

Annual Register, 1845

Brown, Mervyn, *Madagascar Rediscovered – A History from Early Times to Independence* (London, 1978)

Desfosses, Commander Romain, *Dispatches*

Freeman, Revd J.J., *A Narrative of the Persecution of the Christians in Madagascar* (London, 1840)

Howe, Sonia E., *The Drama of Madagascar* (Methuen, London, 1938)

Illustrated London News, 1845

Heseltine, Nigel, *Madagascar* (Pall Mall Press, London, 1971)

Pfeiffer, Ida, *Voyage a Madagascar* (Paris, 1881)

Shaw, Revd G., *Madagascar and France* (London, 1889)

Sibree, James, *Madagascar Before the Conquest* (London, 1896)

Stratton, Arthur, *The Great Red Island* (Macmillan, London, 1965)

The Times

Villars, Captain de', *Establissment des Français dans l'Ile de Madagascar 1638–1894* (Paris)

The Sikh Wars

Annual Registers, 1845–9

Bruce, George, *Six Battles for India* (Arthur Barker, London, 1969)

Burton, R.G., *The First and Second Sikh Wars* (Simla, 1911)

Cunningham, J.D., *A History of the Sikhs* (London, 1849)

Fortesque, Sir John, *History of the British Army* (Macmillan, London, 1927)

Gough, General Sir Hugh, *Dispatches*

Hardinge, Sir Henry, *Dispatches*

James, Lawrence, *Raj – The Making and Unmaking of British India* (Little, Brown, London, 1997)

Khurana, G., *British Historiography on the Sikh Power in the Punjab* (Allied Publishers, London and New York, 1985)

Khushwant Singh, *A History of the Sikhs* (Oxford University Press and Princeton University Press, 1966)

M'Gregor, W.L., *The History of the Sikhs* (London, 1846)

Moon, Sir Penderel, *The British Conquest and Dominion of India* (Duckworth, London, 1989)

Osborne, W.G., *Ranjit Singh – The Lion of the Punjab* (London, 1846)
Ryder, John, *Four Years' Service in India* (Leicester, 1853)
Sandford, D.A., *Leaves from the Journal of a Subaltern* (Blackwood, 1852)
Smith, General Sir Harry, *Dispatches*
Thackwell, E.J., *The Second Sikh War* (London, 1851)

Eureka Stockade

Butler, Richard, *Eureka Stockade* (Angus & Robertson, Melbourne, 1983)
Carboni, Rafaello, *The Eureka Stockade – The Consequence of some Pirates wanting on Quarterdeck a Rebellion* (Ballarat, 1855)
Clark, Manning, *A History of Australia* (Random House, Australia, 1962–87)
Shaw, A.G.L., *The Story of Australia* (Faber & Faber, London, 1955)
Withers, Bramwell William, *History of Ballarat* (Queensberry Press, 1980)
Younger, R.M., *Australia and the Australians, A Concise History* (Hutchinsons, Victoria, 1969)

Kars

Annual Register, 1855
Brant, James, *Official Reports*
Cunningham, Allan, *Anglo-Ottoman Encounters in the Age of Revolution* (London, 1993)
HMSO, *The Siege of Kars – Uncovered Papers*, series edited by Tim Coates (London, 2000)
James, Lawrence, *Crimea: The War with Russia from Contemporary Photographs* (Thame, 1981)
Kinglake, A.W., *The Invasion of the Crimea* (Edinburgh, 1863–87)
Lambert, Andrew D., *The Crimean War – British Grand Strategy Against Russia 1853–56* (Manchester University Press, 1990)
Lake, Sir Henry Atwell, *Kars and Our Captivity in Russia* (London, 1856)
Royle, Trevor, *Crimea – The Great Crimean War 1854–1856* (Little Brown, London, 1999)
Sandwith, Humphrey, *A Narrative of the Siege of Kars and of the Six Months' Resistance of the Turkish garrison, under General Williams, to the Russian Army* (London, 1856)
Shepherd, John, *The Crimean Doctors – A History of the British Medical Services in the Crimean War*, Volume Two (Liverpool University Press, 1991)
Slade, Adolphus, *Turkey and the Crimean War* (London, 1867)
Strachan, H., *From Waterloo to Balaclava* (Cambridge, 1985)
The Times
Williams, General William Fenwick, *Dispatches*
Wood, H. Evelyn, *The Crimea in 1854 and 1894* (London, 1895)

The Fenian Invasion of Canada

Annual Registers, 1866–7
Comerford, R.V. (contrib.), *A New History of Ireland, Volume V: Ireland Under the Union* (Clarendon Press, Oxford, 1989)

D'Arcy, William, *The Fenian Movement in the United States* (Washington, 1947)

Jones, Paul, *The Irish Brigade* (NEL Books, London, 1989)

Keneally, Thomas, *The Great Shame – The Story of the Irish in the Old World and the New* (Chatto & Windus, London, 1998)

Litton, Helen, *Irish Rebellions 1798–1916* (Wolfhound Press, Dublin and Colorado, 1998)

The New York Times

O'Connor, Sir James, *History of Ireland 1798–1924*

The Rochester Union

Rutherford, John, *The Fenian Conspiracy* (1877)

Woodham-Smith, Cecil, *The Great Hunger* (Hamish Hamilton, London, 1962)

Belize

Burdon, Sir John Alder (ed.), *Archives of British Honduras*, Volumes II and III (London, 1935)

Caiger, Stephen L., *British Honduras – Past and Present* (Allen & Unwin, London, 1951)

Dobson, Narda, *A History of Belize* (Longman Caribbean, 1973)

Fowler, Henry, *A Narrative of a Journey Across the Unexplored Portion of British Honduras* (Belize, 1879)

Means, P.A., *History of the Spanish Conquest of Yucatan and of the Itzas* (Cambridge, Mass., 1917)

Merrill, Tim (ed.), *Belize – A Country Study* (Federal Research Division, US Library of Congress, 1992)

Reed, Nelson, *The Caste War of Yucatan* (Stanford, 1964)

Sierra Leone

Alie, Joe A.D., *A New History of Sierra Leone* (Macmillan, London, 1990)

Annual Registers, 1898–9

Bourke, Major H.C., *Dispatches*

Cardew, Sir Frederick, *Response to the Chalmers Report* (London, 1899)

Chalmers, Sir David, *Report by her Majesty's Commissioner on the subject of the Insurrection in the Sierra Leone Protectorate* (Stationery Office, London, 1899)

Cunningham, Lieutenant-Colonel G., *Dispatches*

Denzer, La Ray (contrib.), *West African Resistance – The Military Response to Colonial Occupation* (Hutchinson University Library for Africa, London, 1971)

Fairclough, Captain E.D.H., *Dispatches*

Marshall, Colonel J.W., *Report – Operations in Timini Country* (London, 1898)

Norris, Major R.J., *Dispatches*

Index

Numbers in italics indicate illustrations